New Borders and Old Barriers in Spatial Development

Edited by
PETER NIJKAMP

Avebury

Aldershot · Brookfield USA · Hong Kong · Singapore · Sydney

© Peter Nijkamp 1994

Published by
Avebury
Ashgate Publishing Limited
Gower House
Croft Road
Aldershot
Hants GU11 3HR
England

Ashgate Publishing Company
Old Post Road
Brookfield
Vermont 05036
USA

British Library Cataloguing in Publication Data

New Borders and Old Barriers in Spatial
    Development
    I. Nijkamp, Peter
ISBN 1 85628 906 0

Library of Congress Cataloging-in-Publication Data

New borders and old barriers in spatial development / edited by Peter
    Nijkamp.
    p.   cm.
ISBN 1-85628-906-0 : $67.95 (approx.)
    1. Regional planning. 2. Nijkamp, Peter. II. Title: Spatial
development.
HT391.N443 1994   94-7287
338.9--dc20   CIP

Printed and Bound in Great Britain by
Athenaeum Press Ltd, Newcastle upon Tyne.

TABLE OF CONTENTS

PREFACE

For many people the flying carpet is a dream which symbolizes a world without any borders, a world with free mobility for everybody. Geopolicital and administrative borders are in this perception annoying impediments preventing people from enjoying the fruits of a borderless society.

In our present era we have been witnessing the disappearance of many man-made borders, exemplified by the unexpected opening up and falling apart of the East European power block. At the same time we are observing signs of international cooperation in the EC, EFTA, NAFTA and ASEAN countries which seem to prelude a gradual removal of unnecessary obstacles between the countries concerned. Whether this leads to an open society characterized by the flying carpet still remains to be seen, although popular terms like globalisation, international networking and tele-society seem to suggest that distance does not necessarily mean friction.

Reality however, seems to be fairly harsh, in that vanishing borders do not necessarily imply more openness. Mankind seems to be very keen in inventing new bottlenecks precluding a free movement of people, goods or information. Self interest or group interest is apparently a strong driving force which is often at odds with the social (or global) benefits of a borderless society and may thus destroy the dream of a flying carpet. In the same vein, it is also noteworthy that the past years have demonstrated the inability of large organizations to effectively control individuals, groups and regions via a centralized decision system. Again many examples from Europe, Asia and America show convincingly the failure of the nation-state as a definite model for ruling culturally different people. The recent history of Europe has also demonstrated the potential and viability of the city-state or region-state as an area with a cultural identity which may be more suitable as an efficient decision unit than conventional institutional configurations mirrored in the nation-state. Current geo-political and socio-economic restructuring phenomena tend to eliminate existing borders with the aim to be more competitive in a global economy. Surprisingly, often the removal of political borders provokes the emergence of new barriers to a free exchange of people, goods and services. Borders and barriers are thus key words in understanding the dynamics in our economies which tend to move toward open international networks.

The friction between new borders and old barriers is therefore an important policy and research issue. It was addressed at a workshop recently held at the Netherlands Institute for Advanced Study (NIAS) in Wassenaar, under the auspices of the Network on European Communication and Transport Activity Research (NECTAR). A selection of presentations at this venue supplemented with some additional contributions forms the ingredients of this book. It brings together refreshing views on the above theme and draws also clear policy conclusions regarding European spatial and transportation problems. I wish to thank the NIAS staff for their support in organizing this meeting. Yossi Berechman, Maria Giaoutzi, Dirk-Jan Kamann and Aura Reggiani - all former NIAS fellows - have to be thanked for their intellectual support to the above theme. Finally, I wish to acknowledge the skillful editorial assistance of Myrna Wettke and Paul Geerlings in preparing and completing this volume.

Amsterdam, July 1993   Peter Nijkamp

CHAPTER 1

BORDERS AND BARRIERS: BOTTLENECKS

OR POTENTIALS ?

A PROLOGUE

Peter Nijkamp

1. Borders and Barriers in Space: Introduction

Many spatial development theories take for granted the existence of a uniform space in which a free movement of people or goods is taking place all over. Space is then simply the passive medium for transport and communication flows and does not have an indigenous possibility to influence spatial movements. Classical location theories (Weber, e.g.) provide for example, a stylized representation of a spatial structure, in which only discrete point locations in a continuous space act as signposts for locational behaviour (and locational constraints) of firms.

In recent years the recognition has grown that spatial development processes are shaped through a complex interplay of both a heterogeneous physical space and a multi-layer socio-economic stratum. Barriers and borders are evidently playing a very critical but often neglected role in spatial and socio-economic dynamics. Batten and Johansson (1991) offer various interesting historical examples which show that a removal of bottlenecks may have substantial impacts on the growth of regions or nations. For instance, the expansion of trade and the growth of cities in medieval Europe were prompted by drastic improvements in European transport infrastructures (inland waterways, coastal transport, roads) whose dilapidated state had for long prevented the emergence of an efficient production and trading system. Similarly, the rise of new commercial centres in Japan in almost the same period would not have taken place without the removal of trade barriers and the creation of new distributional concepts (e.g., scheduled periodic markets, new commercial areas in nodal points of the network, protected castle towns etc.). The authors suggest that the transition towards a **network economy** has been of decisive importance for the growth of regions and nations. Thus multi-layer network formation with both interdependencies and hierarchies at all spatial levels seems to become the new model of western economies (see also Camagni, 1993).

Impediments to network formation deserve therefore much attention (cf. Batten and Törnqvist, 1990). Such impediments may take different forms ranging from institutional inertia or bureaucracy to lack of physical resources or missing infrastructure links. It is increasingly recognized that the rise of nations or regions is often the result of overcoming these impediments (cf. Denison, 1967; Olson, 1982). This forms also the background of the deregulation movement which seeks to optimize network performance by removing unnecessary bottlenecks of a regulatory nature. Some authors (e.g., Fukuyama, 1989) speak even of the "end of history" as a stage in the history of the western world in which free competition and liberalism are the ultimate driving forces of the modern network economy.

In any case, the idea of **design** of a network seems to more relevant than the notion of **control:** design is a structuring activity oriented towards change of form (including barriers), whereas control refers to optimization of key parameters under a given set of **fixed** constraints (or barriers).

As mentioned above, a barrier may have different meanings (cf. Nijkamp et al., 1990). According to the Oxford Dictionary a **barrier** is an obstacle or circumstance that keeps people or things apart, or prevents communication. The related term of a **border** has more a geo-political meaning: it is the line separating two political or geographical areas, especially countries. It is now an interesting research question what the relationship is between barriers and borders on the one hand and network performance reflected in regional development in the long run on the other. Furthermore, the removal of old borders - a situation we have witnessed regularly in the past years - provokes the question whether all related impediments are at the same time eliminated (Molle, 1990). It is a fascinating research issue whether new borders may even create new barriers of a different nature.

2.   Networks in Space

Network connectivity seems to become one of the prominent features of industrial economies, as it is able to combine decentralized decision-making with the benefits from synergy. In this respect both economies of scale and economies of scope can be satisfied to a maximum extent.

It is evident that there is a variety of networks. Examples are:
- physical networks (in which physical capacity, links, nodes, spatial configuration and service level are dominant features).
- immaterial networks (in which information plays a critical role through transfer mechanisms such as central facilities, connectivity channels, capacity and receptivity).
- organisational networks (in which people act as nodes with many formal and informal linkages and communication channels, organisational objectives and coalition strategies).
- club networks (in which network externalities, new information technology and connectivity play a basic role).

The above networks can be either planned or spontaneous, but can all be typified according to the following features:
- material (e.g., links, capacity, fixed facilities or connectivity degree)
- structural (e.g., hierarchy, spatial lay-out, spatio-temporal evolution)
- economic (e.g., operational versus capital costs, scale economies, externalities, user charge principles etc.)
- behavioural (formal and informal use, actual versus perceived costs, price elasticity etc.)

- multi-layer (complementarity or substitution with other networks, joint use, overlapping functions etc.)
- decision-making (formal versus informal planning, centralized versus decentralized planning, budget versus profit principles, etc.).

Clearly, a network is essentially based on actor dependency. Kamann and Nijkamp (1991) distinguish in this framework the following dependencies in network relationships: technical dependency, knowledge dependency, continuity dependency, social dependency, logistical and administrative dependency, innovative dependency and financial dependency.

Networks do not have an aim in themselves, but are vehicles for achieving one or more goals of actors using the services or benefits rendered by networks. A necessary condition for the emergence of networks is **interaction** between different actors. Since usually actors are not characterized by spatial iuxta-position, networks have a clear **geographical** component. However, the geographical dimensions of networks are intertwined with order, organisation and coordination of such networks. The design, supply and organisation of networks should thus meet the **needs of the potential users**. Furthermore, these users have different expectation patterns regarding the services provided by a network, and hence in many cases we observe **different layers** of networks (e.g., roads, railways, waterways, airline connections etc.). Such networks follow also the **hierarchical structure** of central and less central places. Since there is no single network which can serve all needs, we observe in reality a complicated system of partly overlapping, partly complementary network segments. **Multimodality** is a good example of the latter phenomenon.

The **supply** side of a network is oriented towards fulfilment of demand conditions (market pull), but it is strongly influenced by technological changes (technology push) and by prevailing property and ownership regimes as well as by geopolitical interest. Since the beginning of this century network supply has often been a public government responsibility, but in recent years - after the recognition of market failures and government failures - we observe an increasingly commercial attitude towards network supply. This means that the organisation of the supply side of networks will likely drastically change.

The current popularity of network concepts is undeniably connected with the declining domain of public policy: networks tend to become the vehicles through which competition is flourishing. Both external megatrends and internal system's forces necessitate a market orientation parallelled by risk minimization strategies. Networks seems to offer more certainty in terms of expected consequences of strategic decisions and hence may be regarded as a major critical success factor in (inter)national competition.

Despite the socio-economic need for well performing networks, we also witness the environmental and safety conditions in network planning, construction and use. Network use will most likely have to materialize within ever increasing narrower limits. The recognition of such barriers requires rigorous social science research on externalities, complementarities and scale economies.

The set of network policy actions that can be envisaged is vast and ranges from direct public supply or intervention to user charge principles or complete laissez-faire. A major challenge of network owners and operators will be to formulate strategic plans that convincingly incorporate non-zero-sum game strategies with gains for all parties involved. This may be illustrated by means of some examples.

The "user charge" principle in transport policy has in particular become a success in those countries where suppliers and users of transport infrastructure were all enjoying benefits (e.g., suppliers by receiving more revenues from road charges, users by increasing their travel speed etc.). Likewise the question of intermodal substitution (e.g., from the car or lorry to the train) will critically depend on the willingness to implement such incentives.

International competitiveness is a necessary condition for enhancing the level of European economic performance after the completion of the internal market. Segmented and nationalistic infrastructure policy may at best serve the short-run interests of infrastructure owners, but is in the long run to the detriment of all network owners (and users) and affects Europe's economic position. Thus transportation and communication policy requires a balanced implementation of actions which ensure a consideration of both private and social costs, and a global orientation which exceeds country-based or segmented policy strategies. The current plans regarding the European high speed railway system are a clear case of creative action-oriented policy analysis, even though the technology policy underlying this system serves mainly the interest of individual countries.

Networks are at the same time vehicles through which nations (or regions) can control part of the international (or interregional) competition. Monopolistic and oligopolistic structures in space are the result. The socio-economic benefits of coordination and harmonisation are often neglected in favour of emphasis on narrow nationalistic interest. This opens much new research on the economic importance of the existence of (deliberate and coincidental) barriers in international networks (including the missing links and missing networks phenomena). This issue will be discussed in the next section.

3. The Role of Borders and Barriers

Borders were traditionally regarded as barriers to economic development: it is not surprising that many lagging regions were found near borders with other countries. Borders were in general creating impediments which hampered the economic gains of trade.

In the past years many old borders have vanished and new maps have emerged. Especially Europe has exhibited a fast dynamics in this respect, but also other continents (e.g., NAFTA in North-America) are gradually following the same trend. This means that the ongoing process of socio-economic integration and economic competition in an open network economy is creating new roles and new possibilities for national states, cities and regions. Barriers related to former borders may disappear, but national self-interest may create new barriers. Thus renewal and establishment are coping with one another.

Governments find themselves in a different position, as the deregulation paradigm prevents them from a direct intervention. Controllability via public agencies becomes thus more and more problematic. Cities and regions tend to form their own strategic alliances without too much consideration for the former borders of nation-states. At the same time it has to be recognized that transborder cooperation may generate unexpected benefits, as the economies of scale of new strategic alliances across the borders are significant (see Ratti and Reichman, 1993). Consequently, borders are no longer barriers to development, but also windows of opportunities. This does not only hold for commercial activities, but also for exchange of information and knowledge (cf. Schott, 1988).

Borders and barriers lead in general to a lower performance of a network; a border because of geopolitical reasons and a barrier because of institutional, physical or human-made impediments. They form an obstacle in a free transfer of people, goods or information. Clearly, some of these impediments are given by nature (e.g., mountains, lakes), but most of them are man-made and created for the sake of convenience or protection or are unintended effects or spinoffs of other barriers. Examples of man-made barriers are: congestion, fiscal constraints, institutional rules, technical conditions, market regulations, cultural inertia, language barriers or information shortage.

Nevertheless, it should be emphasized that barriers may not only be imper-meable and detrimental to development, but also semi-permeable and stimulating for development (e.g., the Swiss watch industry in the Jura) (Ratti and Reichman, 1993).

Bennett and Chorley (1978) distinguish four types of spatial transfer pro-cesses which are relevant in our context:
- barrier processes
- hierarchy processes
- network processes
- contiguity processes

The corresponding spatial patterns are depicted in Figure 1, where a typology of such processes is given.

The removal of bottlenecks in a network may have profound impacts on the spatial perception of distance. For example, if one compares the European railway map of 1987 - in terms of time distances - with the map in 2015 (after the widescale introduction of high speed trains), one obtains an interesting picture of Europe (see Figure 2).

Because of globalization and other factors (including the need for higher and sustained economic growth), transportation in many countries has grown enormous-ly, especially in recent years. As the supply of infrastructure - for various reasons - followed this trend only in part, existing infrastructure bottlenecks have been accentuated. This is a very serious problem, since economic development and infrastructural development have always been strongly interlinked. The full benefits of a network economy will only be reaped in case of effective (physical and non-physical) infrastructural adjustments. What is needed in this context, is supranational - and **not** national - thinking and action in infrastructural policy, based on knowledge

6

of past successes and failures in infrastructural planning and of the future needs of the economy, and the constraints imposed by an (increasingly threatened) (natural) environment.

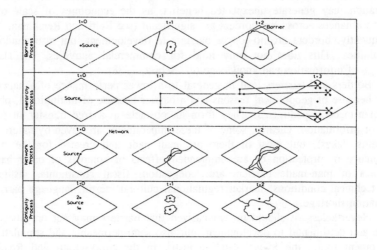

Figure 1: A typology of spatio-temporal patterns
Source : Bennett and Chorley (1978)

Figure 2: Europe before and after the introduction of high speed trains.
Source : Spiekermann and Wegener (1993)

4.   The Changing Scene of Transportation Planning

The role of transport and communication networks for spatial development is rapidly changing. Not many years ago it was possible to argue that - due to underpriced energy and the ubiquity of the road network - accessibility was losing its importance for the organisation of space. Today a number of developments work in the opposite direction, i.e. enhance the key function of transport and communications networks for spatial development:

- New, faster transport networks (high-speed rail and air) superimpose new, higher levels of infrastructure on top of the existing hierarchy of transport networks and create new spatial concentrations of accessibility.
- Strategic megaprojects (such as the Channel Tunnel, the Scandinavian links across the Belt and Sound, the transalpine base tunnels and the conversion of the Iberian mainlines to standard gauge) will create global network connections.
- Despite the reintegration of East-Europe into the European transport network, the difference in accessibility between West and East will for many years remain large.
- New high-speed, high capacity telecommunication networks such as ISDN and satellite communications complement existing communication networks and create areas of high informational accessibility at nodal centres.

The supply-side developments have spawned an unprecedented growth in the demand for international, interregional and intra-regional goods transport, passenger travel and information exchange, led to the globalisation and internationalisation of economic processes and increased the dependency of regions and cities on access to transport and information networks. Borders and barriers are from this perspective a serious threat to a competitive economy.

It does not need much courage nor phantasy to claim that the context and substance of network planning have dramatically changed in the past years.

The **external environment** has a completely different "face" compared to a decade ago. The drastic political changes in centrally planned countries, the return to market oriented societies and the belief in competition and free entrepreneurship have destroyed the idea that public governments were the vehicles par excellence for ensuring "the greatest welfare for the greatest number of people".

Furthermore, the **substance of planning** has changed. A fine tuning to democratic desires of citizens is more and more required, making planning a theatre of democratic operations. Thus external megatrends and internal system's movements force planning towards a client orientation. At the same time, more frictions between wish and reality become apparent, so that planning as a science tends to become the art of conflict resolution. This leads to a re-orientation in terms of scope and research methodology. This is clearly witnessed in European transport planning.

In the light of the previous observations, it is clear that there is a broad spectrum of questions which need to be addressed in policy formulation. The recognition of frictions and bottlenecks is the first stage in a policy life cycle. The policy agenda itself is of course much longer. In the past years where many countries have increasingly been faced with the negative externalities of the transport sector, social science research has been of critical importance for formulating issues that needed to be addressed in policy analysis. A simple illustration may clarify this statement.

The "undesirable" outcome of a highly mobile society is - almost paradoxically - the result of rational and plausible actions of a great many individuals. Social science research has convincingly demonstrated that the neglect of social costs in individual decision-making must by necessity lead to a macro outcome that is far from optimal. This explains worsening quality of life conditions in major cities all over the world. At the same time cities are becoming competitive strategic nodes in a global network (Sassen, 1991), especially because of their information gathering, processing and distributing power (Castells, 1989).

Policy implementation in networks is thus not in the first place a clean application of instruments, but requires a fine tuning between goals, measures and social acceptance.

Such pro-active strategies require creative policy and social research, not only regarding technical solutions or financial means, but also regarding material resources, human responses etc. Those countries which have been able to develop and support such research have been rather successful in their policies. A particularly important, but often neglected factor in this context is the organizational and managerial setting that is necessary for making a policy strategy successful.

5.   Borders and Barriers in European Networks

It does not need much argumentation to claim that in the past years Europe has been showing the signs of an extremely dynamic socio-economic and geo-political development: changes in economic heartlands, opening up of Eastern Europe, closer links between EC and EFTA countries, splitting up of former unified countries, strong tendencies towards regional autonomy and drastic changes of former border areas. Traditional centres of economic activity have to compete increasingly with medium-size locations offering economies of scope based on neofordist and flexible production systems. Besides, recent developments in new information technology may generate substantial benefits for less favoured regions of the Community, as they do not suffer from diseconomies of scale in the congested European heartlands.

The previous observations imply that the imbalances between different regions in the European continent will not only create a more mobile labour pool (including international and interregional labour migration), but will also create a different - and more promising - scene for the European border regions. In this spatial-economic restructuring process two eminent forces call for more strategic attention, viz. the role of infrastructure and the geo-political changes at the regional level.

As far as **infrastructure** is concerned, we have argued above that transport developments place a massive burden and an unprecedented tension on a balanced (co-evolutionary and sustainable) development of regions in Europe. The needs of lagging areas, congestion in the European heartland and in almost all metropolitan areas, an ever increasing mobility of people, environmental stress by increasing transport volumes, landscape deterioration by new infrastructure and absence of politically accepted sound economic market principles in the transport sector necessitate policy-makers at all levels to undertake emergency strategies in which integration and coherence benefits are neglected in favour of short-term successes for a limited territory. The discussion on "missing links" and "missing networks" is illustrative for this situation, even though the implementation off the plans for new transnational European infrastructure begins to bear increasingly the fruits of a coherent network. An important problem is however, that the relative position of lagged (often peripheral) regions is increasingly worsened by the development of high speed links which favour only the economic centres of Europe.

The **geo-political changes at the regional level** do not only concern the position of European centres (e.g., the shift from Bonn to Berlin, or the emergence of new capital cities in the former Yugo-Slavia and USSR), but also the former border areas. The **internal** border areas in the EC are likely to receive a sudden improvement in their competitive position in view of their shift from geographical "dead ends" of a country to new gateways. However, the **external** border areas do not have such perspectives, so that their peripheral position may even be aggravated as a result of more integration and cohesion inside the EC. Furthermore, also rural areas and coastal areas and islands will be facing many new challenges without a clear perspective on a structural better position in the "Europe of regions" (see EC, 1991; Amsterdams Historisch Genootschap, 1992).

6. Scope and Organisation of the Book

The previous sections have pointed out that the current geopolitical and socio-economic dynamics has dramatically influenced the traditional role of borders between regions or nation-states. In many regions and countries the economic meaning of borders is changing, although this does not imply that a "border-less" economy is emerging. Changing borders provoke at the same time new issues which are of a socio-cultural and politico-historical nature, such as the sense of social identity, preservation of life style, economic survival, community sense and language. The pathway towards an open network may thus create new barriers which may shape maps of regions and nations which will differ significantly from former administrative delimitations. In light of these observations the present volume aims to bring together a series of contributions on the changing role of borders, the socio-economic consequences of new border policies and functions, the creation of new transport and communications infrastructures in a "border-less" network economy, and the emergence of new barriers hampering the achievement of the full socio-economic benefits of an integrated network economy.

This volume is organized as follows. In the first part (part A) a collection of reflections on the role of new borders and old barriers from an international perspective is offered. The following issues are dealt with: the negative and positive economic functions of frontiers as semi-permeable borders, the influence of cultural differences between countries as barriers in international business life, the interregional disparities and the changes in the European map after the completion of the internal market, the regional barriers and policies after the economic reform in Russia, the extent and nature of socio-economic frictions (including migration) at the

10

U.S. - Mexico border, and the potential of modern communications technologies in overcoming international barriers.

Next, in Part B the attention is more specifically focused on policies and design of a network infrastructure in Europe which serve to overcome the distance barriers in this heterogeneous region after the elimination of most economic intra-European borders. Topics discussed in this part are: changing European transport infrastructures and their regional implications, borders as barriers in the European road network with a particular view on accessibility of European urban agglomerations, barriers in European road-rail networks and connections, the emerging European high speed railway network aiming at overcoming physical barriers in Europe, the potential of European waterways (inland waterways and coastal transport) in overcoming the problem of missing networks as barriers to European integration, the frictions and possibilities of airline systems and related policies in generating socio-economic benefits from an open international network, the new policies and their bottlenecks in the field of telecommunications, and finally the promises and bottlenecks of advanced road transport informatics aiming at alleviating the external costs of transport.

A final reflective paper addresses methodological issues by calling attention for scientific and mental barriers in our problem-solving capabilities regarding a wide spectrum of modern policy issues.

REFERENCES

Amsterdams Historisch Genootschap, **The United States of Europe**, Amsterdam, 1992.

Batten, D.F. and G. Törnqvist, Multilevel Network Barriers: The Methodological Challenge, **Annals of Regional Science**, vol. 24, 1990, pp. 271-287.

Batten, D.F. and B. Johansson, Origins of the Network Economy, Paper 31st European Congress Regional Science Association, Lisbon, August 1991.

Bennett, R. and R.J. Chorley, **Environmental Systems: Philosophy, Analysis and Control**, Princeton University Press, Princeton, 1978.

Camagni, R.P., From City Hierarchy to City Network, **Structure and Change in the Space Economy** (T.R. Lakshmanan and P. Nijkamp, eds.), Springer, Berlin, 1993, pp. 66-90.

Castells, M., **The Informational City**, Basil Blackwell, Oxford, 1989.

Denison, E., **Why Growth Rates Differ**, Brookings Institution, Washington D.C., 1967.

EC, **Europe 2000**, DG Regional Policy, Brussels, 1991.

Fukuyama, F., The End of History?, **The National Interest**, Summer 1989, pp. 3-18.

Kamann, D.J. and P. Nijkamp, Technogenesis: Origin and Diffusion in a Turbulent Environment, **Technological Forecasting and Social Change**, vol. 39, 1991, pp. 45-46.

Molle, W., **The Economics of European Integration**, Darthmouth, Aldershot, 1990.

Nijkamp, P., P. Rietveld and I. Salomon, Barriers in Spatial Interactions and Communications: A Conceptual Exploration, **Annals of Regional Science**, vol. 24, no. 1, 1990, pp. 237-252.

Olson, M., **The Rise and Decline of Nations**, Yale University Press, New Haven, 1982.

Ratti, R. and S. Reichman, Spatial Effects of Borders, **Europe on the Move** (P. Nijkamp, ed.), Avebury, Aldershot, UK, 1993, pp. 115-138.

Sassen, S., **The Global City, New York, London, Tokyo**, Princeton University Press, Princeton, 1991.

Schott, T., International Influence in Science: Beyond Center and Periphery, **Social Science Research**, vol. 17, 1988, pp. 219-238.

Spiekermann, K., and M. Wegener, **Zeitkarten für die Raumplanung**, Working Paper 117, IRPUD, University of Dortmund, 1993.

Part A

BORDERS AND BARRIERS: A CHANGING INTERNATIONAL SCENE

CHAPTER 2

SPATIAL EFFECTS OF FRONTIERS:

OVERVIEW OF DIFFERENT APPROACHES AND THEORIES

OF BORDER REGION DEVELOPMENT

Remigio Ratti

1.   **Introduction**

The revival of the European construction process has, almost by spellbound, introduced the mythical scenario of a "Borderless Europe". The EC aims to realize this large, single market as of the end of 1992, based on the liberalization not only of the movement of goods and people but also of capital, and above all, the possibility of (re)localization of the economic agents' activities. Furthermore, the East European events have substantially changed frontiers, both politically-institutionally and social-economically. This is an important process that implies the breaking down of barriers and obstacles which create discontinuity or jumps in a normal process of communication and diffusion of people, goods, information or knowledge (Nijkamp et al., 1990). In this new setting, it is necessary to evaluate both the discriminating effects of these barriers (or frontier effects) that should be eliminated and the spatial effects of the existence of institutional borders.

The necessity of resorting to theoretical interpretation keys becomes evident regarding these "frontier effects". It is noteworthy that the existing literature is, apart from case study material, very poor in theoretical spatial economic contributions (Button and Rossera, 1990). Besides, the concept of a frontier appears to be elusive, because such barriers may be of a different kind: cultural, linguistic, institutional, physical, political-economic or social. Frontiers have also a polyvalent meaning: positive for the identity construction of single agents, groups or territorial units and negative when the border is perceived as an hostility factor (Ercmann, 1987).

According to historical situations and contingencies, a frontier can be a separating line or, on the contrary, a contact area. By making this distinction, we will better understand how Europe may eliminate some of its boundaries without turning into a "borderless" Europe. To study frontier effects means to identify and evaluate the modality, particularly the spatial one, of those factors that influence, in a distinct manner, the regional development and the normal process of the spatial diffusion of a good, be it physical or immaterial.

In a first (positional) part of the paper our aim is to give an overview of the different approaches which have been (or could be) applied to study spatial effects of frontiers. Examination of the socio-economic literature (Button and Rossera, 1990) has brought us to distinguish between two different views (or interpretation keys) as shown in Figure 1. A frontier is a dual concept (Reichmann, 1989), generally either representing a border as a region located along the boundary (a line representing the jurisdictional limit of a state), or referring to a marginal or peripheral position. Thus two different views come to mind (see Figure 1):

- first, the traditional view, that is the one of the "border area", defined as the territory immediately close to a fixed frontier line (in most cases institutional) inside which the socio-economic effects due to the existence of a border are felt significantly (Hansen, 1977a);

- second, the view of the "frontier limit", according to which the border is seen less as a demarcation line but rather as an external limit, and moreover as a mobile limit. In economic terms, the border is the place where marginal costs are equal to marginal prices (Di Tella, 1982). Every elimination of obstacles to communication will have an economic impact, apart from a distance friction, on the diffusion processes of material or immaterial goods. The field of interest becomes then extremely wide.

The second part of this article is a specific contribution to the theory of border region development; in fact, border regions are most affected by the changes in the institutional border nowadays, and in this field there is a great need for theoretical improvement.

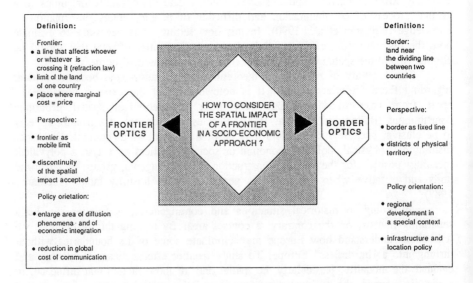

Figure 1: Two different views and interpretation keys in order to evaluate the spatial effects of a frontier

2.   **The Border Area View (Border Region)**

The border view is perhaps the more traditional and is more often found in arguments in empirical studies. As indicated in the English dictionary, the word "border" refers to territories immediately close to the dividing line between two or more countries. The perspective is that of a border territorially defined with a fixed line. This given boundary line is the starting point for the analysis: it offers privileges in particular to the territory close to it. In the areas close to the border line we will observe a series of effects directly connected with the barrier in which the institutional border between two countries is the responsible factor. It is a narrow but rather operational definition of the concept of the border area as treated by Hansen (1977a): "This relates to that part of the natural territory in which economic and social life is directly and significantly influenced by the proximity of an international frontier. We thus consider here only open or potential open regions, excluding regions with a closed natural border situation, like, for example, some parts of the Alps". For what concerns the area to consider, there exist two concepts: the **border area** which extends itself along the boundaries on the national territory (and is therefore an expression of the country's centripetal idea) and the **transbording area** which extends across the political boundary and represents the centrifugal forces (which characterizes the free economy). Yet, even this approach, apparently simple, immediately presents some difficulties: is the border effect exhausting itself in the area territorially adjacent to the border? Evidently not, and it will absolutely always diminish with the progress in telecommunication.

House (1981), for example, already distinguishes a second territory, farther away, which he calls " regional intermediate", by refering to the intermediate area between the border area (coinciding roughly whith the activity area of the "commuters") and the national centers. This concept assumes a typology of relations between national centers, provincial centers and bordering areas supporting an input-output model of transbordering flows.

From the viewpoint of "border region" as the territory immediately close to the dividing line between two or more countries, it is possible to derive four types of approach which, directly or indirectly, can be found or derived from the regional science literature (see Figure 2).

A first economic approach is that of a **"functional"** type (Guichonnet and Raffestin, 1974). For instance, in a case study concerning the regional development of a border area (Biucchi and Gaudard, 1981) one can find, even though it is not always explicitly evident, an attempt at measuring the functions of a frontier (Ratti, 1988); in some cases one will observe real and true flow interruptions (barrier paradigm), in other cases discriminating effects (positive or negative) will be evident which will lead to the phenomenon of man-made differential incomes (manifested, for example, by smuggling), while, again in other cases, one can directly observe some polarizing effects (localization at the border permitting a break in the transport burden).

The rather traditional case, which one often finds in the existing scarce literature on the theory of border effects, is that of the **border barrier** with its corollary of penalizing and discriminating effects. The end thesis is certainly that of Hansen (1983), according to which border areas have traditionally been handicapped

18

and slowed down in their development because of the "principle of separation", in which the central government gives priority to its sectoral policies with respect to the regional and interregional socio-economic relations.

The third theoretical case interprets the "border" in its **filtering role**, as a discriminating mediator between two or more political-institutional systems and between economic systems.

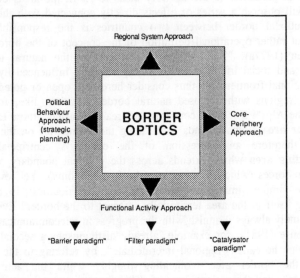

Figure 2: Spatial impact of communication barriers; theoretical approaches in "border optics"

A border separates, in relevant and discriminating terms, two or more systems located in a reciprocal potential tension (House, 1981). Now, accepting the theoretical neoclassical view according to which the economic border is the place where the marginal costs (e.g., of agricultural products) are equal to the selling price (Di Tella, 1982) (i.e., zero profit), the introduction of an institutional border, acting as a filter and changing the economic space, provokes the important concept of differential rent. In other words, the economy of border regions can bring up such income situations, positive or negative, for either side of the border, in which the total net effect - and this is very important - is not necessary a zero sum.

Finally, the fourth theoretical case is that of an **open border** (Courlet, 1988) where the function of contact (and not that of separation) is predominant between two or more political institutional systems or socio-economic subsystems. It is the model of the objective of Europe 1992, of a borderless or open Europe (House, 1980). It is clear that in this context the economic development of the bordering regions will not anymore be determined by the political-institutional differential (i.e., the position rent, positive and negative, due to the effect of membership of a given country), but eventually by comparative advantages of the combination of the two areas. In other words, the "open border" implies (Ratti and Baggi, 1990) the bypassing of the traditional economic concept of the bordering areas (Hansen, 1983) towards that of transborder economies. This situation started in Europe with the new phase of economic reconversion that became necessary after the 1974 crisis; then new repolarizing or specialization processes, new modalities for services and industrial development (e.g., technologically advanced small and medium size enterprises) came into being. In the EC 1992 view, the border effect (Maillat, 1991) is not anymore that of a barrier or that of a screen; the contact function will predominate.

The latter approach for evaluating the development of the border area refers also to the theoretical interpretation key of the "core-periphery" type (Friedman and Weaver, 1979; Giaoutzi and Stratigea, 1991). In fact, in most cases (and almost by definition) the border areas are not only institutional outskirts but also outskirts in an economic sence. Yet, in a world with increasingly complex interrelationships between areas, the dualistic reference to a unique center and to an outskirt appears, most of the time, as a limitation, so that it seems preferable, in view of the dynamic aspects, to develop an interpretation key that uses an explicit referenc to a systematic type of approach (Dauphiné, 1979). The changing form of regional development can be interpreted as a spatial response to changes of a dynamic, but contradictory, economic system (Stillwell, 1991). Thus political disarticulation, like a border, may be identified as specific elements of a regional restructuring process, and it may be shown why there are instabilities in patterns of regional economic development; for example, studies on the evolution of territorial organization of the Canton Ticino have emphasized how, in only one century (or even in a few decades), this area has evolved (Ratti and Di Stefano, 1986) from a situation of a double peripheral area (with respect to the North of the Alps and to Italy) to a spatial position of an intermediate area, where transborder relationships have arisen from the encounter of diverse structures. This observation is also important for strategic planning approaches (Faludi, 1986). If the border really exists, it will influence the individual subjective perception of the economic agents and, particularly, the strategic behaviour of the latter will be influenced (Covin and Slevin, 1989).

There are many questions about this subject (Reichmann, 1989): are people aware of the border existence? Up to what point do the two aspects of separation and of encounter exist in the population's perception? Are there diverging opinions in the perception between two populations separated by a border? "The emphasis is upon individuals, upon their surrounding perception and upon their action space in the specific case of the border region. However, people do not act only following a subjective image of the space but also following the function of external parameters: the economic situation, the internal and external politics of the two bordering countries, and so on. We should therefore integrate (moving towards a regional systems approach) the "microapproach" with a unique study of certain extra-regional processes influencing the bordering region, that is with a "macroapproach" (interconnected environment model). However we realize that the subjective perception, like other individual actions, cannot be aggregated to a unique model of general access" (Leimgruber, 1987).

3. **The View of the "Limiting Frontiers"**

In this view, the border is perceived following the etymology of the English word "frontier", by which the border is seen less as a boundary line but as an external limitation. Thus limitation may be mobile (Turner, 1921). For example, the various constitutive phases of an empire may show mobile borders. The adoption of this hypothesis of a mobile frontier is scientifically meaningful, as it allows to practically operate on a worldwide scale and above all to consider also a discontinuous space (Di Tella, 1982). Our approach refers in particular to the study of barriers to communication with the objective of cost reduction and acceleration of spatial diffusion of innovation, or, in other words, with the objective of the spatial-economic integration (Peschel, 1982). Hence, we also foresee a change in the nature of the function of border areas (Ratti, 1989) and therefore their development modalities.

As shown in Figure 3, it is intended here to simply discuss some of the theoretical approaches that have been suggested or that can be assumed to solve the problem, in the "limiting frontier" view, of the spatial impacts of barriers to communication. Four of these possibilities can be identified.

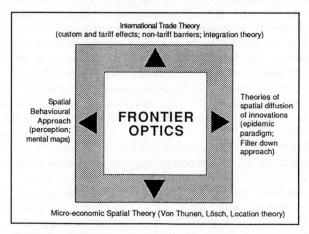

Figure 3: Spatial impact of communication barriers; theoretical approaches in the "frontier optics"

A first approach is the **spatial micro-economic** one (Hansen, 1977b). It dates back to the classical approach in the German School of localization. August Loesch, in his fundamental contribution "Die Raeumliche Ordnung der Wirtschaft" (1940, translated in English in 1954) gives one of the richest images of the border effect on the spatial-economic organization. He distinguishes between two political borders and two economic borders which in rather diverse ways (more incisive for the political borders) have both the effect of interrupting the net of market areas. The political borders have rather the role of "rupturing" the economic space with the consequence of increasing the "holes" in the market areas net, while the economic borders are defined, following the neoclassical concept, as the place where the marginal cost equals the selling price. This border is then determined by the distance, but above all by other barriers to communications, like those barriers that are of real interest in the study such as fiscal, political-cultural, physical and so on.

Moreover, for another classical author, Walter Christaller (1933), the existence of barriers has the inconvenience of limiting the expansion area of commercialized services from central locations. It is interesting however, to see how Christaller enriched his analysis by introducing the dimension "time" and observing how the existence of older centralized locations - therefore, the history - will condition the subsequent spatial organization (for example, the relative decentralized organization of Germany can be explained by traces of centralized locational systems left by the Romans).

Summing up, even though both authors recognize the reality of positive effects, the negative effects - due to the existence of barriers - will determine the spatial effects of distortion and non-integration. The limit of the border is analogous to a desert: "The seam at the boundary gives more or less the impression of a Wasteland; in the far as it is less thickly populated and many products can be obtained only from a distance or not at all." (Loesch, 1940, p.205).

A second approach is that inspired by the theory of **international trade** (Bröcker, 1984). The study of communication barriers plays, therefore, a crucial role in policy of economic integration. The questions arising in this case refer to the effects of economic integration on regional disparity at an aggregate level. The literature, as indicated by Jeanneret (1985), presents only scarce theoretical support: those published around the 1960's as a simulation hypothesis of the integration consequences and those subsequently devoted to provide an interpretation key for the evaluation of the first effects of the trade liberalization of industrial goods in Europe.

As an example of an "ex ante" evaluation we discuss here the contribution of Bourguinat (1961) who also refers to Giersch (1949). Starting from a number of hypotheses referring to the theory of polarized growth, this author concludes that the elimination of barriers - and therefore the modification of economic frontiers - would have an unbalancing effect on the process of spatial growth, as this would be to the advantage of the large centres, i.e., the poles or the central countries. For what concerns the areas at the border, the model of "desert-frontier" would not change, except for those border areas that would also take advantage of the polarization effect, because they belong to the economy of the poles or central countries. The hypotheses used in various empirical verification models of economic integration in Europe refer sometimes to gravitational models of potential. Among the most complete models are those from the regional accessibility as a growth factor (Keeble, 1982) following the traditional expression:

$$P_i = \sum_{j=1}^{n} \frac{M_j}{D_{ij}} + F$$

where
P_i : potential of region i
M_j : activity volume in region j
D_{ij} : global transportation costs between region i and region j
F : customs taxes in the case of the existence of a border between region i and region j

In this case the effect of a barrier modification is simply reflected by the variations of a customs tax. On the basis of such gravity models the theory foresees, at an aggregate level, rather a reinforcement of the central area with respect to pheripheral areas. However, the real situation in the peripheral border areas shows a strong influence by the historical evolution: "If at all, a distance variable can only explain the patterns of production and trade on a aggregate level. This distance variable is neither equivalent to the transportation costs of today, nor does it fully represent the communication of today. It rather reflects the influence of the past on the contemporary spatial pattern of production and trade" (Peschel, 1981).

Among the studies of an international character Herman et al. (1982) adopt a regression analysis in order to quantify the influence of cultural factors and to compare them to those bound to distance. The central hypothesis is that the communication costs have an important weight as much as those connected to the distance. These communication costs exist both at the supply level (knowledge of markets) and at the demand level (consumers information) and are supposed to be lower as the cultural and lingual proximity is better (Maggi, 1989). The existence of this latter proximity effect - and therefore, on the contrary, of linguistic-cultural barriers - is shown by Jeanneret (1985) in his thesis on interchanges of industrial goods and services among the different Swiss lingual regions and the bordering countries.

A third approach relates to the analysis of the **spatial individual perception** (Huriot and Perreur, 1990). The concept of border, interpreted as "limit", is positioned in the center of the interest in new propositions on the "geography of perception". Man owns and perceives a specific territory where extension is, at first, a function of his "vissuto" (timespan lived there). In this context, the border becomes a central notion and enters in strict relation with the action and the perception that man has about space. It is important, therefore, to define "mental maps" (Colledge, 1988); the latter will inform the researcher about the effects of the border at a perception level and of the regional identity. At an empirical level, some authors (Leimgruber, 1980) propose a useful differentiation on a hierarchical level of three spaces: the first level is that of the daily action space (the space that is immediately perceived); the second is the space of the subjective perception (built around a system of values and information) and the third, the largest one, is a "Prozessraum" (a space of processes) inside which, more objectively, the socio-economic and political process are functioning. Now, it is in the confrontation between this third space ("objective") and the individual space ("subjective") that the economist can find an ideal approach for measuring and interpreting the effective role of certain barriers to communication. However, the theoretical and methodological approach is still waiting for further solid contributions.

Finally, a fourth approach to the study of the spatial impact of communication barriers is the one developed in the theories of **spatial diffusion of innovations** (Brown, 1981). The topic of the spatial diffusion of technological innovations (Camagni, 1991) assumes a double centrality; in the first place, because the technological innovation is considered nowadays as a crucial variable in economic development; in the second place, because communication is particularly related to immaterial flows of information and knowledge. In this field, the studies on industrial economics and on geography have tended to follow the tracks indicated by three paradigms: the **epidemic** (or neighbourhood) paradigm, the **hierarchical** paradigm and the **network** paradigm.

The first paradigm, the epidemic one, sees the diffusion of innovation happening by contagion as a function of the communication channels and inversely related to the obstacles due to the distance or other factors of economic, sociological or cultural nature. Following the second paradigm, the hierarchical one, the diffusion of innovations is not happening simply as a decreasing function of distance but more precisely it follows the urban hierarchy. Here we are in the geographical tradition of Christaller and Haegerstrand, but the economist has been able to easily insert specific arguments following the theory of "filtering down". Particularly, it is asserted that the role of the urban media is that of limiting the uncertainty level because of the important economies of agglomeration (Camagni and Cappellin, 1984). Finally, the spatial differentiation in the selection environment is an important aspect of the origin and diffusion of new ideas and innovations. This is to a large extent determined by the network freedom and participation of economic actors. "Network cooperation between actors creates a synergetic surplus. Those actors who succeed to dominate other actors or even entire network segments will consume the synergetic surplus at the cost of others. Dominant actors will therefore, through these network relations, dominate those areas where they are situated. Distribution of power over the participants of a network and the ability to monopolize strategic information in a network are important for the diffusion of innovations and for the related distribution of incomes generated" (Kamann, and Nijkamp, 1991).

In a spatial perspective, the analysis of the diffusion of innovations (Ratti, 1991) - and therefore the analysis of barriers to innovations - should be conducted accounting for various relevant geographical subdivisions, from the national one to the local one, considering particularly the phenomenon at hand as the result of three forces: the hierarchical force, the neighbourhood force (epidemic) and the network component.

4.   **Elements of a Theory of Border Region Development**
The interest in problems of the development of border areas in Europe has distinctly increased after the introduction of the European Frame Convention on transborder cooperation of collectivities or territorial authorities (Conseil de L'Europe, Madrid, 21 May 1980). This convention has on the one hand anticipated the objectives of the communitarian Europe for the year 1992 and the openings toward East Europe and on the other hand started to reassure the period of transition toward a real Europe of Regions. If the political objective relevant to the construction strategy of the Europe of Regions is clearly stated, it appears however more difficult to understand the development modalities of these areas. First, the theory - specially the one about localization - presupposes that these regions be generally dominated by conflicting relations (House, 1980), that is, penalized in their development. Second, emphirical observation shows that some of these border areas are named among those that are developed most (Gaudard, 1971, Ratti, 1971, Hansen, 1983), and also present the characteristics of the emerging peripheral

regions (Ratti and Di Stefano, 1986). Since then, it appeared necessary to abandon the simple static vision in order to examine the development processes bound to these border regions.

In this chapter, we will examine the traditional approach, which considers the border regions as being economically penalized, and those approaches which are based on theories of international division of labour and revenues. The necesssity for new theoretical frameworks geared towards the concept of a "border area of contact" gives us the opportunity to develop an original approach, based on industrial organisation theory and on the operators' strategic behaviour in overcoming the "border obstacle".

4.1 The traditional hypothesis of border region penalization

The interrelated frame between political-institutional and socio-economic subsystems allows us to point out the contribution of two classical authors on spatial analysis.

Christaller (1933) already recognizes the principle of the socio-political separation of the border as the third spatial organization system, from the viewpoint of the economic logic concerning the organization principles of markets and transportation. The border is recognized as an artificial distorting element of market areas and central places which will allow, in those regions where its effects manifest themselves, only a limited economic development. The border is a factor that provokes the segmentation of remote regions from central places. The investment costs increase is tied to the high risk of instability typical of the border areas. In the border regions the accumulation of these negative effects will inhibit the formation of central places having a high degree of complementarity and with a strong capacity of development.

Loesch (1940) emphasizes the conflict between political and economic objectives for this type of regions: to the economic priority order - efficiency, "Kultur" (culture), power, continuity - corresponds a political priority order which is exactly reverse - continuity, power, "Kultur", efficiency - (for example, political issues such as custom's taxes separate sometimes complementary economic areas such that public contracts and military objectives introduce some real barriers). The arising barriers provoke a negative discriminating effect for this type of peripheral areas.

It is true, even in the traditional localization theory, that the border also creates favourable effects, witness the case of border tax abolishment for the transportation sector (Ratti, 1971; Spehl, 1982) and the emergence of "tariff factories" as a response to political protectionism, that is, investments in foreign neighbouring areas in order to more easily penetrate the market of the other country (Peach, 1987). All these elements, together with the economic liberalization period, have disappeared or have seen their nature modified by rationalization, economic integration and new technologies (Ratti, 1988).

The above considerations have pointed out the weakness of localization theory with an essentially static character. Therefore, if the hypothesis of the penalizing effect is plausible, it does not really seem to be confirmed, but if so, mainly in relation with general factors of political and economic order. Regarding the negative effects for peripheral border areas, the case of Alsace, unfairly treated for decades because of instability and political centralization (Urban, 1971), and that of Ticino, penalized first by the constitution of the Swiss Custom Union and next by the foundation of the Italian National State, are eloquent cases in this context.

To conclude, the actual literature on the matter leads us to assert that the simple phenomenon of negative effects due to the border should not be seen as a "theory of border region development". On the contrary, this development must be interpreted in the framework of a joint and dynamic action of the process of political and socio-economic order.

4.2 The development of border regions from the viewpoint of international division of labour

A more promising theoretical framework that is able to interpret the development process of the border regions, is based on more dynamic approaches to localization, which consider these areas not only in their national space but also in the wide context of the emergence of the world economy (Michalet, 1976), accounting for the spatial division of labour. In current production and market conditions, it is the search for a differentiated revenue which drives the process towards a territorial organization made up by a hierachical and spatial distribution of production segments, functionally and sectorally polyvalent (Aydalot, 1986a).

What is then the place of border regions in this process of organized dispersion of activities? Can some intrinsic characteristics in relation to other peripheral regions be defined? If yes, how could the consequences for their socio-economic development be appreciated? Considering the spatial and international division of labour model, the border regions - provided that they are really open - present some attractive characteristics for the localization of specific segments of production activities for three main reasons:

a. Economic order bound to a proximity effect. A border region, even being a portion of a national territory, is necessarily at the same time an area of separation and of contact. It therefore constitutes a tension space but, simultaneously, it acts in some way as a gateway to the other country. An eventual localization in this area - whether in the nationally territory or in the contiguous foreign space - can be very attractive, because it will profit from the proximity advantages, i.e. the presence in the area of economic operators from two or more political-institutional systems and the benefits determined by the logic of spatial delocalisation of activities.

b. Social reasons which are bound to the flexibilty of the labour force availability. The border, because of its legal and control functions, created - even easier than anywhere else - some discriminating conditions in the labour force as a function of the needs proper to displaced production units - discriminations created by law or "de facto" because of different motivations to the workmanship of the border labour force (Doeringer and Priore, 1971).

c. Cultural reasons which are bound to the permeability of local societies. The border region can be considered to have easier permeability due to a series of circumstances: the necessary practice of the adoption spirit, frequent migratory phenomena, different values regarding identities and traditions. The behavioural analysis of the parties (Spehl, 1982) and the perception of the transborder reality (Leimgruber, 1987) plays in fact a significant role in the border-effect manifestation.

If we consider the case of an open border, two types of revenues are created (Di Tella, 1982; Turner, 1921):

a. a differential revenue which is determined, for example, by a discrimination in wages between the areas divided by the border;

b. a position rent which is determined by the effect of proximity that might create some specific comparative advantages.

These two types of revenue have consequences which manifest themselves in an unequal way, both in "sign" and intensity: the global effect can be a positive value, a zero sum or a negative value for the whole transborder region. The fragility and instability of the elements at the base of the revenues lead, without any doubt, to resort to a dynamic approach to these phenomena. We will now try to examine whether these characteristics really position border regions in the logic of the spatial organization process described above.

Numerous case studies seem to confirm a new thesis which may act as a potential catalyst of certain border areas for the localization of distributed activities inside the spatial hierachy of production.

First, the existence of a significant effect of proximity on socio-economic and cultural patterns has been demonstrated. This phenomenon determines for the regions at both sides of the border some privileged relations, inter alia a level of investments and of exchange above average (Jeanneret, 1985). The case of Swiss and German entrepreneurial investments in the Alsace (Datar, 1974) confirms the logic of minimisation of production costs at the level of simple establishments.

Decisive evidence on the existence of a process of spatial and hierarchical division of labour is given by results on the labour market. An empirical study covering all European border-regions shows the existence of important differences in the remuneration level at both sides of the border. This makes up a favourable potential for the creation, maintenance or development in the richest areas of production segments strongly conditioned by workmanship costs (Ricq, 1981). The dualism of the employment market, characterized by the strong presence of transborder workers, becomes then the thermometer of the catalyst role of the border in the process of spatial diffusion of activities. This situation is also noted in studies concerning transborder interactions between Mexico and the U.S.A (Hansen, 1981; Peach, 1987) and in the case of the transborder triangle area "Alsace-Baden Württemberg-Basel", of the axis Swiss-French Jura and Ticino (Biucchi and Gaudard, 1981).

4.3   A new theoretical framework on "borders as contact areas": the network strategy

In the current developments in Europe, it is important to emphasize the theoretical hypotheses that are not only linked to the effects of a barrier existence, but also to the removal of these barriers and the construction of contact spaces allowing inter-regional cooperation (Ratti and Baggi, 1990, Ratti, 1989). For this purpose, we suggest an original approach based on industrial organisation theory. A border, whether institutional or of any other nature, is almost always characterized by a situation of cumulative uncertainty and growing complexity, and often signifies imperfect information or lack of transparency. The profitable management of this uncertainty and related transaction costs needs a necessary connection with modern theory of industrial organizations, particularly the strategy of horizontal integration.

(i) Postulates

*   Beside the "firm" and the "market", there exists a third form of organization and regulation of production: the cooperation between enterprises (Richardson, 1972: "The dichotomy between firm and market, between direct and spontaneous coordination, is misleading; it ignores the institutional fact of interfirm cooperation and assumes away the distinct method of coordination that this can provide").

*   The existence of "uncertainty" requires new functions, particularly of coordination (Camagni, 1991: "The presence of unescapable static and dynamic uncertainty in the real world implies the presence of extra costs and therefore new functions to cope with these costs and new "operators or institutions" organizing these functions and shaping factual behaviour").

*   The concept of "transaction costs" constitutes the discriminating instrument between the functions assumed by the firm, the market or the cooperation (Coase, 1937: "A firm will expand until the cost of organizing an extra-transaction within the firm becomes equal to the cost of carrying out the same transaction by means of an exchange on the open market or the cost of organizing within another firm").

(ii) Thesis

The existence of market distortions and transaction costs constrains the enterprise to adopt two types of strategic behaviour:

*   vertical integration, following the classical reasoning (Williamson, 1975, 1985, 1986);

*   horizontal integration, as an intermediary organization form, more indulgent and based upon a logic of dialogue (Porter, 1980, 1986), particularly attractive for the SME (Small and Medium Enterprises) searching for "synergies" (Kamann and Strijker, 1991).

There is a firm probability that these intermediary forms of cooperation will be territory-dependent, because of the need of performing by following a common code of behaviour (Christensen, 1988: "The distance of dialogue is restricted by the need of common code and the need of face-to-face contacts.....This need for proximity is based on the assumption that a common code is embedded in a contextual macroframe characterized by common language, law, value, social background and joint ability of orientation").

(iii) Corollaries

The existence of a "border" - or any other form of "barrier to the communication" - constitutes immediately a determinant factor of uncertainty and

28

transaction costs. The study of these "borders" or "barriers" becomes then a crucial element in the constitution and dynamic explanation of an intermediary organization of the "réseau (network)" type (See Figure 4).

a. The degree of integration of a firm, constituted by an agreement with other enterprises (from the simple licence agreement to the joint venture to a branch), is a function of the transaction costs or the market access costs (CT-CT or CT'-CT'), or of the control costs of the developed interfirm organization (CC-CC or CC'-CC') and also of a preference curve for integration, corresponding to the demand curve (D-D or D'-D').

b. The transaction costs are an exogenous constraining data. Below a certain level (CT'-CT'), the firm will have an interest in further developing internal organization. Beyond that point, an inter-enterprise cooperation would constitute a less expensive option in relation to the market solution.

c. The control costs are represented by a growing function of the "integration quantity". The points E1 and E2 are situations where there are equivalences between the possibility of recurring to the market and that of organizing certain functions of production with other enterprises.

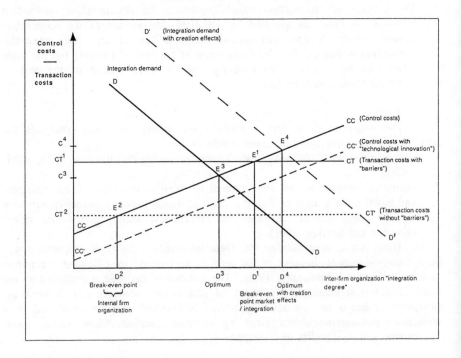

Figure 4: The degrees of integration of a firm (transaction costs, control costs and preference to the integration)

The following remarks are to be made here.

a. The optimum is established by considering the demand curve, that is, the preference curve of the integration. The point E3 is lower than E1, because it is possible to account for a certain fear due to the risks of all external cooperation formulas.

b. The presence of a border or a barrier signifies a line of high transaction costs (CT'-CT'). It will then allow some intermediary solutions for an integration as high as the market distortion. All uncertainty reductions due to the barrier-border would need to be approached by means of market solutions. This indicates that the cooperation solutions are not necessarily stable nor better.

c. The opportunity of the firm to take advantage of a planned solution with other enterprises consists in the lowering of the curve CC-CC toward CC'-CC', by technological innovation and management. This shows the innovative character of the network, but does not necessarily guarantee that it will be advantageous to the firm in absolute terms.

d. Our reasoning has been conducted in terms of minimization of costs. Regarding the objection that the resilient integration requires also a creation effect, it is possible to answer that the preference curve may be displaced upward (from D-D toward D'-D'). This will also determine an optimum (E4) which will even be above the transaction costs, having as a consequence a particularly high integration degree.

Finally, even when for the time being the trend of some transaction costs is leaning downward, following the idea of a new Europe without borders, the relevance and the continuity of an organization in a network depends on its capacity to innovate in terms of both minimizing control costs and of value creation.

In conclusion, in the new context of open borders, the theoretical analysis suggests that the economic development of border areas will not be determined by the political-institutional differential (and therefore by the differentiated position of profits, positive or negative, due to the effect of belonging to a given nation), but more likely by the real net advantages of both border areas. The "open border" implies the passage from the concept of a border area economy to that of a transborder economy. This situation may imply quick and fundamental adjustments. Hence, the strategic behaviour of the partners is particularly crucial. A strategy of supporting such a cooperation network is the most efficient approach to overcome persistent or residual obstacles and uncertainty situations typical of a border area. But, all this needs to be supported by a strategy of funtional synergies, that are able to manifest themselves at a level covering the whole transborder area in a timely manner like in the case of the filter border.

REFERENCES

Aydalot, Ph., Les Technologies Nouvelles et les Formes Actuelles de la Division Spatiale du Travail. **Dossier du Centre Economie, Espace, Environment**, 47, Paris, 1986.

Biucchi, B.M. and Gaudard, G. (eds.), **Régions Frontalières**, Georgi, St.-Saphorin, Switzerland, 1981.

Bourguinat, H., **Espace Économique et Intégration Européenne**, SEDES, Paris, France, 1961.

Bröcker, J., How Do International Trade Barriers Affect Interregional Trade? **Regional and Industrial Development Theories, Models and Empirical Evidence**, Elsevier, Amsterdam, 1984, pp. 134-147.

Brown, L., **Innovation Diffusion**, Methuen, London & New York, 1981.

Button K., and Rossera, F., , Barriers to Communication. A Literature Review, **The Annals of Regional Science**, 24 (4), 1990, pp. 337-357.

Camagni, R. (ed.), **Innovation Networks: Spatial Perspectives**, Belhaven Press, London and New York, 1991.

Camagni, R, and R. Cappellin, **Cambiamento Technologico e Diffusione Territoriale**, F. Angeli, Milano, 1984.

Christaller, W., **Die zentrale Orte in Süddeutschland**, Wissenschaftliche Buchgesellschaft, Darmstadt, 1933.

Christensen, P.R., **Enterprise Flexibility and Regional Networks**, Paper presented at Annual Congress RSA, 1988.

Coase, R.H., The Nature of Firm, **Economica**, 4, 1937.

Courlet, C., La Frontière: Couture ou Coupure? **Economie et Humanisme**, 301, 1988, pp. 5-12.

Covin, J.G., and D.P. Slevin, Strategic Management of Small Firms in Hostile and Benign Environments, **Strategic Management Journal**, 10 (1), 1989, pp. 75-87.

DATAR, **Investissement Étrangers et Aménagement du Terrutiore: Livre Blanc**, Datar, Paris, France, 1974.

Dauphiné, A., **Espace, Région et Système**, Economica, Paris, France, 1979.

Di Tella, G., The Economics of the Frontier, **Economics in the Long View** (C.P. Kindleberger and G. Do Tella, eds.), **Vol. 1: Models and Methodology**, Macmillan, London and Basingstoke, 1982.

Doeringer, P.B and M.J. Priore, **Internal Labor Markets and Manpower Analysis**, D.C. Heath, Lexington, 1971.

31

Ercmann, S., ed., **Cross-Border Relations: European and North American Perspectives**, Schulthess Polygraphischer Verlag, Zürich, Switzerland, 1987.

Faludi, A., Toward a Theory of Strategic Planning, Neth. **Journal of Housing and Environmental Resources**, 3, 1986, pp. 253-268.

Friedmann, J. and C. Weaver, **Territory and Function**, Edward Arnold, London, UK, 1979.

Gaudard, G., Le Problème des Règions-Frontières Suisses, **Cahiers de l'ISEA**, Paris, France, 1971.

Giaoutzi, M. and A. Stratigea, The Impact of New Information Technologies on Spatial Inequalities, **Regional Science - Retrospect and Prospect** (D. Boyce, P. Nijkamp and D. Shefer, eds.), Springer Verlag, Berlin, 1991, pp. 191-210.

Giersch, H., Economic Union Between Nations and the Location of Industries, **Review of Economic Studies**, 17, 1949, pp. 87-97.

Colledge, R., **Behavioural Modelling in Geography and Planning**, Croom Helm, London and New York, 1988.

Guichonnet, P. and C. Raffestin, **Géographie des Frontières**, Presses Universitaires de France, Paris, 1974.

Hansen, N., Border Regions: a Critique of Spatial Theory and a European Case Study, **Annals of Regional Science**, 11, 1977a, pp. 1-14.

Hansen, N., The Economic Development of Border Regions, **Growth and Change**, 8, 1977b, pp. 2-8.

Hansen, N., Mexico's Border Industry and the International Division of Labor: Abstracts, **Annals of Regional Science**. 15, 1981, pp. 255-270.

Hansen, N., International Cooperation in Border Regions: an Overview and Research Agenda, **International Regional Science Review**, 8 (3), 1983, pp. 255-270.

Hermann, H. et al., **Kommunikationskosten und Internationaler Handel**, Florentz, Münich, FRG, 1982.

House, J.W., Frontier Studies: an Applied Approach, **Political Studies from Spatial Perspectives** (A. Burnett, and P. Taylor, eds.), Wiley, Chichester, 1981.

House, J.W., Frontier Zone. A Conceptual Problem for Policy Makers, **International Regional Science Review**, 1 (4), 1981, pp. 456-477.

Huriot, J.M. and J. Perreur, Distance, Espace et Représentations, **Revue d'Economie Régionale et Urbaine**, 2, 1990, pp. 197-237.

Jeanneret, Ph., **Régions et Frontières Internationales**, EDES, Neuchatel, Switzerland, 1985.

32

Kamann, D. and P. Nijkamp, Technogenesis: Origin and Diffusion in a Turbulent Environment, **Diffusion of Technology and Social Behaviour** (N. Nakicenovic and A. Grübler, eds.), Springer Verlag, Berlin, 1991, pp. 198-222.

Kamann, D. and D. Strijker, The Network Approach: Concepts and Applications, **Innovation Networks: Spatial Perspectives** (R. Camagni, ed.), Bellhaven Press, London and New York, 1991.

Keeble, D., P.L. Owens, and C. Thomson, Regional Accessibility and Economic Potential in the European Community, **Regional Studies**, 16, 1982, pp. 419-432.

Leimgruber, W., Die Grenze als Forschungsobjekt der Geographie, **Regio Basiliensis**, 21, 1980, pp. 67-68.

Leimgruber, W., **Il Confine e la Gente**, Lativa, Varese, Italy, 1987.

Loesch, A., **Die Raumliche Ordnung der Wirtschaft**, G. Fischer, Jena, 1940.

Maggi, R., Towards an Economic Theory of Barriers to Communcation, **Papers of the Regional Science Assocation**, 66, 1989, pp. 131-142.

Maillat, D., Transborder Regions between Members of the EC and Non-Member Countries, **Regional Development Trajectories and the Attainment of the European Internal Market**, (M. Quevit, ed.), GREMI, Paris, France, 1991.

Michalet, Ch. A., **Le Capitalisme Mondial**, Presse Universitaires de France, Paris, 1976.

Nijkamp, P., P. Rietveld, and I. Salomon, Barriers in Spatial Interactions and Communications. A Conceptual Exploration, **Annals of Regional Science**, 24(4), 1990, pp. 237-252.

Peach, J.Z., US-Mexican Border Workers: A Review of Selected Issues and Recent Research, **Cross-Border Relations: European and North American Perspectives** (S. Ercmann, ed.), Schulthess Polygraphischer Verslag, Zürich, Switzerland, 1987.

Peschel, K., International Trade, Integration and Industrial Location, **Regional Science and Urban Economics**, 12, 1982, pp. 247-269.

Peschel, K., On the Impact of Geographic Distance on the Interregional Patterns of Production and Trade, **Environment and Planning**, 13, 1982, pp. 605-622.

Porter, M.E., **Competitive Strategy: Techniques for Analyzing Industries and Competitors**, Free Press, New York, 1980.

Porter, M.E. (ed.), **Competition in Global Industries**, Harvard Business School Press, Boston, USA, 1986.

Prescott, J.R., **Political Frontiers and Boundaries**, Unwin Hyman, London, UK, 1990.

Ratti, R., **I Traffici Internazionali di Transito e la Regione di Chiasso**, Editions Universitaires, Fribourg, Switzerland, 1971.

Ratti, R., Development Theory, Technological Change and Europe's Frontier Region, **High Technology Industry and Innovative Environments: the European Experience** (Ph. Aydalot & D. Keeble, eds.), Routledge, London & New York, 1988.

Ratti, R., Economia di Frontiera: l'Evoluzione di Unconcetto. Barriera Filtro o Luogo d'Incontro?, **Insieme Cultura**, 12, 1989, pp. 37-40.

Ratti, R., Small and Medium-size Enterprises, Local Synergies and Spatial Cycles of Innovation, **Innovation Networks** (R. Camagni, ed.), Belhaven Press, London and New York, 1991.

Ratti, R. and A. Di Stefano, L'innovation Technologique au Tessin, **Innovative Environments in Europe** (Ph. Aydalot, ed.), GREMI, Paris, France, 1986.

Ratti, R. and M. Baggi, Strategies to Overcome Barriers: Theoretical Elements and Empirical Evidence, Working Paper, Workshop NECTAR, Lund, 1990.

Reichmann, S., Barriers and Strategic Planning - **A Tentative Research Formulation**, Paper Presented at NECTAR Meeting, Zürich, Switzerland, 1989.

Richardson, G.A., The Organisation of Industry, **The Economic Journal**, vol 82, 1972, pp. 883-896.

Ricq, Ch., **Les Travailleurs Frontaliers en Europe: Essai de Politique Sociale et Regionale**, Anthropos, Paris, France, 1981.

Rossera, F., Discontinuities and Barriers in Communications. The Case of Swiss Communities of Different Language, **The Annals of Regional Science**, 24 (4), 1990, pp. 319-336.

Spehl, H., Wirkungen der Nationalen Grenze auf Betriebe in Peripheren Regionen - Dargestellt am Beispiel des Saar-lor-lux-Raumes, Report University of Trier, FRG, 1982.

Stillwell, F., Regional Economic Development: an Analytical Framework, **Revue d'Economie Regionale et Urbaine**, vol 14, 1991, pp. 107-115.

Turner, F.J., **The Frontier in American History**, New York, USA, 1921.

Urban, S., L'integration Économique Européenne et l'Évolution Régionale de Part et d'Autre du Rhin, **Economie et Société**, vol 5, 1971, pp. 603-635.

Williamson, O.E., **Markets and Hierarchies. Analysis and Antitrust Implications**, Free Press, New York, 1975.

Williamson, O.E., **Economic Institutions of Capitalism: Firm, Market, Regional Contracting**, Free Press, New York, 1985.

Williamson, O.E., **Economic Organization: Firms, Market and Policy Control**, Wheatsheaf Books, Brighton, 1986.

CHAPTER 3

SPATIAL BARRIERS AND DIFFERENTIATION

OF CULTURE IN EUROPE

Dirk-Jan F. Kamann[1]

1.   One Europe, One Culture?

The unification of Europe coincides with an increased internationalization of activities. More and more companies and organizations have frequent and intensive contact with other organizations from other member states. Sometimes, this happens because of mergers or takeovers. The increase in co-operative agreements and alliances is another cause. The increased internationalisation implies increases in communications between managers, employees and civil servants of different countries. In this **process** of communication people become aware that other people, from different cultural backgrounds, sometimes have different interpretations and implementations of rules and regulations. Our partners abroad interpret our messages in a different way than we originally intended. Many managers find that "they" will interpret uniform EC rules and regulations in a different way. These managers also find that people behave in a different way than they are used to; in negotiations, in business talks and social interaction like over drinks at the hotel bar in the evening. It may be that certain behaviour is considered to be "not done," or "very aggressive," while this was not meant at all. What is noticed, is a **different way of doing, a different way of looking at things**, both in the private and the non-private sector. In other words, many misunderstandings are due to differences in the **cultural background** of the actors concerned.

Our contribution addresses the following two issues:

(1)   **communication problems**
    What is the cause of people not understanding each other very well, even when they speak the same language. This concerns the role of the cultural context for a message.

(2)   **cultural differences between member states**
    This component consists of the following elements:
    (a) how to visualize culture, measure and model it;
    (b) how can we demonstrate a number of differences between member states;
    (c) what does this mean for the management style in a given country;
    (d) what does it mean for international take-overs and alliances.

36

The sequence of topics to be discussed is determined by the following path. We will start with a more general discussion about **communication in the cultural context** (Section 2). In Section 3, we will discuss the possibility of **modelling** culture in a spatial context. We will then continue our discussion of culture with an illustration of the relation between the **national** culture and the management style in a country, where we will use the example of France and the Netherlands (Section 4). Since, according to this example, national differences are rather important, we will go deeper into national differences in Section 5. Given the differences found, we will, in Section 6, deal with its opposite: **cultural congruence**. The reason for doing so is, that in cooperative agreements, mergers, joint-ventures and so on, combinations between partners with a high cultural congruence may lead to less mis-communication problems. Further attempts to set up an actual measurement instrument of "culture" are given in Section 7. We will end this contribution with some conclusions and recommendations in Section 8.

2. Communications and the Cultural Context

2.1 Communication
Communication between persons is represented in Figure 1.

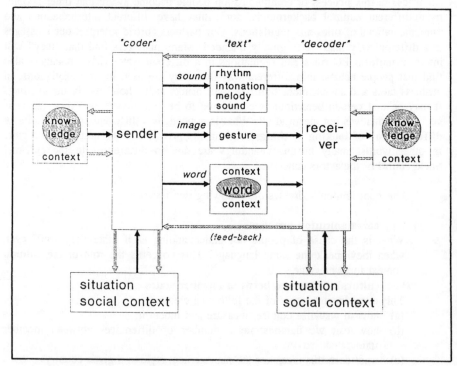

Figure 1: Communication, text and cultural context

The **sender** codes his message from his knowledge, his interpretation of his role, his interpretation of what is suitable in a certain situation, at a certain moment, in a certain place, in a certain social context. He does this in a way he **is used to**, based on his **experience of routines**. He chooses, again based on what he **thinks** is adequate and suitable, a certain mode - face-to-face, telephone, telex, fax, letter, memo, advertising, t.v. commercial or cinema advertising. When he chooses face-to-face communication, he then communicates his message using three elements: word, gesture and sound. He puts the words (what most readers would call text) in a certain form and style and he accompanies this block with a set of so-called additives (sounds, melody, intonation and gesture). The receiver will **decode** the message and interpret it in a certain way, based on his interpretive schemes, the **cognitive maps** that he possesses as a result of his process of socialisation. Again, given the particular social context, place, time and role of the receiver.

As long as sender and receiver work from the same interpretive schemes, there is no problem at all and the message will be decoded and interpreted as it was meant to be. However, as soon as interpretative schemes deviate from each other, or are dissimilar, we will have problems.

2.2 Interpretative schemes: culture.

A difference in interpretative schemes means that we will value a gesture, a word, a role situation in a different way. These different interpretative schemes coincide with differences in culture. By culture we mean **the conditioned way people look at things**, the way they solve problems, which aspects they focus on when they have to solve a problem, or what they look at. It also refers to the issue "what is good or bad"? Not only as a value judgement, but also in a practical sense; which methods are the **usual** methods and which are the **unconventional** methods? This leads to the collective mental programming (Hofstede, 1991), the common belief set (Kamann and Jagersma, 1993). The experiences we have within a culture in a specific way, become routines. They become an integrated part of our way of responding to things. Sometimes this is so automatic that we are terribly disturbed when somebody else responds in a different way. What then occurs, is miscommunication, misunderstanding, frustration and, sometimes, pure anger.

3. Modelling Culture in a Spatial Context

3.1 Organisational man

A present day person is not only part of society in general, with its socialising forces, but is also an **organisational man**. This means, he is conditioned by that organisation, but, at the same time, as part of that organisation, also determines the nature of that very same organisational culture. Therefore, we say that the organizational culture of an enterprise in a certain area arises in exchange with the - spatially differentiated -environment of that organization. The transient society in that area is influenced by the past of that society and the impact of higher level societies (national, supra-national) (Boog, et al., 1991, p.5). Of course, the organisation also has a life cycle, with crises and shifts in generally accepted ways of solving problems. What we presently observe in an organisation, is the resultant of this all, grown from a historical pattern.

3.2 Spatial differences in culture

Given the spatial dimensions we want to emphasize, we may ask "what determines the behaviour in action and thinking of such an actor in a certain area". Apart from everybody's **personal** genetic properties and personal socialization, we will find the following factors in the process of socialization[2]:

(1) the national culture[3];
(2) the regional or sub-national culture;
(3) the branch culture of someone's profession;
(4) the skill-level and type of work (managerial, administrative, or production work).

Since people usually work in firms, semi-state bodies or public agencies, they are influenced by the organisational culture. In its turn, the organisational culture is influenced by the cultures of its organisational participants. Some of these have a stronger influence than others; very few organisations have participants with identical personalities and no sub-cultures.

The typical company - organisational culture therefore is determined by:

(1) the corporate culture of the parent company (Kilman, 1985);
(2) the life cycle and stage in the life-cycle of the firm (Schein, 1985);
(3) the technology/product market combination in which the company is working (Kamann and Jagersma, 1993), mixed with the influence of the branch culture;
(4) the outcome of the various sub-cultures of the participants in the organisation; and as a result of this: the above mentioned national culture, regional culture, branch culture, skill levels.

3.3 A general model

Figure 2 shows the elements mentioned in a general model for companies or, more general: organisations[4]. We propose a LISREL type approach for further testing and estimating the model[5]. Figure 2 shows a case with country 1 with a company **a** which is the subsidiary of Parent **A** in country 2.

The **exogenous** (latent) variables in the model are:

Xi_1 and Xi_2 for the two national cultures

Xi_3 for the Branch culture

Xi_4 and Xi_5 for the Product/Market Combinations (PMC) of the parent and subsidiary

Xi_6 for the Transnational culture (e.g. EC regulations)

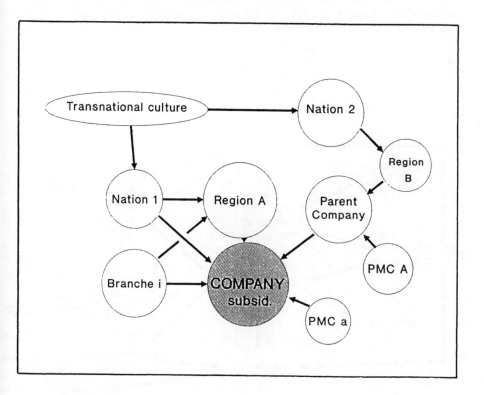

Figure 2: The general LISREL model for spatial organisational culture

The **endogenous** latent variable is:

Eta₁ for the Company culture of the subsidiary

The **mesogenous**[6] latent variables of the model are:

Eta₂ for the Culture in the Region of the subsidiary;
Eta₃ for the Culture of the Parent Company

For cases where the parent company works on the same PMC as the subsidiary, we may eliminate variable Xi_5. Each latent variable is based on a set of observable - measurable - variables. In Section 5, we will give some examples of

40

these observable variables that can be used. A more specified model is given in Figure 3. Two companies, in different trades, are established in two different regions. Each company has three subsidiaries, branch-plants or "locations", spread over the two regions.

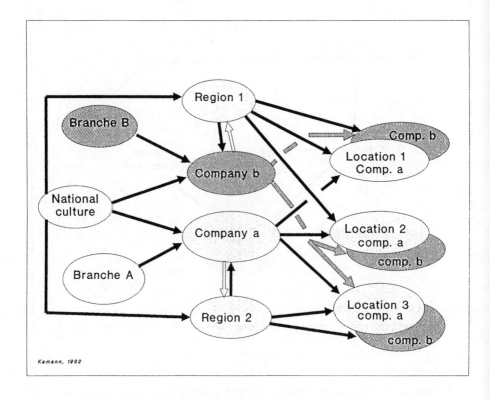

Kamann, 1992

Figure 3: Two-region LISREL-model for 3 locations and 2 companies

The latent variables in the model are:

exogenous (latent) variables[7]:

Xi$_1$ = the national culture
Xi$_2$ = the culture of Branch **A**
Xi$_3$ = the culture of Branch **B**

mesogenous latent variables:

Eta_1 = culture of Region 1
Eta_2 = culture of Region 2
Eta_3 = the culture of Company a
Eta_4 = the culture of Company b

endogenous latent variables:

Eta_5 = the culture of Location 1, in Region 1, of Company a
Eta_6 = the culture of Location 1, in Region 1, of Company b
Eta_7 = the culture of Location 2, in Region 1, of Company a
Eta_8 = the culture of Location 2, in Region 1, of Company b
Eta_9 = the culture of Location 3, in Region 2, of Company a
Eta_{10} = the culture of Location 3, in Region 2, of Company b

The measurement - through observable variables - required to estimate the model, is still under construction and in development. In the rest of this contribution, we will report on the state of this art and the recommended direction of further research.

4. National Culture, Management Style and Cultural Centrism - an Example: France and the Netherlands

4.1 Introduction

The first step in de model is based on the assumptions, that **national cultures** will be reflected in the management styles practised in such a nation, i.e., in organisational cultures of the companies inside a nation. In addition to this, we state that managers from a particular country will attempt to **reshape** the culture of a subsidiary abroad along the nature of the culture they are familiar with: their own. We could name this type of behaviour "**cultural centrism**". To illustrate this, we will give an example, based on a study by Nijborg (1992; see also Nijborg and Kamann, 1993). It describes how cultural differences between France and the Netherlands result in differences in management styles, and in organizational behaviour. Such differences are **transferred to, or implanted into** the organisational culture of the foreign subsidiary.

4.2 The differences between France and the Netherlands

The differences between France and the Netherlands can be summarised as follows. France is a more hierarchical society than the Netherlands. In the Netherlands, the egalitarian idea plays an important role. Because of this, the French are more inclined to obey authorities. The Dutch are more inclined to revolt to authority. The French society has experienced more revolutions, more violence. Within the Dutch society, violence and conflicts are rejected. The motto is, to cooperate and negotiate in harmony, until a compromise has been reached.

In **education**, we find that in France, competition, the result, the ability to show you are better than the rest, plays a central role. In the Dutch system, social adaptation and the ability *not* to deviate from the group, are key elements.

The **political** system of France allows for a much larger distance between the "national leader" and the common man than in the Netherlands.

As to the **trade unions**, we also find differences. France shows both divided employers' associations and trade unions. Lack of mutual trust prevents a close cooperation, both between groups of the same nature, and between the opposing camps. Described in a somewhat over-stated way, we could say that the Netherlands show a close cooperation between all parties involved and a relation based on loyalty, while the French relation is one based on mistrust.

4.3   The results: differences in organizational behaviour

The next result[8] gives a summary of the culturally related differences in organizational behaviour between French and Dutch employees. In the example four dimensions are used to show these differences: (1) co-operation; (2) leadership; (3) decision-making; (4) interpersonal relations.

Cooperation

FRANCE	THE NETHERLANDS
cooperation, based on authority	cooperation, based on loyalty
little willingness to cooperate	large willingness to cooperate
less delegation	more delegation
conflicts in the organisation are normal	conflicts are avoided
less cooperation according to (un)written rules and procedures (abstract)	more cooperation based on (un)written rules (concrete)
employees less scared to disagree with superior	employees afraid to disagree with boss
confrontation occurs more frequent	harmony-oriented behaviour dominates; confrontation avoidance
more group-oriented/responsible attitude and commitment inside the group (department)	individual duty bound behaviour, with one's own responsibility and commitment

Leadership

FRANCE	THE NETHERLANDS
intense supervision is appreciated	intense supervision meets a negative valuation
a directive, persuasive superior is appreciated more	a participative superior is appreciated more
higher and lower skilled employees share the same values about authority	higher skilled employees value authority as less important than lower skilled employees
mixed feelings of superior about sharing leadership and initiative	ideological support by superior in sharing leadership and initiative
obeys authority	authority resistant

Decision taking

FRANCE	THE NETHERLANDS
autocratic, paternalistic	consultative
independent decision making	group decisions
mixed feelings superior to participation subordinates in decision making	ideological support superior to participation by subordinates; participative
shorter process of decision making: - less participation all parties - using lobby and pressure - confrontation (discretely) - verbal violence	longer process of decision making: - all parties participate - consultation and exchange of views; - conflict avoidance; harmony; consensus; compromises

Interpersonal relations

FRANCE	THE NETHERLANDS
status and recognition important	interpersonal relations important
formal work relations are determined by hierarchical levels and status; relations determined by department	informal work relations less determined by hierarchy; egalitarian; not determined by department
result/"self-realisation" central with superior	social adaptation central to superior

4.4   Conclusions: it really makes a difference

The example shows that national cultural differences do make a difference and *are* translated into different ways in which managers and employees in organisations from different national backgrounds deal with each other and go about things. In the empirical part of her study, Nijborg (1992) analysed a Dutch company, which was taken over recently by a French company. Indeed, she found that

* both Dutch and French managers became aware of the differences;
* both nationalities had criticism;
* already, there were misjudgments among the French, based on interpreting Dutch behaviour as if it were the French way;
* a mixture of the two cultures was arising; the French "top" was planning to impose the French way of doing (culture) to the Dutch subsidiary; especially in decision making procedures.

5.   Measuring Differences Between Countries

5.1   Introduction

Accepting the fact, that indeed, **national** differences in culture result in differences in management style, we will now describe **how** managers and employees from different countries differ in their views of certain aspects. These aspects are only a selected part of the total set of **observable variables** to be used in our models of Section 3. The variables discussed here are:

* **work related:**
(1) the **meaning** and importance of work/labour;
(2) **values** derived from work;
(3) **motivation** for work and related aims in life;
(4) risk behaviour;
(5) attitudes towards group decision making;

* **general attitudes:**
(6) masculinity;
(7) power distance-work/labour.

5.2   The meaning of work

George England and his group researched the **meaning of work** for people. They defined "labour centrality" as "the meaning of work in the life of an individual at whatever moment". (England and others, 1984, p.4). The importance of things like leisure, community, religion and family were related to the importance of work. In addition to this, managers were asked to express the importance of work on a hundred point scale. The total result was assembled into one score. Figure 4 gives these results for eight countries. The figure shows that, for instance, the scores of persons in England and Germany are quite close. In other words, people in these two countries consider work at a similar level of importance.

England and his colleagues also looked into what people thought of the **role** of work: "what does it mean to you?" Table 1 gives the result of the replies. In this table we see that test persons from rather similar countries, like Germany and the Netherlands who thought work to be equally important, still differed in **why** they think work is important. Especially if we look at the deviations related to the average of the whole group we see that:

(1) Germans are more inclined to see work as a source of income than the Dutch. The Dutch consider work to be something interesting and satisfying compared to the average, while the Germans are below that average.

(2) The Dutch consider work much more as a way of establishing contact with other people, while Germans see this as less of an element.

(3) The Dutch see work more as a way of making oneself useful to society than the Germans. The Germans focus to a much larger extent on the status and prestige derived from work.

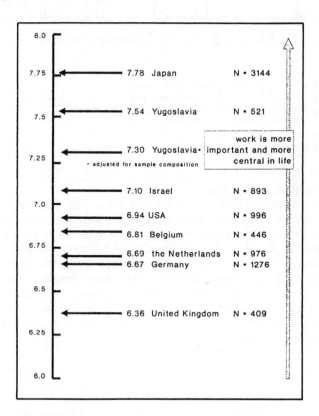

Figure 4: Work centrality according to the group of England

46

Country	N	Income 1	Interest 2	Contacts 3	Serve 4	Occupied 5	Status 6
Japan	3180	45.4	13.4	14.7	9.3	11.5	5.6
Germany	1264	40.5	16.7	13.1	7.4	11.8	10.1
Belgium	447	35.5	21.3	17.3	10.2	8.7	6.9
United Kingdom	471	34.4	17.9	15.3	10.5	11.0	10.9
Yugoslavia	522	34.1	19.8	9.8	15.1	11.7	9.3
United States	989	33.1	16.8	15.3	11.5	11.3	11.9
Israel	940	31.1	26.2	11.1	13.6	9.4	8.5
Netherlands	979	26.2	23.5	17.9	16.7	10.6	4.9
ALL COUNTRIES[9]	8792	35.0	19.5	14.3	11.8	10.8	8.5

Table 1: The role of work according to England's MOW Group (1985)

where:
1 = working provides you with an income that is needed
2 = working is basically interesting and satisfying to you
3 = working permits you to have interesting contacts with other people
4 = working is a useful way for you to serve society
5 = working keeps you occupied
6 = working gives you status and prestige

5.3 Motivation: aims in life

Bass and Burger (1979) carried out a survey of over three thousand managers in twelve countries. They asked them to rank the numbers of aims and priorities in importance. The subjects were asked to give a score of 1.0 to the highest priority, and a score of 11 to the lowest one. From Table 2 it transpires that self-realisation scores highest among the whole group, although the Netherlands significantly deviates from the group. There, "expertise" is the most important aim. Additionally, the Netherlands and Germany have rather different views on the role of leadership. France, in a number of aspects, coincides with the Netherlands, while in others it coincides with Germany. So, there seems to be no systematic congruence or incongruence between these three countries.

Country or National Grouping	N	Self-realization	Leadership	Expertness	Wealth	Independence
Anglo-American						
USA						
Britain	272	3.33	4.33	6.00	7.33	5.13
	618	4.14	5.18	5.73	7.93	5.36
Low Countries						
Netherlands						
Belgium	441	6.08	6.02	4.40	8.90	4.82
	248	3.83	5.57	4.72	8.33	4.83
Nordic						
Germany/Austr.						
Scandinavia	284	3.40	3.96	4.81	7.71	3.56
	253	3.95	5.90	5.18	8.49	5.07
Latin						
France	154	3.30	6.22	4.33	7.64	5.05
Italy	368	3.45	5.58	6.14	9.12	4.19
Iberia	166	3.02	5.64	4.44	8.96	6.07
Lat-America	142	3.74	5.25	4.73	8.00	5.63
Asiatic						
India	88	4.95	5.65	4.40	7.57	5.24
Japan	48	2.79	3.96	4.13	8.84	3.83

Country or National Grouping	Prestige	Affection	Service	Duty	Security	Pleasure
Anglo-American						
USA	7.42	5.38	6.32	7.66	6.35	6.26
Britain	8.01	4.98	5.88	8.33	4.95	5.54
Low Countries						
Netherlands	7.72	5.70	5.80	5.16	5.15	6.30
Belgium	7.79	5.26	5.89	6.00	6.18	7.60
Nordic						
Germany/Austria	7.25	6.06	6.95	8.88	5.58	7.82
Scandinavia	8.43	4.91	5.44	7.85	4.67	6.14
Latin						
France	8.47	4.43	5.89	6.85	6.46	7.37
Italy	7.76	4.23	6.85	6.81	5.21	6.68
Iberia	7.38	5.31	4.79	6.38	5.58	8.44
Lat-America	5.94	5.73	5.81	7.12	6.25	7.82
Asiatic						
India	6.23	5.89	5.46	5.17	6.57	8.85
Japan	8.44	5.69	7.19	5.32	6.39	8.59

Table 2: Aims in the lives of managers (1.0 is highest; 11.0 is lowest)
Source : Bass and Burger (1979, p.62)

48

5.4   Risk tolerance

In the same survey, Bass and Burger showed to what extent managers are prepared to take risks (Table 3). Dutch managers belong to the category with the highest risk tolerance. German managers clearly show a more distinct risk-avoidance behaviour - they score lowest, together with the Austrians. French managers have identical scores to the Dutch, while the Belgians have identical scores to the Germans[10].

United States	89%	United Kingdom	50%
Japan	67%	India	50%
The Netherlands	61%	Italy	44%
France	61%	Spain/Portugal	44%
Scandinavia	61%	Belgium	39%
Latin America	60%	Germany/Austria	39%

Table 3:   Average risk-tolerance after Bass and Burger (1979, p.91)

Hofstede (1991), in his survey of 116,000 employees of worldwide IBM establishments, also   researched risk attitudes. He defines risk-avoiding behaviour (p.144) as "the degree that members of a culture feel threatened by uncertain or unknown situations". This feeling is expressed in nervous tension and a desire for predictability, "a desire for formal and informal rules and regulations". He calculated the risk-avoiding index for 50 countries and three groups of countries. Table 4 gives a selection from this set. This research indicates a slightly different ranking than the previous one we showed. For instance, also in this table the Belgians are much more hesitant to take risks than the Dutch, but according to this result the Belgians are in the same group as the French, while the Germans continue to show a larger risk-avoidance than the Dutch, although the difference is much smaller. The question here is when talking about the Belgians: are Flemish and Wallonians equally represented in the two survey groups? It would be interesting to divide the Belgians into the two language groups.

ranking	country	score	ranking	country	score
1	Greece	112	29	Germany	65
2	Portugal	104	33	Switzerland	58
5/6	Belgium	94	35	The Netherlands	53
7	Japan	92	38	Norway	50
8	Yugoslavia	88	43	United States	46
10/15	France	86	47/48	Great-Britain	35
10/16	Spain	86	49/50	Sweden	29
23	Italy	75	51	Denmark	23
24/25	Austria	70	53	Singapore	8

Table 4:   Scores on the Uncertainty-avoidance Index by Hofstede (1991, p.145)

5.5   Individuality versus collectivity; deciding alone or in groups.

The last result of Bass and Burger we will show, relates to the degree to which people are willing to be dependent from others in their decision-making, and to what degree people are in favour or against group decision-making. Table 5 shows two double columns. The first set of double columns gives the scores for the dependency on others, both the actual and the preferred situation. The second set gives the scores for group decision-making, again, the estimated actual situation and the preferred situation. The scores show that the German managers would like to be more dependent of others in decision-making than the Dutch and the identical scoring French. The evaluation of the actual situation shows that they think they are less dependent than their Dutch counterparts. French managers think that they are even more independent than others in their decision-making. In contrast to this, German managers would like to be less involved in group decision-making than they actually are.

From this table we can see that the Dutch have a significantly higher score than the Germans. The British and American are at the top. Inhabitants of less developed countries, with lower gross national products, score lower. Singapore is the lowest scoring country. The question is, what does a difference in scores on the individuality index actually mean? The next two tables, again from Hofstede, will explain more about this.

Country	Dependence of others		Individual versus group decisions	
	actual	desired	actual	desired
United States	5.1	6.1	5.7	5.7
Unites Kingdom	4.5	4.8	5.5	5.1
The Netherlands	5.2	5.4	4.9	5.0
Belgium	4.5	5.2	4.9	4.2
Germany/Austria	4.7	6.3	4.7	4.0
Scandinavia	5.5	6.8	4.8	4.5
France	4.2	5.4	4.5	4.2
Italy	4.2	4.8	4.0	3.4
Spain/Portugal	3.6	4.3	4.3	3.3
Italy	4.7	5.6	5.3	4.2
Japan	5.0	6.5	5.1	4.8

Table 5: Dependency on others and opinions about group decision-making.
Source : Bass and Burger, 1979, p.131

Related to this topic, Hofstede developed the so-called **"individuality index"**.
Table 6 gives part of his results.

ran-king	country(groups)	sco-re	ranking	country(groups)	sco-re
1	United States	91	14	Switzerland	68
3	Great-Britain	90	15	Germany	67
4/5	The Netherlands	80	18	Austria	55
7	Italy	76	20	Spain	51
8	Belgium	75	22/23	Japan	46
9	Denmark	74	30	Greece	35
10/11	Sweden	71	33/35	Yugoslavia	27
10/11	France	71	33/35	Portugal	27
13	Norway	69	39/41	Singapore	20

Table 6. Scores on the Individuality Index (Hofstede, p.73)

Collectivistic	Individualistic
People are born into extended families who protect them in exchange for loyalty	One is conditioned to take care of oneself and one's immediate family
Identity is based on the social system	Identity is based on the individual
Children learn to think as "we"	Children learn to think as "I"
Harmony must be preserved; avoid direct confrontation	An honest man should say what he thinks
Expertise, order, duty and security are provided by organisation or clan	Autonomy, variety, pleasure, and individual financial security are sought in the system
Strong context communication	Weak context communication
A mistake leads to shame, loss of face for the individual and his group	A mistake leads to feelings of guilt and loss of self respect
Purpose of education: learn how to do	Purpose of education: learn how to live
Diplomas are entries to groups of higher status	Diplomas increase the economic value and/or self respect
The relation employer-employee is considered as a moral obligation, similar to a family tie	The relation employer-employee is seen as a contract with mutual benefit
Selection of personnel and promotions are determined by the group one belongs to	Selection of personnel and promotions are to be based only on quality and rules
Management means leading groups	Management means leading individuals
Personal relations are more important than duty	Duty is more important than personal relations

Table 7: Differences between collectivistic and individualistic.
Part 1 - general norms, family, school and work.

Collectivistic	Individualistic
Collective interests supersede private ones	Individual interests rank higher than the collective
Private life is subordinate to group life	Everybody is entitled to have privacy
Opinions are determined by group membership	Everybody is supposed to have his own opinion
Laws and rights differ between groups	Laws and rights are equal for everyone
The State plays a dominant role in the economy	The State only plays a limited economic role
The economic system is based on group interests	The economic system is based on individual interests
Lobbies and interest groups dominate politics	Voters are the political power
Media controlled by the state	Freedom of press
Harmony and consensus in society as ideal	Self-realisation for everybody is the ideal

Table 8: Differences between collectivistic and individualistic.
Part 2 - politics and ideas (Hofstede, p.99)

5.6   Masculinity

Hofstede also looked into the degree of masculinity in a society. The next elements are typical for a **feminine** society:
* dominant values are the care for others and the environment.
* people and personal relations are important.
* everybody is assumed to be modest.
* both men and women may be gentle and pay attention to human relations.
* in the family, both father and mother deal with both facts and feelings.
* both boys and girls are allowed to cry but neither are allowed to fight.
* sympathy for the weak and losers.
* the average pupil at school is the norm.
* poor study results at school are no disaster.
* friendly teachers are most valued and appreciated.
* boys and girls choose the same studies and fields.
* you work to live.
* managers use their intuition and aim for consensus.
* emphasis on equity, solidarity and life quality.
* conflicts are solved by compromise and negotiation.

The typical **masculine** society usually had the polar possibilities as their main features.
* money and possessions are important.
* men must be assertive, ambitious and hard.
* sympathy for the strong and winners.
* people live to work.
* emphasis on wages related to work.
* ambitiousness and competition.

Translated into politics and ideas, people in a feminine society are more tolerant than in the more repressive masculine society. There is also more emphasis on environmental questions in a feminine society whereas in the masculine society economic growth has the highest priority.

If we look at the *scores* on the masculinity index, Japan is number 1 with a score of 95, followed by Austria with 79. Italy and Switzerland share the fourth and fifth place (79). Great Britain and Germany share a ninth and tenth place (66). The United States scores lower with 52, Belgium with 54 holds 22nd place. France is thirty-fifth (43). The lowest scores go the Netherlands (14), Norway (8) and Sweden (5). Again, we see a significant difference between Germany, France and the Netherlands. Remarkable is the shared place of Germany and Britain.

5.7   Power distance

Power distance is the degree at which less powerful members of institutions and organizations in a country expect and accept that power is divided (Hofstede, 1991,p.31). This reflects the reaction by people of a country that people in that country are fundamentally unequal. Hofstede found high scores for Roman language countries and in Asian and African countries. The United States and the non-Roman part of Western Europe score significantly lower; Germany and the Netherlands are respectively on the 42nd/44th and 40th place, with scores of 35 and 38. Only Denmark (score 18) and, remarkably, Austria, score lower.

According to Hofstede the score on the power-distance index varies by functional groups. If we compare six functional groups, then the lowest three categories in education score 65 to 90. People with a university or higher polytechnical education score 22 and their managers score 8! In other words, the higher the education and functional levels, the lower the score for power distance.

5.8   Differences

All our examples show quite some differences between national attitudes, norms, values etc. It means that two partners in an alliance from rather different cultural backgrounds may expect some differences in decision making, in interpreting information and communication, in organising activities. Because of this, we will take the next step in Section 6: **given** the fact that cultures differ, which cultures are closest to "us". In this case, "us" being a Dutch organisation.

6.   Cultural Congruence

6.1   The role of national cultures in alliances

When we study international alliances between companies, we find that in many cases non-financial arguments play a role. In other words, (financial) business economics cannot explain why certain potential alliances failed or rather were a success. For instance, during the negotiations for a merger between KLM and British Airways the Dutch trade unions were worried about what in their eyes was the inferior company culture of the British company. Still, in financial circles, it is said that these partners are the ideal partners because of the assumed cultural congruence[11]. Reason why a merger is still considered to be possible *and* likely[12]. Talks about close cooperation between the Belgian airline Sabena and the Dutch KLM were blocked by the French speaking Walloons. A little later, Air France effectively took over Sabena and eliminated its executive powers.

This type of "nationalistic" behaviour implies that in alliances, mergers and takeovers the cultural factor **should** be weighted as important, together with the financial aspects. The next question is then, that if a company has a choice of potential partners from different countries, which partner - from which country - it should prefer, given the slightly unrealistic assumption that all potential partners are equally attractive from a business economic perspective[13].

In the rest of this section we will deal with the question from the perspective of a Dutch company, that tries to minimise "cultural" incongruence with potential foreign partners.

54

6.2 The congruency coefficient

In order to assist in such a decision process, we used a number of international comparisons of managerial attitudes to compute a so-called **congruency coefficient**. Taking the Netherlands as a basis, we expressed the cultural difference of each of the other countries with the Netherlands. To prevent occasional or incidental differences relating to the way of computing the congruency coefficient, we used three different ways of computing the coefficient.

The first way is based on weighted differences and can be written as:

$$CC_{i,1} = \sum_{s=1}^{4} \sqrt{(\frac{x_{1,s}-x_{nl,s}}{x_{nl,s}})^2}$$

where

$cc_{i,1}$ is the Congruency Coefficient #1 of country i

$x_{i,s}$ is the score of a country i on scale s

$x_{nl,s}$ is the score of the Netherlands on scale s

The second coefficient is based on ratios and calculated as:

$$CC_{i,2} = \frac{1}{4}[\sum_{s=1}^{4} \frac{x_{i,s}}{x_{nl,s}}] \; if \; x_{i,s} > x_{nl,s}$$

$$CC_{i,2} = \frac{1}{4}[\sum_{s=1}^{4} \frac{x_{nl,s}}{x_{i,s}}] \; if \; x_{i,s} < x_{nl,s}$$

Finally, the third coefficient is based on the average of absolute differences and calculated as:

$$CC_{i,3} = \frac{1}{4}\sum_{s=1}^{4} (x_{i,s}-x_{nl,s})^2$$

The final results are given in Table 9.

We see in Table 9, that the Scandinavian block belongs to the category "most congruent countries", that is, according to the scales of Hofstede. Canada in some cases, also belongs to that category. When we look at the scores, based on the scales of Bass and Burger, Britain and Belgium are the most congruent, directly followed by the Scandinavian block with France. Both measurement methods indicate a high congruence with Scandinavian countries. Great Britain, according to Hofstede, is only a "fourth category" country which means that when using our criterion it goes into either the fourth block or the fifth block. For Germany the results are quite different depending on the measurement criteria used, i.e., the third, fourth of fifth category. France scores third, and twice in the fourth category. The Germans, relative to other countries almost differ maximally from the Netherlands. The French are in between the Germans and the British.

Scales Hofstede   *Scales Bass & Burger*

criter. 1		criter 2		criter 3		criter 1*		criter 3*	
Netherlnds	0.00	Netherlnds	1.00	Netherlnd	0.00	Netherlnd	0.00	Netherlnd	0.0
Norway	0.81	Norway	1.30	Norway	6.8	Grt Brit	0.66	Belgium	3.5
		Finland	1.35	Finland	10.0	Belgium	0.70	GrBrittan	3.8
Denmark	1.31	Denmark	1.66	Canada	11.0	Norway	0.72		4.1
Finland	1.31	Canada	1.71	Sweden	12.3	Denmark	0.72		4.1
Sweden	1.39	Sweden	1.75	Denmark	14.5	Finland	0.72		4.1
Yougoslav.	2.82	Australia	1.89	Australia	15.3	Sweden	0.72		4.1
Canada	2.83	France	1.90	U.S.	17.0	France	0.80		4.2
Chili	2.99	Spain	1.92	Switzerl.	19.3	U.S.	1.01	Italy	5.4
Thailand	3.07	U.S.	1.94	SouthAfr	19.8	Italy	1.14	U.S.	5.4
Spain	3.49	SouthAfric	2.03	Germany	20.0	Chili/Uru	1.30		6.3
Australia	3.57	Yougoslav	2.03	GreatBrit	20.5	Germany	1.31	Span/Port	6.6
France	3.60	Germany	2.06	Italy	23.5	Span/Port	1.37	Germany	6.6
Korea	3.74	Switzerlnd	2.10	France	25.3				
U.S.	3.75	Belgium	2.10	Spain	27.3				
Uruguay	3.76	Great Brit	2.11	Belgium	28.3				
SouthAfric	4.05	Uruguay	2.11	Thailand	29.3				
Turkey	4.09	Turkey	2.18	Chili	32.3				
Germany	4.18	Chili	2.19	Yougoslav	33.3				
Great-Brit	4.25	Italy	2.20	Turkey	33.5				
Switzerl.	4.35	Portugal	2.20	Uruguay	34.5				
Belgium	4.40	Thailand	2.33	Korea	35.3				
Italy	4.78	Greece	2.51	Portugal	36.5				
Costa Rica	5.09	Korea	2.60	Costa Ric	37.6				
Greece	5.33	Costa Rica	3.15	Greece	42.3				

* For Scandinavia, Iberia and South-America, only group scores were available

** clustering of blocks on pragmatic grounds

Table 9: Most congruent countries with the Netherlands

6.3 Conclusions so far

We have shown that there are differences between national cultures - differences in attitudes. We also demonstrated that an objective way of measuring and weighting the differences seems to be rather difficult. Some of these differences may be explained by differences in the population researched and the methodologies applied. In spite of this, we tend to conclude that:

(1) there are national differences;
(2) managers from Scandinavian countries show the highest cultural congruence with their counterparts from the Netherlands.

7. Further Attempts to Make Differences Measurable and Visible

7.1 Introduction

In the previous sections, we showed that there are differences between national cultures and how they are reflected in different behaviour of people inside organizations. We just saw in Section 6, how difficult it is to **objectively** measure these differences. Because of these noted problems, an objective measurement instrument is presently under construction. The results of it are meant to feed into our models, described in Section 3. In this section, we will describe the methodology used for the instrument. First, we will go into the required level of aggregation (7.2). Then, we will discuss the various methods and concepts used (7.3).

7.2 The desired level of aggregation

What we require, is a methodology that

(1) reflects the relevant aspects and dimensions of **culture**;
(2) indicates differences between the way different actors from different **areas or regions** score on these aspects and dimensions.

The methodology proposed here, has been tested at the level of large multi-site organizations. The method we will describe is called the "**culture sketch**" (Kamann and Jagersma, 1993). The culture sketch is a particular selection of measurement techniques and aspects studied. Therefore, it should be seen as a composite layered method. The weaknesses of one layer are compensated by the advantages of other layers in order to reach a balanced result.

7.3 The culture sketch

The culture sketch, as a layered method, is based on:

(1) the cultural profile;
(2) the six dimensions by Sanders and Neuijen;
(3) the onion model, or layer model;
(4) the four aspects of Hofstede;
(5) the theory of Mastenbroek.

The cultural profile

The cultural profile is based on a full-scale questionnaire among all members of an organization -location, branch etc. It results in scores on 18 theoretical dimensions[14]. The score reflects the way people in an organization perceive a situation related to that dimension. It does not give an absolute score but a perceived situation[15]. The 18 dimensions that we deal with are:

(1) information;	(10) education;
(2) confrontation;	(11) quality orientation;
(3) delegation;	(12) management;
(4) decision-making;	(13) reward;
(5) work pressure;	(14) modelling;
(6) initiative;	(15) training and introduction;
(7) communication;	(16) co-operation;
(8) support;	(17) commitment and
(9) regulation;	(18) a "special"[16].

An example

Figure 5 shows "raw" scores on the dimension "co-operation" by a number of branches of a company[17]. The branch "location A" scores higher than average. The branch "location B" scores significantly lower than average. This location apparently deviates from the other branches. It indicates a potential problem[18] (see further Kamann and Jagersma, 1993).

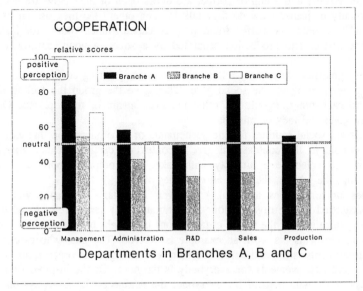

Figure 5: Scores on the Dimension Co-operation

The dimensions by Sanders and Neuijen

Sanders and Neuijen developed 6 dimensions in order to make a typology for companies. This typology relates to the daily affairs inside the company and organization. The dimensions are as follows: (1) process oriented versus result oriented; (2) human oriented versus work oriented; (3) organizational oriented versus professional; (4) open versus closed; (5) rigid control versus loose control; (6) pragmatic versus normative. On each dimension a score on a five point scale is given[19].

The layered onion model

The onion model assumes, that in order to change an organization, one should start with the outside layer. By going inside, one will finally reach the core. The different layers - or features - are:

*   symbols;
*   gossipers and story-tellers;
*   rituals
*   heroes and anti-heroes;
*   values and norms.

Symbols are artifacts, acts or words that apart from having day-to-day meaning, will represent what the organization wants to be or wants to show. Apart from that they are relatively simple to recognize. Examples of these are the colour of the interior of the building, the architecture, the reception, do you need a pass or not? A seat for visitors and a cup of coffee, are doors open or not? How are people dressed - formally or jeans? How do they talk to each other? Do they use christian names or "sir"? Is there one coffee room or a co-called "lunch room" for higher personnel. Are offices and production separated by a street, a pond, a railway or whatever?

Priests, gossipers and story-tellers are those who, during coffee breaks and other social events, bring on the social glue. They give the group the feeling that they belong to each other. People are often not even aware of these priests. Only when they are gone will they be missed.

Rituals are social routines for the participants of an organization that express something essential in the context and give a context to certain events. Drinking coffee together to celebrate a birthday with cake, the company sports day, the personnel outing, the jubilee, these are all examples of it.

Heroes or anti-heroes are real - or even imaginary - persons who are admired or disgusted by the organization. Ideas about (anti) heroes refer to what in parts of the organization (or the whole organization) is thought of as desirable. From the way a hero performs his work an example is derived. The man who carelessly stopped all investments is the anti-hero. The man who changed the organization with great changes and improvements for everybody is the hero. Or the inspired founder who is always ready with a word for everyone, the engineer who is always on the road to help customers in need.

We can obtain more information from three elements:

(1) language, text, and regulation;
(2) behaviour;
(3) rites and ceremonies.

In all three elements we find something of the **modus operandi** (Bourdieu 1972-77, Kamann and Jagersma, 1993). The **modus operandi** refers to the way people solve problems, the way people deal with each other and what people think is important. All the features we have mentioned refer to a relatively stable pattern of values and ground-rules. Values have a "thou shall" or "thou shall not" character that relates to the thinking and behaviour of people. Based on this they judge what is good, bad, rational, and so forth. Ground-rules coincide with what is silently accepted to be true. For instance, "somebody from Company X works hard and never complains". Ground-rules and values are only to be reached after all the other layers are passed and therefore are difficult to change. Some parts you cannot even talk about. Some parts can only be changed after a difficult process of awareness that things can be done in a different way. Successful change of values and ground-rules means a simultaneous manipulation at all levels of the organizational culture in all its features.

The dimensions by Hofstede
We have already discussed four of Hofstede's aspects: power distance, uncertainty avoidance, individualism and masculinity. His fifth dimension - long-term versus short-term -we have allowed to coincide with Goddard's division into various types of contacts which will be included in what we call the "scanning by walking around", participative observations inside the organization and during conversations, resulting in scores[20].

Mastenbroek's theory
Mastenbroek considers organizations as networks, and in his book "Conflict Dealing in Organizational Development" (1986), he goes deeper into various types of relations. He makes a difference between four types of relational aspects in so-called "tension balances"[21]. According to Mastenbroek, the tension-balance in these four fields form the structure in the culture of an organization.

8.   Conclusions and Recommendations

8.1   Developing a better proto-type measurement instrument
The culture sketch described above is a combination of approaches and is a methodology that we originally tested out on its soundness, validity and reliability[22] on the level of multi-site (multi-regional) organisations[23]. Presently, it is expanded to suit the purpose of our models of Section 3. In conclusion: the need for more

quantitative data to test the measurement model forces us to focus on the development of adequate scales and methods to acquire data. The "culture sketch" looks promising, in that it combines a number of approaches and techniques.

8.2 Research and policy recommendations

While scientists are still looking for the best method to chase and measure differences in culture and weaknesses in organisational cultures, managers cannot wait. We have reached the point, that we can demonstrate that there **are** differences and that these differences result in a different way of doing things and a different way of interpreting things. But what are the managers supposed to do? Managers have to learn so-called multi-cultural behaviour which means that they have to be aware that their business partners look differently at things as what they expect their partners to do. That they should treat their partners in a different way if they want to prevent misunderstanding in communication. That their partners may well have different procedures in decision-making. That you cannot simply transplant the usual routines, procedures and attitudes on partners and establishments in other regions and areas. That you cannot simply, by regulations and rules, change the behaviour and thinking of an organization.

The important element at this stage is that people become *aware* that there may be differences. And, that there are methods to visualise those differences in order to take action to prevent annoyance, misunderstanding or frustration in dealing with partners in other European regions.

Notes

1. The author wishes to thank the Netherlands Institute for Advanced Study (N.I.A.S) in Wassenaar for providing the social and scientific environment for writing this paper.

2. For a more detailed discussion in this context, applying Bourdieu's **habitus** on organisational culture, see Kamann and Jagersma (1993).

3. We assume for the time being, that trans-national influences are filtered through the national culture.

4. Two exogenous variables have been left out. First of all, the past of the company -its stage of development or its position at the life cycle. Secondly, the skill level of the department studied. In later more detailed models, these can be added quite easily.

5. See Kamann (1989).

6. A mesogenous variable is endogenously related to the exogenous variable, but, at the same time, is exogenously related to the endogenous variable(s) of the model (see Kamann, 1989).

7. "Optional extra are Xi_4 and Xi_5 for the Product/Market combinations of the two companies 'a' and 'b'; Xi_6 for the Transnational culture (e.g. EC regulations).

8.   Derived from Nijborg (1992).

9.   The combined totals for all the countries weigh each country equally, regardless of sample size or number of inhabitants.

10.   A remarkable aspect of this research is that all managers are **prepared** to take more risks under uncertainty than they were actually taking at that moment.

11.   They point at the successes of other Anglo-Dutch combinations, like Royal Dutch Shell and Unilever. However, these combinations came into being in a time where assumingly the cultures of the UK and the Netherlands were closer than presently. While the Netherlands developed into a modern welfare state, the UK kept many of its feudal institutions and thinking, especially in its industrial relations. The example of BA and KLM also illustrates that the Trade Unions apparently look at different aspects to assess cultural congruence, than 'financial circles'.

12.   As usual in these cases, a change in the top of BA, where the new man seems more willing to team-up with KLM, illustrates the usually underestimated role of **personal** behaviour and features. Another example of personal influence is the Fokker-DASA case. There, we read that the chairman of Dutch aircraft producer Fokker "rather liked the German DASA guys", while the largest shareholder, the Dutch Minister of Economic Affairs, showed rather a dislike of the Germans involved. A tough battle in negotiations between the department and DASA followed.

13.   If this assumption is not met, the company has to make a trade-off, which is a difficult task because of problems in quantifying the effects of poor cultural congruence.

14.   When the scores of the questionnaires are analysed, using Factor Analysis, new latent constructs can be constructed. These may - and in many cases will - deviate from the 18 theoretical dimensions mentioned.

15.   For instance, "work pressure is high", means that people in a unit or a department perceive the work pressure as being high. In real terms, the work pressure in that department may be very low, or relatively low.

16.   This special relates to some circumstances or conditions where a particular organization at the moment of research was faced with, for instance, a merger, reorganization, becoming independent, a closure, a take-over, etc.

17.   "Raw" in the meaning of subject to only primitive statistics, such as taking the unweighed average, in stead of computations, taking inter-correlations and so forth, into account.

18.   Either people in branch B are not satisfied with the level of information, while the other branches are satisfied with that level or, branch B receives less information than the other branches and is therefore not satisfied.

19.   This intermediate result can be used in the following way for practical purposes. Using the information gathered, a so-called **profile** can be drawn up. After that, we can compare the actual profile with an ideal profile, given the technology product market combination where the particular unit is working. Then we can see whether the profile compares favourably or unfavourably with the partner of other units.

62

20. The original Goddard (1973) measurement is, of course, more accurate in this respect. It is a matter of time management whether researchers can afford a more accurate - and more expensive -measurement here.

21. These dependencies are described as:

   (1) **Power and dependency** relations that give direction to mutual behaviour according to a tension-balance:
   mutual dependency < ... > **autonomy**

   (2) **Negotiation relations** where employees have to divide between them all types of scarce commodities. Here, the tension-balance is:
   maximalisation total revenue < ... > **maximalisation one's own revenue**

   (3) **Instrumental relations** where employees consider each other as a means of production. Here the tension-balance is:
   consensus < ... > **own preference**

   (4) **Social/emotional relations.** Between employees emotional relations exists which are sometimes very personally oriented in the form of sympathy or antipathy. Here a tension-balance exists according to a:
   "we-feeling" < ... > **"own identity".**

The power and dependency aspect is, according to Mastenbroek, a so called **"1,2,3 model"**. In this model he describes three patterns of power relations which have a close resemblance to behavioral tendencies and problems where specific interventions are required. These levels are:

   (a) **equal versus equal;**
   the parties involved are generally in balance.
   (b) **high versus low;**
   in this case there is a more and a less powerful party.
   (c) **high versus medium versus low;**
   here we find three different levels.

22. We have to admit, that the results and use of the previous tests - with the exception of the cultural profile - still are rather qualitative, rather than quantitative. Only the profile has been subject to analysis in a LISREL model sofar. It proved useful.

23. The method is developed for organization, profit and non-profit making, that have more units at various locations and where the organization is assumed to hold various so-called "blood groups" as a result of mergers and/or reorganizations. Because of this, the survey we used in such a multi-location organization also includes two geographical variables. One for the location or city itself and one for the province. However, our analysis using two sets of about 400 questionnaires each, did not result in an acceptable level of significance to show geographical - sub-regional - differences in the way people responded (Kamann and Jagersma, 1993).

REFERENCES

Bass, B.M. and P.C. Burger, **Assessment of Managers: An International Comparison,** Free Press, New York, 1979.

Boog, C.L., P.K. Jagersma and D.J.F. Kamann, **De Cultuurschets** (The Culture Sketch), Kamann Consultancy B.V., Groningen, 1991.

Bourdieu, P., Esquise d'une Théorie de la Pratique, précédé de Trois Etudes d'Ethnologie Kabyle, Librairie DOS S.A., 1972; translated as **The Outline of a Theory of Practice** by Cambridge University Press, Cambridge, UK, 1977.

England, G. et al., MOW International Research Team, **The Meaning of Working: an International Perspective**, Academic Press, London, 1984.

Goddard, J., Office Employment, Urban Development and Regional Policy, in **Office Location and Regional Development**, An Foras Forbartha, Dublin, 1973, pp. 21-36.

Hofstede, G., **Allemaal Andersdenkenden**, Contact, Amsterdam, 1991.

Kamann, D.J.F., **The Spatial Differentiation of the Social Impact of Technology**, Avebury, Aldershot, 1989.

Kamann, D.J.F. and P.K. Jagersma, **Cultuur en Strategie** (Culture and Strategy), Charlotte Heymanns Publishers, Groningen, 1993.

Kilman, R.M.J. Saxton, R. Serpa et al. (eds.), **Gaining Control of the Corporate Culture,** Jossey Bass Publishers, San Francisco, 1985.

Mastenbroek, **Conflicthantering en Organisatieontwikkeling** (Conflict treatment and organisational development), 1986.

Nijborg, A., Master Thesis Economic Faculty/Faculty of Languages University of Groningen, 1992.

Nijborg A. and D.J.F. Kamann, **Clashing Cultures in Take-overs**, 1993 (forthcoming).

Sanders, G., and A. Neuijen, **Bedrijfscultuur: Diagnose en Beïnvloeding**, van Gorcum, Assen, 1987.

Schein, E.H., **Organizational Culture and Leadership: A Dynamic View**: Jossey-Bass, San Francisco, 1985.

CHAPTER 4

A SPATIAL POLICY PERSPECTIVE

ON BORDERS AND BARRIERS

Kai Lemberg

1. Concerns on Mobility

Over several decades a process of internationalisation of trade, economy and policy making has been developing. This has amongst others caused increased mobility and traffic, primarily motor vehicle traffic, stimulating on the one hand economic growth, but producing on the other hand a number of social costs that are heavily counteracting the positive effects on wealth, efficiency, comfort and ease. These main negative factors are deteriorating transport conditions, especially in cities and on major motor ways, increased fossil fuel consumption, decreased safety, several types of environmental damages and nuisances, long-term ecological imbalances, exclusion of underprivileged people, and physical traffic barriers between neighborhoods.

As a result, transportation planners, town planners, ecologists and political circles are increasingly becoming aware of the limits to the current transport trends.

Some are primarily concerned with physical insufficiencies in transeuropean transport systems, such as lack of capacity regarding fast road and rail connections, or simply missing (fixed) links across the Channel, the Soúnd and the Baltic Sea (separating Scandinavia from the European continent) or tunnels crossing the Alps. This is the perspective of, for instance, the Round Table of European Industrialists (1984), lobbying for new huge investments in bridges and tunnels for road and rail to offer fast, secure and comfortable transport supply "just in time" for an ever increasing goods production and traffic of persons.

Others, notably many citizens in large cities, are more concerned about the negative side effects of economic growth and increasing motor vehicle traffic through externalities, like urban congestion, pollution and noise, traffic accidents and destruction of landscapes. Such social costs are usually neglected by individuals and firms when making decisions on transportation.

So despite the general political move towards market orientation and free (unrestricted) competition, there is a growing need for a new type of transportation planning and strategy. The need to seek for a balance between mobility, safety and life qualities calls for new organisational and managerial approaches in transportation policy.

2. **Barriers and the Common Market**

Regionally and nationally different types of barriers do still exist in Europe: physical barriers in the form of waters and mountains etc., but also political and administrative barriers at national borders, imposing high costs and long lasting bureaucratic procedures for passage of persons, goods and services. Coinciding with national borderline barriers are cultural and language barriers causing different habits, attitudes and tastes.

Physical barriers may be overcome by infrastructure construction like bridges and tunnels or express ferries, while other barriers need definitely a political approach to be removed.

The Cecchini report on the creation and the consequences of the Single Market of the European Communities discusses the problems and the effects of removing these "bureaucratic" obstacles to the free movement of goods and services within the EC (see Cecchini, 1989).

The new concept of the Single Market of the European Communities, discussed from 1985 onwards, aims at eliminating all unnecessary political and administrative barriers implied by national borders. This was essentially already part of the original philosophy of the removal of tariffs and quantitative restrictions on trade between EC countries. Later on this idea was extended also to EFTA countries (and some others). The main intention is to further economic growth through the free forces of the market, economies of scale, concentration of production at the most efficient producers, and specialisation.

But exactly this concentrated effort towards economic growth creates more mobility and transport, primarily as lorry and car transport, and thereby more environmental nuisances, social costs and ecological threats. It is a poor consolation to add that the higher economic growth at the same time creates financing capacity for instruments to fight its negative effects.

As part of the preparation of a new treaty for a European Union the EC Commission set up a Working Group "Transport 2000 plus" to examine the medium and long term transport and communication problems in the Community. In its report " Transport in a Fast Changing Europe" (1991) the group described and analyzed the problems and made a wide variety of considerations and proposals for a new European transport strategy, based upon a number of "main objectives" for the EC, including economic growth, the principle of subsidiarity, free flows of persons, goods and services, competitiveness, mobility, free choice of modes of transport, accessibility and cohesion (within the EC). The links between the transport sector and other policies were illustrated in the diagram, shown here as Figure 1. Transport should - as part of a common EC policy - act as an instrument for regional development and open up and link peripheral regions.

The Maastricht Treaty introduced a wider goal than the Treaty of Rome by creating a Union of a federal nature between the EC member countries with a simultaneous elimination of all internal political or administrative borders. With the final goal of a common currency, a common European Central Bank System, a unified monetary, economic and financial policy, labour market policy, claims towards member countries are practically speaking fully obliterated as barriers in any political meaning of the word. Thus what then may be left, will only be the existence of cultural and language barriers, which may tend to lose their importance in the economic integration process.

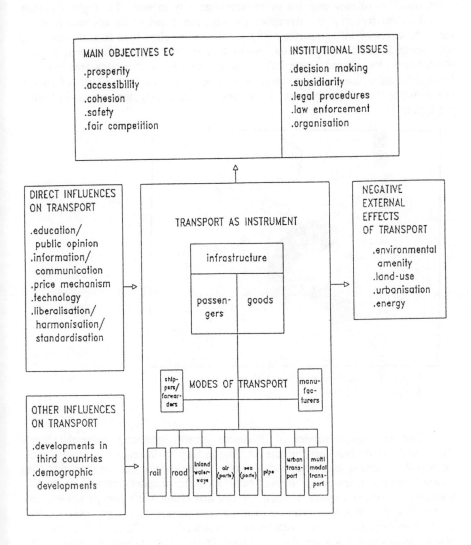

systemic approach

Figure 1: Transport policy as part of a broader European policy

3.   **Spatial Dynamics in Europe**

The EC fundamental goals of economic growth and an (internally) open market intends to stimulate economic rationality and efficiency and to benefit from large-scale production and operation. This efficiency strategy would normally work in the direction of concentration of economic activity in those EC regions already being the most powerful and dynamic. Thus economic and social advantages would mainly be expected in the heartland of the EC, the so-called Blue Banana, stretching from South England over Benelux, North France, Nordrhein-Westphalen, etc., to Württemberg, Bayern and North Italy. A secondary "Sunbelt" growth area might be the Mediterranian coast areas of Italy, France and northern Spain. This, of course, will influence the competitiveness of the various large city agglomerations in Europe (see Figure 3).

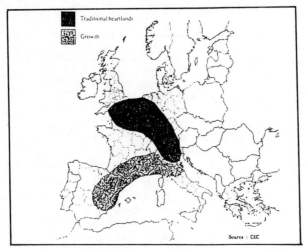

Figure 2: The European "Blue Banana"
Source : CEC (1991)

The expected dynamics of economic growth stemming from the Single Market and the establishment of the EC Union tend to increase - without a strict regional development and infrastructure policy - the inequalities between this Blue Banana area (plus a few large "outside cities") and the peripheral regions of the EC, especially the poorer regions in South Europe and North West Europe (Ireland and Scotland). The Commission is aware of this risk in its report "Europe 2000. Outlook for the Development of the Community's Territory" (see CEC, 1991), which is another preparatory study for the EC Union Treaty. The intensified growth in the core areas will create environmental and health problems there, while at the same time peripheral countries, regions and islands may experience problems of poverty, unemployment, isolation, one-sided economic growth and lack of the attractions of (urban) civilisation. To a minor degree, Denmark may also become a peripheral region.

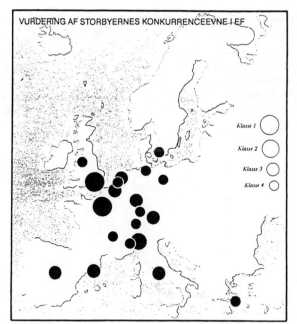

Figure 3: Degree of competitiveness of some major European cities

Consequently, the Commission has proposed huge increases of EC grants to less favoured regions and a coordinated EC regional policy, including transeuropean network investments to "peripheral member countries": Greece, Portugal, Ireland and Spain. However, extension of transport facilities, energy and tourism to such regions may increase economic growth, but at the costs of the environment, ecology and local identity.

Of course, this aim of eliminating the national borders within the EC has to be followed up by an elaboration of the common transport policy of the Treaty on Transeuropean Networks (Art.129 B-D) in order to ensure that barriers in transport are removed (also physically) and to connect peripheral regions of the EC with central regions. The Union may support infrastructure construction by offering studies, guarantees and subsidies, including grants from the new Cohesion Fund to be created before 1994 (Art, 130 D).

With a heavy emphasis on motorways (besides new high speed rail connections) this programme of transport investments will stimulate long distance car and truck traffic, thereby aggravating the environmental, energy and other damages caused by motor vehicle traffic.

4.   Implications for Northern Europe

Mainly for the sake of illustration we will give here an example of borders and barriers policy from the Nordic countries

In Denmark important consequences of this EC transportation policy have become visible since the mid 1980s. Denmark is a country of many islands and one

70

peninsula, Jutland, which interrupts national as well as international transportation by sounds and belts. This has been overcome by a large number of ferry connections, of which many - covering small distances - have been substituted by bridges for road and (the more important) rail. Up to now however, the three most important connections, each constituting a distance of about 20 km, have remained ferry lines: the Great Belt between Sealand and Funen, the Sound between Sealand and Sweden (Scania), and the Fehmarn Belt between Lolland and Germany (Fehmarn) (see Figure 4).

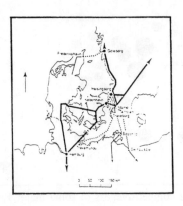

Figure 4: Transit lines through Denmark

In 1984 the Round Table of European Industrialists pointed out the two last mentioned connections among the Missing Links in Europe in their report of that title. They found it necessary to construct these (and several other) missing transeuropean links for road as well as rail - contrary to the exclusive railway tunnel crossing the Channel. A special lobby organization, Scandinavian Link, was set up (supported by the EC Commision) in each Scandinavian Country by large-scale trade companies and industries, including large banks, to secure political support. They had however, to start by advocating the construction of a Great Belt combined road and rail bridge and tunnel - knowing that for Danish regional policy this project (which is of minor international interest) was sort of a flagship for the Danish provinces outside Copenhagen. Without the Great Belt bridge the Sound Belt project would face heavy opposition. Scandinavian Link succeeded in turning an original majority in the Danish Parliament (Folketing) in favour of a railway tunnel into a majority for the combined Great Belt bridge and tunnel, by converting liberals and social democrats to vote in 1987 against their original positions.

Only then it was possible to start arguing for a corresponding fixed connection crossing the Sound between Copenhagen and Malmoe in Sweden, which was also successfully carried through by Scandinavian Link to Danish and Swedish Parliament decisions in 1991. Both cases - Great Belt and the Sound - were accompanied with heavy political and expert protests (on economic, traffic, environmental and maritime ecological grounds) and with criticism on dubious prognoses and economic calculations, but the conservative-liberal-social-democratic majority turned all objections down, claiming the combined bridge to give best profitability, highest employment and hopefully not too many environmental damages. In 1993, however, new doubts have been expressed especially from Sweden, against the environmental consequences for the Baltic Sea, etc., of the combined motorway and rail bridge. The third connection: the Fehmarn Belt bridge (or tunnel?) for road and rail, is now being prepared by the same economic interests for political decision in a few years time.

The City of Copenhagen strongly supported the issue of building a combined Sound bridge in order to counteract Copenhagen's somewhat peripheral position in the EC - outside the central - mid-European growth region and to create a new "Sound Region" combining the forces of the Metropolitan Copenhagen Region and the Swedish Southwest Scania Region with several medium-sized towns. Together with Copenhagen airport the bridge should "put Copenhagen on the map of Europe" as an economic power centre.

To strengthen the attractiveness of this new "Sound Region" to foreign investors - including international institutions and organisations - an amendment was prepared to the Communal (Development) Plan for Copenhagen, proposing a new town with a concentration of offices and service trades on an empty green area on part of the reclaimed land of West Amager - the so-called Ørestad (Sound City).

This plan however, generated a storm of protests from nature conservationists, environmentalists, people living on the inhabited part of Amager, while also the organisations of building constructors declared its scepticism, because already more than 1 million floor square meters for trades and industries are empty in existing buildings and already large projects have been adopted for new offices etc. in old, obsolete harbour areas. This conflict is still going on.

5. A General European Reflection

The EC economic philosophy is - besides neo-liberalism and monetarism - based upon the theory of comparative advantages in international trade: each country should specialize in those export products in which the country is relatively most competitive. With national currencies the country has the possibillty of devaluation to increase its competitiveness and increase import prices. However, in the EC Union with one common currency, this is ruled out, like most other national economic policy instruments. Only two strategies are then left: wage reticence and cuts in public expenditures. So, with no barriers left and no legal resort (according to the Maastricht Treaty) to large budget deficits in the EC Union, the country with low competitiveness will likely have to reduce standards of living, but with some possibilities for emergency support from certain EC funds.

The theory of comparative advantages has been criticized as a dangerous advice, because it makes the country dependent upon scale of a few export commodities and their internationally determined prices. A less vulnerable policy would be to focus on a broader selection of domestic products to replace import goods; but this would not be in agreement with major EC principles.

Exclusion of most independent economic policy instruments from national governments in the EC Union and the impossibility of adaptation through change of foreign exchange rates (devaluation) of the individual EC member countries will increase the necessity of a coordinated EC regional policy. This is the aim of Art. 130 A-130 E in the Union Treaty and the inclusion in Art.3 of a new Regional Committee among the main EC institutions.

A reform of the EC regional policy through the EC Structural Funds was carried out in 1989 with a main emphasis on stimulation of the development of backward regions and a secondary emphasis on regions in industrial decline. The Union Treaty will establish before 1994 a new Cohesion Fund to finance environmental and transport infrastructure in the poorer member countries, i.e., the Mediterranian, Portugal and Ireland. At the same time however, the Commission wants the exceptions from the prohibition against (national) state subsidies in Art.92 of the Treaty of Rome to be concentrated to a few high-tech manufacturing industries like the car industry, electronics and medical technology. It is noteworthy in this context that especially Spain has claimed high compensation sums to be transferred by the EC through the Structural Funds and the Cohesion Fund to the less favoured southern member countries (and Ireland), amounting to an annual order of magnitude of some 30 billion ECU, in order to counteract increasing disparity between rapidly growing and stagnant regions in the EC. Clearly, a side-effect of this may be that a disproportionate large part of development aid from the rich EC Union may remain within its own area instead of favouring the developing Third World or the chaotic Second World of East European ex-communist countries. For these global regions only sums of around 6 billion ECU are foreseen for the time being.

REFERENCES

Cecchini, P., **The European Challange 1992**, Gower, Aldershot, UK, 1989

The Treaty of Rome, 1987 edition, EC, Brussels.

Round Table of European Industrialists, **Missing Links**, Brussels, 1984.

Scandinavian Link, Main Report, Copenhagen, 1987.

Group Transport 2000+, **Transport in a fast Changing Europe**, EC, Brussels, 1991.

CEC, **Europe 2000, Outlook for the Development of the Community's Territory**, Brussels, 1991.

CHAPTER 5

REGIONAL BARRIERS

IN ECONOMIC REFORM IN RUSSIA

Alexander Granberg

1. **Present-Day Regional Development and the Tasks of a Regional Development Policy in Russia**

A program of reforms cannot be confined to a set of measures for Russia as a whole. In view of vast differences in natural-geographic, socio-demographic, economic and other conditions in Russia's regions, unified approaches and recommendations - especially in a transitional period - are doomed to fail practically in every region, since Russia has no regions with median conditions. This was convincingly demonstrated by previous attempts at reforming economic and social conditions in the country.

The required reform on regionalization signifies:
- a: taking account of the specificities of regions in implementing an all-Russia structural, investment, fiscal, social, and foreign economic policy;
- b: transferring a number of reform initiatives largely towards a regional level (particularly in small-size enterprises, social conditions, nature protection and use of natural resources);
- c: decentralization of the processes of reform guidance and stepping up economic activity in localities;
- d: the need for developing special programs for inducing reforms in regions with particularly distinctive conditions (regional blocks of the all-Russia program).

At the same time the reform program should include special measures for space integration of Russia's economy. These include the creation of a mechanism of vertical and horizontal interactions of the subjects of economic management and administrative bodies, promotion of an all-Russia territorial division of labour and a single market space, development of measures to prevent and surmount disintegration of interregional economic ties, economic and political separatism.

The need for sustaining stability in all regions and the system of interregional interactions (preservation of unity through multiformity) influences the development of all directions of the reform, but imposes also limitations on the content, intensity, sequence and time limits of implementing principal policy measures.

The dramatism of the present-day situation in most of Russia's regions is conditioned by the combination of
- a general economic crisis;
- intensifying disintegration of economic space;
- differing starting conditions for entry in the market place;

- incompleteness and inconsistency in the transformation of Russia's national-state set-up and delimitation of the terms of reference of federal and regional bodies of management;
- political instability and inter-ethnic tension in some regions;
- geopolitical and socio-economic consequences of the USSR's breakup and the emergence of Russia's new foreign neighbours.

Especially hard problems are nowadays faced by regions:

a. with a high concentration of stagnant and conversion industries as well as uncompleted investment programs;
b. that are largely dependent upon supplies of foodstuffs, raw materials, production technology equipment, hence having limited possibilities for self-sustenance and self-regulation;
c. with a sizeable share of producing industries controlled by the state (through price setting and other marketing conditions)
d. with a critical ecological situation requiring the closure of many production facilities and special measures of social protection.

As a consequence, Russia's entire territory is presently characterized by different types of problem regions where the level and quality of life have steeply declined over the past two or three years. A critical socio-economic situation is characteristic of almost the entire zone of the North (particularly the habitation areas of numerically small populations), old industrial and the more militarized regions of the Centre, the Urals, the south of Siberia and the Far East. Also included here are social disaster areas where up to 90 percent of the population, or even more, live below the poverty line (Tuva, Kalmykia, the North Caucasian republics, certain regions of the Non-Black Earth Zone).

The historically shaped heterogeneity of Russia's economic space manifests itself as a singularly negative factor in the changeover to market relations. If Moscow's agglomeration entered the post-industrial stage of development with prevalent service types of activity, there is a marked difference, say, with Kalmykia and Tuva which still remain at the pre-industrial stage in regard to the structure of production and employment. Russia's regions vary considerably by the pace of agrarian reform, development of civilized commercial structures and market infrastructure, external economic activity and penetration of foreign capital (over two thirds of operational joint ventures fall on Moscow and St. Petersburg). Sociological surveys point to substantial distinctions in the market mentality of the populations of industrial and rural regions, largely Russian regions and republics in Russia.

Manifesting themselves at the modern stage are several regional behavioural patterns displayed by management bodies and economic subjects:

1. Regions with an advanced agricultural sector, whose farm output meets their population's requirements, are distinguished by attempts at containing the fall of consumption and the growth of prices for foodstuffs at the expense of reducing interregional economic ties and their change towards a barter basis.
2. Regions of a largely industrial orientation, possessing an appreciable scientific-

technological potential, but much emphasis on rapid privatization, creation of market structures, joint ventures, and conditions for foreign investments.

3. Regions with predominantly extracting industries and feebly developed agriculture are seeking to organize barter both with industrial and agricultural states and regions, and thereby to cushion the social consequences of the crisis and transition to a market system.

4. Certain republics, territories and regions, possessing natural resources and receiving rights to materialize the economic effect from their utilization, are becoming leaders of movements for unlimited sovereignty and Russia's conversion into, in effect, a contractual state or confederation.

The space disintegration of Russia's economy is manifested not only in the reduction and breakup of former economic ties between regions and former republics of the USSR (irretrievable by external commerce) and replacement of a normal goods turnover by barter. No less dangerous (because of long-term consequences) is the transformation of regional economic and legal mechanisms giving an additional impulse to disintegration trends: introduction of "ersatz" currencies, transition to a single-channel taxation system limiting the consolidation of federal and regional budgets, or adoption of numerous exlusions from general legislation on external economic activity.

Regional progress is substantially affected by an altering geopolitical situation resulting from the dissolution of the USSR and formation of new independent states. Previously, out of 11 economic regions of the Russian Federation, only 6 had an outlet to state frontiers and the ocean. At present only the Volga-Vyatka Economic Region has no such outlet. Out of 76 present-day republics, territories and regions, 29 were previously border areas. At present their number has risen to 46. These changes gave rise to new problems of production specialization, the structure of goods turnover, protection of the local market from rouble intervention coming from neighbouring states, population migration (including Russian-speaking migrants), redislocation of armed forces, etc., which by virtue of their unpreparedness lie as an additional heavy burden on the economy and social sphere of new border areas.

The aims of the contemporary regional policy in the social sphere consist of ensuring a worthy level of wellbeing in each region, creating nearly equal vital opportunities for all citizens regardless of their birthplace and residence, and implementing the right to free choice of residence and work. Excessive regional contrasts in social conditions represent a threat to the very existence of a democratic state, something resulting in its breakup. The regional policy is thus called upon to slacken internal social tensions, preserve the country's integrity and unity. The aims of regional policy in the economic sphere consist of rational utilization of various economic possibilities of regions, of effects of regional agglomeration, objective advantages of territorial division of labour and regions' economic cooperation. The regional policy's harmony lies in reaching a fair balance between economic effectiveness and social justice, between all-Russia and regional interests. The tasks of regional policy implementing principal social and economic aims are, as a rule, inertial and essentially long-term. Many of them come from the past, but change in keeping with new conditions, alter their priorities, and call for new approaches to their solution. Qualitatively, new tasks of regional policy are conditioned by three circumstances:

1. Russia, like all former republics of the USSR, has become an independent state. This has fundamentally altered the geopolitical situation of many Russia's regions, the conditions and objectives of their economic and social development, and their ties with other regions;

2. the Federation Treaty has changed the principles of mutual relationships between the Federation and its subjects, expanded the economic terms of reference of the republics, territories and regions, and ethnic districts. At the same time, what has become a topical task is preserving the integrity of Russia as an object of state (including regional) policy;

3. transition is being effectuated from the previous administrative system of management to a system of largely market regulation on the basis of autonomous economic subjects, including regions. Such transition should be effectuated to a full extent, considering regional specificities.

The strategic tasks of regional development are the following:

- reconstruction of the economy of old industrial regions and large urban agglomerations by way of conversion of defense and civilian industries, modernization of infrastructure, amelioration of the ecological situation, destatization and privatization;

- surmounting the depressive state of the agrarian-industrial regions of the Non-Black Earth Zone, the southern Urals, Siberia, the Far East; resurgence of smaller towns and the Russian country-side, accelerated restoration of the lost habitat in the countryside, development of the local production and social infrastructure, as well as of abandoned agricultural and other lands;

- stabilization of the socio-economic situation in regions with critical natural conditions and predominantly raw materials specialization; creation of conditions for the revival of numerous small communities (above all the regions of the Extreme North and related localities, highlands);

- continued formation of territorial-production complexes and industrial agglomerations in northern and eastern areas, largely at the expense of non-centralized investments and with priority development of industries engaged in comprehensive utilization of extracted raw materials and observance of rigid ecological standards;

- stimulated development of export and import substituting industries in areas distinguished by the more auspicious conditions for this;

- establishment of free economic zones and technopoles as regional centres for the application of the achievenments of national and world scientific progress, and accelerated economic and social progress;

- re-specialization of new border areas, creation of new jobs there and accelerated development of the social infrastructure with regard for potential migrants and redislocation of army units from the countries of Eastern Europe and the former republics of the USSR (Western regions bordering on Ukraine, Byelorussia, the Baltic countries, regions in the North Caucasus, southern Urals and West Siberia);

- development of interregional and regional infrastructure systems (transport, communications, informatics), ensuring and stimulating regional structural shifts and regional economic effectiveness;

- a federal infrastructure is to become in the next few years a priority sphere for the state's investment activity;
- surmounting an excessive lag in the level and quality of life of the populations of certain republics and regions.

The implementation of the strategic tasks of regional development is closely associated with the current structural, investment, external economic and other all-Russia policies, the implementation of one or another scenario (variant) of development. Thus, in case of preserving Russia's resources - raw materials specialization on external markets and a slow pace of saving energy and resources, production - investment activity will shift northwards and eastwards. The policy of removing dependence on foodstuffs import will require a shift into fertile and labour- available southern areas as well as accelerated intensification of farming in the Non-Black Earth Zone. Staking on modern high technologies and accelerated conversion enhances the role of major urban agglomerations and scientific-technological centres in European regions and the Urals.

The state cannot and should not assume direct control over all aspects of the development of regions of different levels. A major proportion of the tasks of the regional policy will shift directly to the level of regions in keeping with their expanding terms of reference. But this process should not be spontaneous. To handle the tactical tasks of the regional policy, a socio-economic mechanism will be created to combine indicative state regulation and regional self-administration.

2.   **Methods of State Control of Regional Development**

The state will influence regional development and distribution of production forces through various administrative and (chiefly) economic methods. The principal forms of the state's direct participation in regulating regional development will be the expense of the state budget, individual structure-forming investment projects, placement of orders for the supply of output to meet nation-wide needs (including support for problem regions) through a contractual system. The number of federal regional programs will be insignificant. They will be worked out and funded solely for regions with especially involved (critical) socio-economic and ecological problems, like the ones existing in the zone of the North. Of fundamental importance is dovetailing the processes of developing and adopting programs with forming and implementing the budget policy. There is a need to make an inventory of programs already started on Russia's territory. This should be coupled with revising the priorities, time-limits and sources of their provision with resources. The more large-scale comprehensive programs, like documents reflecting the Russian Federation's state policy, should be considered and endorsed by top legislative bodies. In conditions of market relations the implementation of state regional programs should not be confined to the existing organs of executive power. To this end, special (state, private) joint independent companies, consortia, agencies with special powers and responsibility can be approved on a contractual basis. The implementation of the reform presupposes a broader application of methods of

economic regulation of distribution of productive forces and regional development:
- creation of special funds of regional development;
- implementation of the policy of subvention for enterprises operating in difficult socio-economic and ecological conditions;
- involvement of private domestic and foreign investors in implementing the tasks of regional policy;
- compensation of additional expenditures borne by certain economic subjects in placing their enterprises in regions with complicated conditions;
- granting a tax cut for "minerals depletion", representing tax exemption in respect to a certain percentage of profit in connection with a possible depletion of natural resources, which is especially relevant for regions with critical conditions;
- setting preferential renting rates in sequestering plots of land for the construction of enterprises of major importance for improving the economy's industry and territory structures;
- introduction of regional-differential amortization enabling enterprises located in regions with complicated conditions to fund accelerated modernization of their own production facilities;
- application of incentive prices for ecologically clean products; introduction of ecological sanctions against enterprises polluting the environment, particularly in the more critical regions.

Regional development funds (federal, republic, regional, etc.) will accumulate financial resources to handle unorthodox tasks of the respective levels of territorial hierarchy. The principal sources of forming the federal fund should be a territorial rent partially sequestered from enterprises and regions using auspicious natural conditions, geographic location, and the effect of previous state investment. The priority tasks, on which the activity of the regional development fund is concentrated, are as follows:
- implementation of regional investment programs of individual territories directly or indirectly promoting structural changes in the economy;
- evening up the levels of regions' social development at the expense of the economic growth of backward areas; reconversion of ecologically polluted zones, etc.
- discrediting of the fund's means among regions should be effectuated by allocation of subventions and subsidies as well as funding of state regional programs and major investment projects.

State regulation of regional development with the help of an economic mechanism will be effectuated at different levels of administration - federal, interregional, regional and local.

Federal organs will regulate, above all, the processes of production organization in pioneering and critical areas, the implementation of large-scale ecological and social programs, organization of interregional (and interstate) economic ties. Regional administrative bodies will concentrate on using local resources, rationalization of the economic structure as well as ecological and social problems. An ever increasing role will be played by amalgamations (associations) of republics, territories, on regions contributing to the creation of interregional market structures.

The parameters of economic regulators as well as the total limits of their impact on economic subjects are defined by legislative and norm-setting acts of the Russian Federation and its constituent republics, territories and regions. However, all component systems of state regulation for each region schould be considered within the framework of a comprehensive regional economic mechanism. Regional specificities predetermine the expediency of using a concrete case. It will comprise elements defined at a federal level too, but responsibility for forming and effectively applying the region's economic mechanism rests with republic, territorial and regional organs.

The effectiveness of the state regulation system of regional development directly depends on the extent to which decisions taken at a federal level are supported by republics and local bodies of authority and administration. Such concerted actions are essential in forecasting the regions' economic and social development, and implementing the program of economic reforms and concrete measures of state regulation.

To carry out a target-oriented regional policy in 1992-1993, it is necessary to prepare a comprehensive outlook for the development and distribution of the Russian Federation's productive forces for a period until the year 2000 with a more detailed elaboration of a period until the year 1995. Such a strategy should take account of new political and social-economic realities, including renunciation of a hypertrophied centralized and departmental planning and of the economy's changeover to market relations. Also, it is necessary to work on industrial and territorial (through Russia's constituent republics, territories, regions, autonomous entities) patterns of development and distribution of productive forces with an eye on new conditions of economic development in the country and its regions. The above scientific studies should provide a substantiation of long-term regional economic and social development ensuring:

- rational specialization of Russia's regions fully matching the conditions and resources of territories and the interests of the state and regions' populations;
- structural reorganization of production with regard to the processes of destatization, privatization, demonopolization, as well as the needs of the economy and regions' populations;
- enhancing the standard of living and progress in servicing the population of all regions in Russia, surmounting a lag in socio-economic development of individual territories;
- development of interregional and external economic ties with an eye on the market situation and long-term trends of the domestic and world markets.

What represents an organic component of the science-based state regulation of regional development is the general pattern of population distribution. This is being worked out in close conjunction with a comprehensive outlook for the development and distribution of productive forces, territorial patterns and district plans. The application of these guidelines should contribute to a balanced solution of the problems of developing settlements at local, regional and federal levels. They are also needed for urban planning, layout and building. Forecasts of patterns underlie the elaboration of an economic mechanism ensuring required changes in the of productive forces, in the regions' economy as well as the implementation of the reform program.

To coordinate the actions of the federal, republic, territorial and regional bodies, it is necessary to utilize indicative current and medium-range plans, mutual exchange of information, regular consultations, coordination of regional programs of economic reforms and inter-regional treaties.

3.   **Regional Factors in an All-Russia Policy**

Successful implementation of economic reforms calls for a comprehensive consideration of regional specificities in effectuating the basic directions of the nation-wide policy. In the area of fiscal and taxation policy this is planned in keeping with the extension of the economic independence of the Federation's subjects - to increase the share of the budgets of the republics, territories and regions in overall budget resources. Simultaneously, it is necessary to ensure all across Russia the operation of a single taxation system with federal, local and municipal taxes, a mechanism of horizontal and vertical redistribution of income between regions. The availability of a multi-channel system is determined by the need to have autonomous and stable sources of federal budget revenues to address tasks that, in keeping with the Federative Treaty, come within the competence of the federal bodies of authority.

Simultaneously, proceeding from the level of economic and social development, unemployment and the ecological situation in regions, there is a possibility of regional differentiation of rates regulating taxes that remain in localities. Centralized means (subventions) from the federal budget are envisaged to be allocated to regions only for the attainment of aims that cannot be attained at the expense of other sources of funding (surmounting the aftermath of natural calamities and critical situations, handling of critical social problems) as well as for the implementation of state regional programs.

The principal objective of the regional aspect of social policy will consist of preventing sharp regional social conflicts, and of removing tensions in regions with heightened social dangers. The areas calling for special attention include newly emerging economic districts with constrained natural conditions, old industrial areas with structural unemployment and general economic depression, agrarian over-population (North Caucasus), territories with an inadequate fiscal-economic basis for stable social development (Trans-Baikal area, Tuva, Kalmykia, Dagestan). Particular attention is also planned to be paid to the social development of regions inhabited by the great many small local communities.

The budgets of the republics, territories, regions, and local budgets, become the principal source of funding regional social programs. To support low-income groups of population, the Republic's federal and territorial funds have already been set up to render social support to the population. The social policy will chiefly be implemented through granting budgetary and extra-budgetary subsidies, setting higher pay rates for workers of budget-funded industries, pension and allowance increments, etc.

In the area of investment policy, in conditions of a reduction of state centralized capital investments, particular emphasis should be placed on the creation of conditions attractive for private and foreign investors, and joint-stock companies. It is necessary to stimulate projects making it possible to rationalize the territorial structure of production, and promoting a higher level of complexity of the region's economy and the solution of major national economic tasks.

To enhance investment attitudes in regions, it is appropriate to resort to payment of investment premiums for implementing projects, guarantee subsidies, render assistance in acquiring lands for building sites, help grant preferential credits for investment activities, create territorial and inter-enterprise consortia, and joint-stock societies for the completion of previously launched projects territories are interested in.

Investment taxation crediting will stimulate economic progress in conditions of economic crisis. It will help enhance the pace of production growth and encourage capital investments in weaker areas and progressive industries requiring new investments. Particular attention is paid to tax and amortization privileges for the purposes of stimulating the structural reorganization of the regions' economies.

The regional aspect is of major importance for reforming external economic activity. A situation has now developed in this context, where under the presure of the leadership of certain republics and regions the Government grants certain local administrations a number of privileges and special rights in relaxing the export of commodities, payment of export duties and mandatory sale by exporters of a portion of currency earnings to executive bodies. As a result of such inadequately regulated activity, the budget becomes substantially unbalanced and an all-Russia regulation of external economic activity turns complicated. Hence the need to revise the conditions of the regions' operation on the foreign market by creating nearly equal opportunities for all regions. This does not imply infringing on the rights of the federation's subjects in independent implementation of external economic activity. Just the reverse, it is designed to ensure Russia's economic security. Exceptions should chiefly apply to newly emergent free economic zones.

Considering that the impact of the regional factor is bound to intensify, it is necessary to adopt already now special legislative or norm-setting acts establishing uniform rules of granting, in exceptional cases, privileges and advantages to individual regions in the sphere of external economic activity. The drafts of such acts should be discussed by legislative organs as well as federal and local organs of executive power. Major importance is likewise attached to working out mutually coordinated programs for developing the export opportunities of Russia's regions, and their integration in a nationwide program of development of external economic activity.

In conditions of a transformation to the market and freedom of entrepreneurship particular importance is attached to state regulation and rigid control over environmental conditions and rational utilization of natural resources. This problem should be handled in practise by republic and local bodies of authority and administration. As regards federal bodies, they should concentrate on working out interrepublic and interdistrict ecological programs and on organizing their implementation. Above all, it is necessary to carry out measures to maintain a minimally required level of ecological security. The urgency of implementing these measures is determined by the need to fulfil commitments stemming from international treaties and conventions on the protection of unique natural zones, the protection of seas from pollution, as well as by an acute ecological situation in many regions of the country.

Delimitation of the terms of reference in the area of nature utilization is formalized by respective legislative acts as well as treaties between the Federation and its subjects. They should reflect limitations on the use of natural resources and objects necessitated by the need to observe common economic and ecological interests.

The regions' social-economic specific features do not only require developing regionally differentiated measures for the implementation of economic reforms but condition also minimal requirements concerning the centralization of resources at a federal level and their interregional redistribution. This is one of the necessary conditions of the stability and reliability of the Russian Federation's socio-economic and political system. Thus, the need for state support of crisis-affected and feebly developed regions as well as ensuring interregional communications predetermines a rather sizeable volume of centralized investments. The need for maintaining the minimal standard of living of the population in all regions (even regardless of their economic situation) calls for accumulation and interregional redistribution of bugetary means and relevant shaping of a federal taxation system.

4.   **The National-Territorial Aspect of Economic Reform**

Economic reform cannot be effectuated without considering the interests of numerous nations and nationalities, and complex interethnic relations in many multinational regions. The program supports:

-   the process of sovereignization and extended selfadministration of the national state and autonomous entities of the Russian Federation within the framework of the Federative Treaty;
-   a desire of all nationalities in Russia to use the process of transformations for ensuring an auspicious medium of habitation, the economic and social base of vital activity, political and state-legal guarantees as well as cultural conditions for the survival and development of ethnic-cultural entities comprising the country's population;
-   the need for attaining and strengthening interethnic concord, trust and partnership of people, elimination of causes of contradictions and ethic conflicts, observance of the principles of the parity and equality of conditions for representatives of different nationalities;
-   measures to remove obvious interethnic disproportions, to even up the level of development of people, taking account of historical and cultural conditions in the area of economic activity, to implement programs and projects in the ethnic-cultural sphere.

The economic reform's ethnic aspect should include a clear-cut course toward combining the processes of federalization and self-determination with a program of economic transformation. Reviving ethnic tradition and preserving the economic specific features of different people in the course of economic reform should not form an obstacle in the way of modernizing the mode of life, and cultivating civilized achievements. Nor should it become a means to conserve obsolete and ineffective economic structures and social institutes.

To prevent the use of progressive changes exclusively in the interests of individual ethnic groups (as a rule, representatives of title nationalities) and to the detriment of the interests and rights of the rest of the population, it is necessary to set up public control councils monitoring the cource of the land reform and made up, on a parity basis, of representatives of different nationalities residing in the republic or a region. Also, there are similar structures operating at a local level. Their job is to monitor, work out recommendations and settle disputes and conflicts arising in the course of the reform.

In the process of auctioning and privatization of large industrial enterprises in republics like Tatarstan, Bashkortostan, Yakutia-Sakha, Buryatia and others, it is necessary to carry out measures of meaningful representation of individuals of title nationalities and other ethnic groups amongst stock-holders and proprietors, in addition to the collectives of enterprises themselves whose staffs comprise, as a rule, "Russian-speaking people". At the same time, the Government should work out special measures of economic support for regions with predominantly Russian residents (the Non-Black Earth Zone, The Urals, the European North) with negative demographic and socio-cultural processes.

The economic reform comprises a complex of special measures and programs designed to ensure the specific interests and rights of minorities residing in a fragile ecological environment and retaining the traditional systems of life sustenance. Such groups enjoy special protection from the state, and market-economy principles and conditions cannot fully apply to them. Therefore, these people of the North and related areas - with the participation of local bodies, ethnic associations and communities - are allotted territories of predominant and exclusive possession and utilization. These are placed under the control or possession of territoral communities and groups of family cooperation. The state gives its support not only to traditional industries, hunting and trades, but helps involve these people in modern forms of economic management, including the development of independent communal enterprises.

The land reform and privatization program will take account of a specific situation that has developed in connection with the rehabilitation of repressed peoples. Stage-by-stage restoration of the statehood of Russia's Germans presupposes - by arrangement with local authorities (particularly in the Saratov and Volvograd regions) - allotment of certain territories and farm lands for their compact settlements.

In the North Caucasus, land reform and privatization will be effectuated on the basis of intercommune dialogue and regional cooperation, with an eye on historical-cultural factors and the political situation. This requires a sub-program worked out with the participation of representatives of the authorities, business community and national movements in the North Caucasus.

5. Formation of a Common Economic Zone - a Common Market of Russia

The danger of the devastating distintegration of Russia's economy remains real nowadays. Therefore, the Government intends to work, above all, on the solution of a minimum task to preserve the domestic market, the common monetary-crediting system, and the unity of key infrastructure systems (power engineering, transport, communications). It is necessary to retain the crictical level of control over food supply, taxation and crediting systems, export and import activities.

Successful implementation of the economic reform in Russia is possible only in combining the multiformity of concrete approaches to handling problems in individual regions with the unity of common principles of market operation over the entire territory, including common rules of interaction of all economic subjects. Locomotive and outsider regions will inevitably crop up in the course of reforms. But what is important is that they all should move in one direction, not opposite ones.

The Government cannot allow an introduction by regions of a single-channel taxation system, total decentralization of the economic mechanism of nature utilization, non-involvement in all-republic socio-economic programs, refusal to fulfil contracts for delivery of products to other regions, and similar moves leading to dismantling economic federalism.

In shaping a single economic space in conditions of developing market conditions, the following principles should be observed:
- freedom of economic, scientific-technological and other contractual relations between enterprises; each enterprise in any region has the right to freely negotiate contracts with any enterprise in any other republic, region or foreign state with regard for operational legislation;
- free movement of merchandise, capital and labour between regions; unconditional observance of human rights in respect to the choice of residence and work;
- preference to the monetary form of goods turnover over exchange in kind;
- refusal to seek bilateral balance in interregional exchange;
- uniform principles of goods taxation regardless of their production place or marketing;
- guaranteed freedom of transit shipment of goods and transportation means within the boundries of the Russian Federation; transit shipments must not be held up or be liable to local duty-levying by regional bodies of authorities;
- accelerated demonopolization of production, and goodfaith competition between producers of different forms of ownership.

In organizing a commodity market, all barriers in interregional ties should be removed. To surmount contradictions between regional interests, measures are planned to regulate interregional economic ties with the help of federal contracts on deliveries to regions performing major state functions (to northern areas, above all) through raising regional profits from the export of goods, and other incentives. A special mechanism is envisaged to protect the market of border areas. In conditions of deepening economic reform, major problems include shaping a labour market and regulating employment processess.

"Risk" factors for regions in the sphere of employment include:

- population reproduction specificities in certain regions;
- a high share of heavy and defense industries which are particularly exposed to production of slump;
- a narrow specialization of the economy;
- scattered settlements and inadequate transport;
- concentration of military units.

These characteristics help distinguish three main types of problem regions;
- those with excessive labour (North Caucasian republics, the Stavropol and Krasnodar territories, Rostov Region);
- regions with predominantly defense industries (St.Petersburg, Nizhny Novgorod Region, the Urals, industrial centres in southern Siberia, etc.);
- single-industry and depressive regions (a major part of the North zone).

In respect to the first type of problem regions, it is recommended to encourage the development of small-scale commodity production in both urban and rural areas. This will help substantially to cushion the problems of unemployment. Considerable support from the state is envisaged for the second type of regions, because the problems of conversion and structural adjustment can hardly be handled without centralized capital investments there. Broad vistas may open up here with the planned creation of conditions to attract foreign capital. In the third type of regions, a policy combining the granting of preferental credits, subventions, etc. is more effective for the creation of jobs and stimulation of initiatives and enterprise. In depressive areas it is necessary to create an especially favourable regime for entrepreneurship through partial tax exemption, accelerated amortization and other economic incentives.

The program for the development of the North envisages a set of measures stimulating and ensuring resettlement of released labour in regions with better climate conditions and employment opportunities.

The problem of meeting the needs of forced migrants can be solved through mechanisms of current and long-term regulation at the level of central management structures, administrative bodies of the republics (making up Russia), territories, regions, local bodies of government, enterprises, organizations and commercial structures.

Developing Russia's single resettlement system in conjunction with territorial economic development is a major condition for strengthening a single economic space. Ensuring the integrity of the economic space, and developing and strengthening comprehensive economic ties presuppose the establishment of a market of capital and free movement of financial resources. The state promotes the development of a system of open joint-stock companies, interregional economic associations and organizations, stock exchanges and commercial banks.

A cut in state investments in production and social overhead will be offset through a considerable increase in the number of institutional investors (funds to support production, enterprise, pensions, insurance, regional funds) operating in keeping with the principle of trust funds. Unlike other economic measures, trust funds are particurarly in need of territorial "attachment" for ensuring their effective operation. The following regional funds will take shape under the trust principle: compensatory funds for the extraction of nonrenewable resources on a given territory, ecological funds, social funds (of housing, insured medicine, education, etc.). Trust mechanisms will be introduced, stage by stage, into the system of economic regulators.

Multi-industry structures of the holding type are endowed with considerable possibilities of integrating the efforts and resources of regions in such issues as providing the population with food and enterprises with material-technological resources.

Further expansion and deepening of the practise of interregional treaties and agreements will serve as an organizational-legal instrument in shaping the Russian Federation's single economic space. It would be expedient to concentrate them on handling problems connected with coordinating regional programs for changing over to the market, privatization of state property, participation in joint programs, joint utilization of natural resources and environmental protection, population migration, personnel training, budget-fiscal and credit relations, and information exchange.

Various forms of interregional economic integration will further develop in the shape of territorial associations as well as on the basis of interregional agreements. Territorial associations of economic interaction, comprising national state, national-territorial and administrative-territorial ones, are being set up for a coordinated solution of major tasks of the regions' socio-economic development:

- formulation and implementation of programs of economic and social development of regions and creation of required funds;
- implementation of a set of measures to enhance the effectiveness of the territorial division of labour, development in condition of "destatization of enterprises" and privatization of property;
- pooling efforts and means for the practical application of the achievements of advanced technologies, expanded production of equipment for farmer households and personal subsidiary holdings;
- studying the labour market in a region and assistance in employment and retraining of personnel;
- formulation and implementation of joint programs for the revival of villages, small towns, historical and cultural monuments, sanctuaries, environmental protection,
- assistance in establishing mutually advantageous economic agreements with other regions;
- assistance in setting up territorial funds of commodity and raw materials resources.

Territorial associations will give impetus to the solution of the old problem of administering large economic areas whose habitation patterns chiefly match the eight territorial associations. Hence the need to speed up revising the existing scale of economic division into districts. Unfortunately, Russia has no adequately integral economic division into districts, for the existing scale is part of the system of economic division of the state that is no more.

CHAPTER 6

BARRIER EFFECTS

IN THE U.S.- MEXICO BORDER AREA

Niles Hansen

1.   Introduction

One might justifiably regard the U.S. - Mexico border region as unique because it is a place where one of the world's richest nations abuts the Third World. To be sure there are other places where this phenomenon occurs - Singapore and Hong Kong being obvious cases - but these are typically enclave situations in contrast to the 2000 mile boundary that separates the United States and Mexico. Despite the numerous political and economic asymmetries that exist between the two countries, large numbers of persons in both countries have gained some advantage by moving freely to the border area that extends from the Pacific Ocean to the Gulf of Mexico - an area that was scarcely inhabited at the beginning of this century. In part, this has resulted from the fact that the two sides of the boundary are not always typical of their respective countries. Mexico's northern border cities are poor by U.S. standards but they are relatively prosperous by Mexican standards; in some cases the per capita income is 50 percent above the Mexican national average (Peach, 1984). On the U.S. side, San Diego and Tucson have per capita income levels that do not differ greatly from the U.S. average. Yet most U.S border cities and towns are among the poorest in the nation, especially in the largely Hispanic Texas borderlands. It should also be recognized that there is a distinct difference between transborder movements that are national in scope and those that are primarily concentrated in the border area. For example, international trade is national in scope on both sides of the border. And the large asymmetric movement of people from Mexico to the United States - both legally and on an undocumented basis - is directed only marginally to the U.S. borderlands. The U.S.- Mexican interactions that are of major concern here are those that are primarily played out in the borderlands. Thus, after describing the long-term growth that has taken place on both sides of the boundary, this chapter deals with the nature and significance of the recent rapid expansion of U.S.-controlled assembly plants in the Mexican border area; environmental issues with international externalities; and the development of transborder cooperation between U.S. and Mexican local authorities.

2.   Growth of the United States Mexico Borderlands

2.1   The United States

The present-day boundary between Mexico and the United States resulted from the military conquest of Mexico by the United States in the War of 1846 - 1848. The imposition of this line of demarcation in 1848 - it has been modified only slightly since then - meant that Mexico lost about half of its territory to an alien people who were aggressively pushing westward under the banner of Manifest Destiny (see Map 1). However, at that time few people lived in what was to become the U.S. Southwest; and of the 80,000 Mexicans who did become instant Mexican Americans, fully three-quarters were concentrated in the upper basin of the Rio Grande River, well away from the border. The great westward surge of population following the Civil War (1861-1865) tended to bypass the borderlands, which, in terms of non-Hispanic settlement, largely grew from west to east over time. Indeed, until the coming of the railroads in the 1880s, both sides of the border remained very sparsely settled.

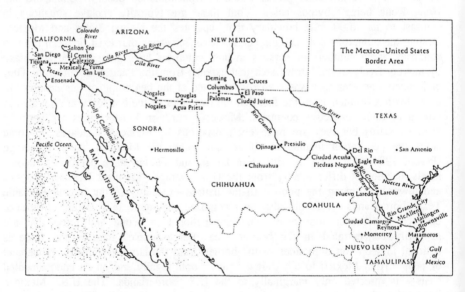

Map 1:   The Mexico United States border area.

The seven Metropolitan Statistical Areas (MSAs) shown in Table 1 account for approximately 95 percent of the total current U.S. population in counties bordering Mexico. The MSAs are divided into three groups. The first group consists of the four Texas MSAs, which have long histories of symbiotic relationships with adjacent Mexican communities. Most of the people who live in these MSAs are of

Mexican descent. Although the second group - the Las Cruses and Tucson MSAs - consist of border counties, the respective urban cores of these areas are relatively distant from the border. And while these cores have numerous interrelations with Mexico, they are not as intense or pervasive as those along the Texas - Mexico border. Finally, the San Diego MSA - which alone accounts for over half of the total U.S. border population - is clearly in a class by itself.

1980 - 1990

Area	Population 1990	Population 1980	Absolute change	Percent change
Brownsville TX	260,120	209,727	50,393	24.0
McAllen TX	383,545	283,323	100,222	35.4
Laredo TX	133,239	99,258	33,981	34.2
El Paso TX	591,610	479,899	111,711	23.3
(Subtotal)	(1,368,514)	(1,072,207)	(296,307)	(27.6)
Las Cruces NM	135,510	96,340	39,170	40.7
Tucson Z	666,880	531,443	135,437	25.5
(Subtotal)	(802,390)	(627,783)	(174,607)	(27.8)
San Diego CA	2,498,016	1,861,846	636,170	34.2
Total, border MSAs	4,668,920	3,561,836	1,107,084	31.1
United States	249,632,692	226,504,825	23,127,867	10.2

Table 1: Populations change in United States Metropolitan Statistical Areas on the Mexican border, 1980 - 1990
Source : United States Department of Commerce

San Diego grew relatively rapidly once it became accessible by railroad. Even so, as recently as 1910 it was still essentially an agricultural and resort community with fewer than 40,000 inhabitants. Since then it has become a major naval base and a major location for electronics; ship, aircraft and missile building; manufacturing; avocado shipping; education; health, oceanographic and biomedical research; and tourism. Although proximity to Mexico has been an advantage for tourism, the rapid growth of San Diego in this century would no doubt have taken place even if the Mexican side of the border did not exist.

The development of the Tucson and Las Cruces MSAs has also been relatively independent of interrelations with Mexico. Tucson originally evolved as a mining, agricultural, and commercial center for southern Arizona. It is the home of the University of Arizona, and has become increasingly prominent with respect to high-technology manufacturing and resort activities. Las Cruces is situated in a large farming area irrigated by the waters of the Rio Grande River. Government employment related to the White Sands Missile Range and the presence of New Mexico State University has also contributed significantly to its expansion.

El Paso del Norte was established by the Spanish along the major transportation route from present day Mexico to Santa Fe, now in northern New Mexico. El Paso remained solely Mexican until it surrendered to U.S. forces in 1846. In 1848 it was divided between what is now Ciudad Juárez, Mexico, and what was to become El Paso proper. Spanish and English are still mutually spoken in both cities. In recent decades El Paso has developed as a manufacturing center with over 400 plants in such activities as clothing, oil and copper refining, and food processing; it has also become a major military training site and one of the world's largest air defense centers. Laredo, McAllen and Brownsville are the three poorest MSAs in the United States. Laredo, where over 90 percent of the population is Mexican American, and Nuevo Laredo, on the opposite side of the Rio Grande River, have more intense family, business, and cultural ties than anywhere else along the entire border. Laredo is the most important United States gateway to and from Mexico for rail, highway and tourist traffic. And even though Laredo is poor by U.S. standards, its per capita retail sales regularly rank at, or close to, the highest in the nation because of purchases made there by Mexican citizens. McAllen and Brownsville are contiguous MSAs in the Lower Rio Grande Valley, on the Gulf of Mexico. This fertile agricultural area is also the home of the most prominent shrimp port in the United States. "The Valley," as it is called in Texas, is a base for thousands of Mexican American farm workers who not only toil in the local fields, but also fan out, on a seasonal basis, to much of the central United States to harvest crops. In recent years the Valley's low labor costs have attracted manufacturing activities at the standardized, low end of the product cycle. In contrast to the Valley's Third World aspects, South Padre Island, on the coast of the Gulf of Mexico, is a world-class resort area particularly favored by the wealthy residents of Mexico's second largest city, Monterrey, which is only a three-hour drive from the Texas Coast.

As shown in Table 1, the rate of population growth during the 1980s ranged from 23.3 percent in El Paso to 40.7 percent in Las Cruces. During this period, the population in all border MSAs grew by 1.1 million or by 31.1 percent; this was over three times the corresponding United States growth rate. San Diego alone grew by 34.2 percent and its increase accounted for 57 percent of the overall absolute growth in border MSA population.

2.2 The Mexican side

Disillusionment resulting from the War of 1846-1848 encouraged Mexico to leave its northern border area relatively undeveloped. The prevailing philosophy for many decades was to maintain a virtual desert between Mexico's heartland and the United States so that Mexico might be spared further harmful consequences of American expansionist zeal. As recently as 1920, Tijuana and Mexicali, both on the border with California, had populations of 1,000 and 7,000 respectively. In 1940, they still had modest populations of 17,000 and 19,000, respectively. But by 1970, these two cities, as well as Ciudad Juárez, on the border with Texas, ranked among the ten largest cities in Mexico. By 1990, these three cities together had over 2 million inhabitants and accounted for over half of the 4.1 million population residing in Mexican border municipalities (see Table 2).

Municipality	Population 1990	Population 1980	Absolute change	Percent change
Ciudad Juárez	797,679	567,365	230,314	40.6
Tijuana	742,686	461,257	281,429	61.0
Mexicali	602,390	510,664	91,726	18.0
Matamoros	303,392	238,840	64,552	27.0
Reynosa	281,618	211,412	70,206	33.2
Ensenada	260,905	175,425	85,480	48.7
Nuevo Laredo	217,912	203,286	14,626	7.2
San Luis	111,508	92,790	18,718	20.2
Nogales	107,119	68,076	39,043	57.4
Piedras Negras	98,177	80,290	17,887	18.2
Total, ten largest	3,505,499	2,627,292	878,207	33.4
Total, border	4,115,419	3,134,307	981,112	31.3

Table 2: Population change in border municipalities in the north of Mexico, 1980 - 1990.
Source : Mexican Population Census

Rapid urbanization on Mexico's northern border has been strongly conditioned by the proximity of the United States, and it has been both a cause and an effect of migration from the interior. For many decades, border cities have been staging grounds for persons who have sought relatively well-paid employment in the United States, either legally or on an undocumented basis. Here a brief historical review is in order. The Bracero Program, a contract labor agreement negotiated by Mexico and the United States in 1942 and officially prolonged until 1964, was a major catalyst for northward migration of Mexicans to and across the border. Between 1942 and 1960, some 4 million Mexican braceros worked temporarily in U.S. railways, agriculture, and food processing. Encouraged by the prospect of earning dollars, campesinos swarmed to the border cities seeking bracero certification. However the program could not accommodate the vast labor supply, which resulted in illegal migration whose magnitude surpassed that of the Bracero Program itself. An estimated 4.7 million Mexicans underwent forced or voluntary expulsion from the United States between 1942 and 1960 for having entered the country illegally (Martinez, 1978). Although many former braceros returned to the United States to work illegally, many remained in Mexican border cities. This, together with continuing migration from the interior and the arrival to prime working age of the population cohort born during the demographic explosion of the 1940s, created severe labor market problems.

In response to the border crisis of the 1960s, the Mexican government created the maquiladora (assembly plant) program. This initiative merits detailed consideration because it illustrates how official development policy has evolved from one based on reaction to dependency in favor of willingness to embrace participation in the international marketplace. From the 1940s to the early 1980s, development policy was based on industrialization by import substitution, as well as a prominent role for the national government in the ownership and operation of numerous key industries. The maquiladora sector, which, as will be seen, was (and still is) heavily dependent on linkages with major U.S. enterprises, was tolerated but not actively encouraged by the Mexican government (James and Peach, 1991). In contrast, during the past decade the import substitution strategy has been increasingly replaced by a model characterized by Sklair (1989) as export-led industrialization fuelled by foreign investment and technology (ELIFFIT). It is a model that has embraced the maquiladoras.

3.   **The Maquiladora Industry**

The maquiladora industry has taken advantage of U.S. tariff code provisions allowing foreign-based subsidiaries of U.S. firms to assemble products whose components were originally produced in the United States, and then export the products to the United States, with duties being imposed only on the value added outside the United States. It also has taken advantage of Mexican government inducements to create jobs and attract foreign investment: duty-free entry of machinery and materials, tax-free export of finished products, and exemption from once-rigid prohibitions against foreign ownership of Mexican firms.

The advantages of the maquiladora program for U.S. firms have been the low cost of Mexican labor, the fact that import duties applied by the United States concern only inexpensive labor inputs, and the proximity of Mexican border cities in relation to other world sources of inexpensive labor. The advantages Mexico has expected to gain are greater employment, more foreign exchange, and an expanded industrial base for border cities - although maquiladoras have now been allowed throughout the country.

In the late 1960s, most maquiladoras were small, utilizing converted old buildings and little capital. Since then there has been a steadily increasing trend in favor of greater capital intensity and the utilization of large new plants in modern industrial parks. In 1982 approximately 100,000 workers were employed in maquiladoras. However, mounting competition from lower-cost Asian manufacturers threatened the future growth of the industry. Then massive peso devaluations made Mexican wages among the lowest in the newly-developing world, resulting in an explosive growth of maquiladora plants and employment. Major U.S. corporations have been primarily involved. They include General Motors, Ford, Chrysler, RCA, Zenith, Honeywell, General Electric, and Westinghouse, among others. Large Japanese and European corporations have also been establishing maquiladora branches with the aim of penetrating the U.S. market through low-cost production facilities in Mexico.

Between 1981 and 1987, the average hourly compensation cost for maquiladora production workers fell from $ 1.67 to $ 0.81 (Shaiken 1990). In the wake of this decline, the industry production grew to 672 plants and 200,000 workers by 1984; to 1,125 plants and 300,000 workers by 1987; and to 2,000 plants and 450,000 workers by 1990. By the end of 1990, value added in the maquiladora industry amounted to $ 3.5 billion (Mexico Business Monthly, 1991a). The electrical equipment and electronics sectors accounted for 36 percent of total employment and for 38 percent of the total value added; and transportation equipment accounted for 23 percent of total employment and for 25 percent of total value added. The textile and apparel and furniture sectors ranked next in importance. The number of maquiladora plant declined to 1,870 in early 1991 due to the economic recession in the United States, but this phenomenon was not just a recent occurrence. Maquiladora activities also dropped significantly between 1975 and 1977 and again between 1980 and 1982 because of U.S. recessions. However in each case subsequent growth resumed at a faster rate than before (Mexico Business Monthly, 1991b). The dependence of the maquiladora industry on the United States is also indicated by the fact that only about 3 percent of the relevant inputs are purchased within Mexico (Banco Nacional de México 1990). Although maquiladora inputs are overwhelming supplied from the United States, the low-wage, labor-intensive activities performed in Mexico are definitely viewed as a threat by U.S. labor unions. The most careful econometric analysis of this issue suggests that maquiladora growth is about as sensitive to differentials between Mexican wages and those in the newly industrializing countries of the Pacific Rim as it is to differentials between Mexican and U.S. wages (Gruben, 1990). In other words, Mexican workers compete as much with Asian workers as they do with those in the United States; and while maquiladoras no doubt take U.S. jobs, these jobs would probably have gone to Asian or other newly-developing countries if the maquiladoras did not exist.

Nevertheless, it might be supposed that there would be numerous actual, or at last potential, opportunities for U.S firms near the border to supply inputs to the maquiladoras. Moreover, such opportunities would seem to be particularly great along the Texas-Mexico border area, where symbiotic transborder relations are particularly pronounced. The Mexican state of Chihuahua, which borders far-western Texas, accounts for over a third of the employment and of the value added in the entire maquiladora industry; and the vast majority of this acitivity is concentrated in Ciudad Juárez, which is immediately adjacent to El Paso, Texas. Indeed, the Economic Analysis Center of the Texas Controller of Public Accounts (1988, p.6) recently reported that "The border continued a strong trend spurred by twin-plant expansions in Mexico. Twin plants involve factories in Mexico that assemble parts made in Texes". Again, it was asserted that "Growth in increasingly capital-intensive twin plants, such as automotive suppliers, will boost related manufacturing and support services located on the Texas side of the border (Texas Comptroller of Public Accounts, 1989, p.3) But the fact of the matter is that twin plants have never really appeared to any significant extent on the Texas side of the border; maquiladora inputs have typically come from U.S. areas far beyond the border (Molina and Cobb, 1989)

Although a substantial number of maquiladoras would like to have local Texas suppliers, border area manufacturing firms in Texas have not been capable of handling large volume contracts with tight tolerance and delivery time requirements. To overcome their present handicaps, Texas border firms will need to deal not only with shortages of skilled production workers, but also with deficiencies in areas including cost analysis, financial analysis, procurement and marketing (Patrick, 1989). It seems to be an issue of so near yet so far. It is probable that inadequate education and training opportunities for the majority Mexican-American population in the Texas borderlands, and a lack of producer-services support networks for Texas borderlands manufacturing firms represent a continuing drag on the ability of Texas border firms to supply not only the maquiladoras, but also their ability to participate in expanding opportunities in the U.S. economy.

Although the maquiladora industry has largely produced outputs at the tail end of the product cycle - with all that this implies for wages and the quality of labor inputs - it can be argued that development must start somehow, and that the experience of South Korea, Taiwan, Singapore and Hong Kong clearly demonstrate that it is possible to begin at the low end of the product cycle and then move up to more sophisticated activities and better-paying employment opportunities. In fact, many maquiladora plants have been moving up the technology ladder, especially in such sectors as electronics, transportation equipment, pharmaceuticals and plastics. Shaiken (1990) notes that the number of technical workers as a percentage of all maquiladora workers rose from 9 percent in 1975 to 12 percent in 1987, while the percentage of administrative workers rose from 5 percent to 7 precent. In the electronics sector, technical workers comprised 14 percent and administrative workers 8 percent of the work force in 1987. Nevertheless, even technologically-advanced maquiladoras have very few backward linkages with Mexican suppliers and they continue to rely upon labor-intensive processes. While Japanese-style production methods have become more commonplace with respect to flexible machinery and just-in-time inventory practices, such flexible labor practices as job rotation, quality circles and worker self-supervision have been less in evidence. The developmental success of Asian newly industrializing countries has been based not only on more sophisticated equipment, but also on a considererable upgrading of workers' skill, education, and training levels, which in turn has resulted in higher wages. The picture in this regard with repect to the maquiladora labor force has thus far not been promising.

In 1989 the Mexican government announced new regulations that extended many of the benefits enjoyed by the maquildoras to other Mexican industries and liberalized the conditions under which maquildora outputs could be sold within Mexico. The continuing opening of Mexico to foreign investment will no doubt further blur distinctions between various kinds of export-oriented industries. Nevertheless, proximity to U.S. markets and to U.S. sources of inputs will still make the northern border area relatively attractive for the location of many manufacturing activities.

4.   **Environmental Issues**

The rapid growth of the maquiladoras and the increasing sophistication of the goods they produce have generated a huge array of such chemical wastes as acids, thinners, alcohols, oils, degreasers, and toxic metals and solvents. Of the hundreds of thousands of tons of chemical wastes that maquiladoras produce annually, only a small fraction is returned to parent companies in the United States, as required by Mexican law (Tomaso and Alm, 1990). Because the enforcement of Mexico's environmental laws is lax and the cost of disposing of waste in the United States is high - from $ 200 to $ 2000 per barrel - the incentive to dump the waste in Mexico is great. In many instances maquiladoras stockpile wastes at plant sites, sell them to questionable Mexican "recyclers," flush them down sewers, or dump them in the desert. In the slums of Ciudad Juárez, where thousands of families have no running water, 55-gallon drums that once held deadly solvents and other chemicals are used to store water that people use for washing and drinking. Studies in Nogales, Sonora, suggest that maquiladoras have been dumping toxic chemicals directly into municipal drains; this is also likely to have occurred in Tijuana though thorough studies have yet to be carried out there (Farquharson, 1991). A recent agreement to pursue free trade negotiations between the United States and Mexico was nearly blocked by U.S. environmental groups who argued that free trade would result in further environmental degradation along the border. The U.S. government finally split the environment movement by promising to include pollution issues in the negotiations and to work toward cleaning up the border area.

The dumping of industrial wastes into municipal collection systems and the failure of Mexican sewage systems frequently result in highly toxic sewage washing across the border. Sewage treatment plants on the Mexican side of the border are rare. Ciudad Juárez does not have any and Tijuana built its first one only recently. More than 12 million gallons of untreated sewage and chemicals still run into the Tijuana River each day, with much of it ending up on Imperial Beach on the California coast, which has been closed for ten years. The San Pedro River, which runs northward from Sonora into Arizona, is frequently contaminated by the large copper works at Cananea, Sonora. Arizona farmers have long been concerned about damage to their land and crops, and residents are disturbed about the potential health hazards. The New River, which rises south of Mexicali and flows northward to the Salton Sea in California, is perhaps the most polluted stream in the United States. The flow, normally some 3.5 million gallons an hour, consists largely of irrigation drainage and drainage from Mexicali's main municipal dump, untreated slaughterhouse and industrial wastes, and the inadequately treated sewage of over 600,000 people. Local residents along the 55 - mile course of the river have long known to keep away from the water, but because of the increasing flow of tourists through the Imperial Valley, signs have been erected warning of the dangerous situation. The stretch of the Rio Grande River at Laredo, Texas is one of the most polluted along the river's entire 1800 mile course because, on an average day, adjacent Nuevo Laredo, Tamaulipas, pours 24 million gallons of untreated wastewater into the stream - which both cities use for drinking water. Nuevo Laredo's capital budget for sanitation is used to install pipes to get raw sewage out of streets and neighborhoods, but it is not sufficient to construct a sewage treatment plant (Alm and Tomaso, 1990).

In addition to surface water problems, there are impending groundwater shortages in many locations along the border. In recent years at least twelve U.S. border municipalities have been completely dependent on groundwater, and another four partially so. Ciudad Juárez and a number of smaller Mexican border cities are almost totally dependent on groundwater, while Mexicali, Tijuana, Reynosa and Matamoros have been variously dependent upon this source for up to half of their water. Along the entire border there are at least twenty locations where groundwater has become or could become a source of international conflict (Mumme, 1982). Waters in underground basins located partly in the United States and partly in Mexico have never been legally apportioned between the two countries; and sensitve sovereignty issues associated with subsurface land rights have made both sides reluctant to deal with the problem. The consequent race to see which side can withdraw water most rapidly is particulary pronounced in the El Paso - Ciudad Juárez area, where there is mutual dependency on an underground aquifer whose withdrawal-to-recharge rate is approximately twenty-to-one (Utton, 1989). Clearly there is a pressing need for cooperative international strategies for managing the utilization of increasingly scarce groundwater along - and under - the border.

Population growth, industrial development and agricultural activities have all contributed to air quality problems along the border. Although the U.S. side has many more motor vehicles, the average age of Mexican vehicles is much greater and they frequently are not equipped with pollution control devices. Carbon monoxide, hydrocarbons, and nitrogen oxide emissions pose particular problems in the densely-populated international urban areas. Although the U.S. side of the border generates more solid waste matter, most of the 9700 tons of refuse that are produced daily in ten major Mexican border cities is not treated or stored in municipal garbage dumps; exposed to the open air, it becomes a source of air as well as water pollution and contributes to a great deal of gastrointestinal illness.

In the San Diego - Tijuana basin it is common for the prevailing winds to carry pollutants from Tijuana to San Diego during the morning hours, whereas during afternoon hours the opposite occurs. Moreover, it is not uncommon for temperature inversions to prevent the dispersal of pollutants. Similar conditions exist elsewhere along the border, especially in the El Paso - Ciudad Juárez region. El Paso is currently in violation of U.S.- mandated emission standards for total suspended particulates, ozone, and carbon monoxide. Ciudad Juárez is also in violation of these standards as well as those established by the Mexican government. The major cause of the increase in pollutants has been vehicular traffic, which can only increase in the future. The border itself directly contributes to this situation. Drivers in the long lines of stop-and-go traffic that wait to clear customs controls typically leave their engines running, thus producing large quantities of ozone and carbon monoxide (Applegate and Bath, 1989).

Pollution control efforts are particularly difficult to implement in border areas when the respective countries concerned have markedly differing levels of development as well as different attitudes and values with respect to environmental issues. For example, the adoption of common air quality standards would imply that the relatively poor country would have to devote a higher proportion of its resources to pollution reduction than would the relatively rich country. Apart from abstract questions of justice, this circumstance would not lend itself to agreement between the two countries.

On paper, Mexico has impressive legal regimes for environmental protection, but as in many developing countries the government in fact accepts high levels of pollution as part of the price that must be paid for economic development. The situation on the U.S. side of the border is more heterogeneous, but there, too, conflicts between development and environmental objectives are apparent. Most indicators of economic welfare decrease from west to east along the U.S. borderlands. For example, per capita income in the San Diego metropolitan area is above the national average, whereas the three poorest metropolitan areas in the United States - Brownsville McAllen, and Laredo - are located on the Texas-Mexico border. In keeping with this pattern, the constituency on behalf of environmental causes has been relatively strong in San Diego, while in the Texas borderlands, environmental polution "as a problem ranks far behind others such as unemployment, health care, industrialization, lack of development, and a host of others" (Bath, 1978, 183).

Despite differences in preferences and standards - or at least enforcement of standards - the United States and Mexico have been developing a legal framework concerning environmental protection in the border area. The La Paz Agreement, signed by the respective national presidents in 1983, stated that the two governments would adopt appropriate measures to prevent, reduce, and eliminate sources of land, water and air pollution in the territory 100 kilometers from the boundary on each side. In fact, the agreement did lead to some successful projects with respect to water quality improvement, air pollution abatement, and harzardous waste reduction. Recently joint arrangements have also been made for dealing with the sewage problems of Tijuana, the New River, Nogales, and Nuevo Laredo.

But while Mexico did place environmental issues on its national policy agenda, it still allocated few resources to the enforcement of the relevant policies. And, with the exception of San Diego, U.S. border communities have still been slow to demand action on environmental matters. A fresh impetus to cooperative international environmental policies has come about as a result of free trade negotiations. In response to criticisms that a free trade agreement could result in increased pollution - by creating pressure for relaxed standards in the United States in the face of possible plant relocations to the more tolerant Mexican side of the border - the United States and Mexico released a major new draft plan in 1991 to improve the quality of the environment along the border. The plan contains proposals to build on and expand ongoing programs; to improve the environmental data bases on both sides of the border; to expand planning, training and education programs; to strengthen enforcement of existing laws; and to reduce pollution through new initiatives. Six regions where population and economic activity are particularly concentrated in adjacent U.S. and Mexican cities are accorded special attention. The regions and the key problems to be addressed are Tijuana - San Diego (sewage, air pollution); Mexicali - Calexico (sewage and air pollution); Nogales - Nogales (sewage and air pollution); Ciudad Juárez - El Paso (air pollution); Nuevo Laredo - Laredo (sewage); and Matamoros - Brownsville (sewage and water supply sources). Despite the positive intent of the draft plan, at this writing a suit has been brought by U.S. environmental groups against the Office of the U.S. Trade Representative charging that the proposed free trade agreement lacks a formal environmental impact statement, and that the draft environmental plan contains no commitments with respect to staffing and spending levels. Thus, pressures at the national level in the United States may well bring about improvement in the environmental quality of the border area despite a great deal of relative indifference in this regard within the area itself.

5.   Transboundary Cooperation

Although industrial development and environmental issues have received particular attention in recent years, numerous transborder interactions also take place in the U.S.- Mexico border area with respect to health, education, cultural events, fire protection, law enforcement, tourism, transportation and communications, and commercial relations. Given the history of U.S. - Mexican political relations as well as the economic disparities that exist between the two countries, it is commonly argued that asymmetric interdependence has placed Mexico in an unfavorable state of dependency. Be that as it may at the national level, the eminent Mexican scholar Victor Urquidi (1979, 27) argued that "The only area where there is perhaps a balanced mutual dependence is along the 2000 miles of the fairly open U.S.- Mexico border. A way of life has developed there that benefits inhabitants and businesses on both sides of the border." Thus, over the years, border residents have evolved a wide variety of informal arrangements to deal with transborder facets of their daily lives. Examples of informal, but regular, "microdiplomacy" include the cooperation of fire departments, health authorities, and police to handle emergencies without federal government intervention on the part of either side (Ganster and Sweedler, 1990).

Proponents of even closer cooperation across the border have stressed the mutual benefits to be gained, but they have also pointed out that cooperative efforts have frequently been hindered by policies in the respective distant national capitals, where the nature and significance of actual and potential transborder symbiotic relations are not understood. Indeed, it has been argued that the U.S. and Mexican national governments have in fact created many of the problems that exist in the borderlands (Hansen, 1986a; Stoddard, 1984.) Despite a large growing literature on international interactions along the U.S.- Mexico border, the relevant studies have been based on a priori socio-political perspectives, anecdotal evidence, or case studies of particular cooperative undertakings. In contrast, survey research by Hansen (1986b) obtained evidence concerning attitudes and perceptions about cooperative interactions from persons on both sides of the border who were engaged in a variety of cooperative efforts. The results of the research, which was carried out in Brownsville, Laredo, El Paso, San Diego, Ciudad Juárez and Tijuana, are summarized here.

Respondents from both sides of the border tended strongly to agree that transborder cooperation did in fact help to achieve the objectives being sought. There also was a high degree of common agreement that both economic development and the presence of friends and relations on both sides of the border were a stimulus to transborder cooperation. Respondents from each side tended to stress the need for close personal contracts as well as for more information from the other side. U.S. respondents in particular expressed the view that transborder cooperation was hindered by lack of continuity of government officials on the other side of the border. On the other hand, the Mexican respondents had a significantly lower perception that transborder cooperation was made more difficult because of problems arising from one side's lack of understanding of the language and customs of the other side in either direction across the border. Mexican respondents tended to view the cooperative process in more formal terms than did the U.S. respondents; the latter also had a relatively stronger tendency to believe that informal relations represent the best approach to transborder cooperation.

There was widespread agreement among respondents on both sides that transborder cooperation benefited both sides, and to about the same degree. Among those who felt that one side benefited more than the other, most held that the Mexican side received the greatest benefit. This was the case for both Mexican and U.S. respondents. There was also widespread agreement among both Mexican and U.S. respondents that the benefits of transborder cooperation were spread among a broad spectrum of the border population on each side, rather than being mainly confined, for example, to business interests. It should be pointed out that this result is not merely a reflection of self-serving responses on the part of respondents from the business community. Only 30 of the 79 U.S. respondents were primarily involved in transborder cooperation concerning commerce and industry. And only 13 of the 54 Mexican respondents were engaged in this type of cooperation

For the most part, neither side viewed transborder cooperation as a threat or potential threat to national sovereignty or independence. Similarly, there was a strong tendency on each side to reject the notion that the border relationship resulted in economically adverse consequences for the respondents' side of the border.

Repondents from both sides tended to believe that the respective national governments do not understand the nature and significance of transborder problems.

The U.S. side had a more negative view of each national government in this regard than did the Mexican side; this was especially the case with respect to Washington, D.C. In a very similar way, both U.S. and Mexican respondents agreed that local governments should be given more responsibility for transborder cooperation; and that such enhanced cooperation would benefit both sides in about equal degree.

It should be pointed out that while a significant portion of the literature on the U.S.- Mexico borderlands has stressed the supposedly negative aspects of Mexico's "dependence" on the U.S. side, the responses obtained here from Mexican as well as U.S. participants in transborder cooperation do not support such allegations. Moreover, it should be stressed again that most of the respondents were not engaged in commercial or industrial cooperation (and this was especially the case on the Mexican side), so response patterns cannot be dismissed as reflective of capitalist elites with a self-serving view of transborder cooperation.

Finally, the principal policy implication to be derived from the results of this study is that local governments should be given more responsibility for initiating and carrying out transborder cooperation efforts. Relatively unfettered transborder cooperation at the local level benefits the respective border populations without threatening the principle of national sovereignty.

6.   **Barrier Effects in the U.S.- Mexico Border Area: A Summary Overview**

To borrow the terminology of Nijkamp, Rietveld and Salomon (1990), the U.S.- Mexico border area represents a complex barrier with respect to spatial interactions, having both discouraging and stimulating effects as well as varying degrees of symmetry and asymmetry, depending on the phenomenon being considered.

When the present boundary was established in the mid-nineteenth century, few people lived in its vicinity because the area was remote from centers of population in both countries and in any case had few valuable resources. For decades the Mexican government did little to promote development in its northern borderlands, believing that this would discourage any further U.S. attempts to acquire Mexican territory. Nevertheless in this century - and espacially in the last fifty years - the border area has become a zone of attraction for population and economic activity on both sides. Today over 10 million people reside in the area and population growth on each side exceeds the respective national rates of growth. It is likely that most of the growth on the U.S. side would have occurred whether or not Mexico were in proximity - San Diego and Tucson alone account for most of the U.S. border population and their development has been largely independent of any Mexican connection.

While the boundary is not a discouraging barrier for U.S. citizens traveling to Mexico, this is not the case for millions of Mexicans wishing to enter the United States. However, the boundary is permeable to considerable undocumented Mexican migration. In 1986, for example, 1.6 million deportable Mexican aliens were located by the U.S. Border Patrol (U.S. Bureau of the Census 1989, p. 175), even though a large number of undocumented Mexicans still live and work in the United States. Proximity to the United States has thus made the Mexican border cities staging areas for persons seeking to enter the United States, either permanently or on a cyclical basis. Mexican border cities also provide employment in activities catering to U.S. tourism and, especially in the last decade, in activities related to the maquiladora sector.

The maquiladoras originally represented a compromise with one of the principal legacies of the Mexican Revolution, namely, a commitment to avoid asymmetric dependence on U.S. capital and capitalists. And the maquiladoras were originally strictly a border phenomenon. They could bring in from the United States machinery, and components to be assembled by Mexican workers, but they could not sell their products in the protected Mexican market. Mexico's recent opening to the international marketplace will diminish the significance of the border enclave aspect of the maquiladoras. Nevertheless, the proximity of the Mexican borderlands to U.S. markets and to U.S. sources of components inputs to be assembled in Mexican plants will no doubt continue to make the area an attractive location to many U.S. corporations. Japanese and other foreign firms will also be well represented in the region because of the opportunity to utilize cheap but productive labor to produce goods for sale in the U.S. market. In other words, the Mexican borderlands will be a zone of increasing attraction to manufacturing firms as the scope for free trade between the United States and Mexico widens. To the extent that this activity creates employment on the U.S. side of the border related to the processing and financing of international trade flows, the boundary will increasingly represent a symmetric stimulating barrier.

Mexico accounts for 7 percent of U.S. exports and for 6 percent of U.S. imports. Fully 73 percent of Mexican exports and 68 percent of Mexican imports involve the United States. Between 1986 and 1990 the value of U.S. exports to Mexico rose from $15 billion to $28 billion, while imports increased from $13 billion to $30 billion. The average U.S. tariff on Mexican goods is now less than 4 percent, whereas the average Mexican tariff on U.S. goods is 10 percent. The anticipated free trade agreement between the two countries will no doubt substanially increase the trade volume of items on which tariffs are still high at the present time. This in turn will further exacerbate congestion barriers at the border. Zlatkovich (1991) argues that the most marked impact of the free trade agreement will be on the transportation system between the two nations, particulary at the border and in northern Mexico. Border crossing formalities are already a significant barrier to the flow of goods. Waits of more than an hour are not uncommon and are usually caused by U.S. efforts to reduce contraband traffic, e.g. drugs and undocumented workers. With few exeptions, two-lane roads between the border and the interior of Mexico are the rule, and routes through cities and towns are slow and congested. Although some efforts are being made to alleviate some transportation bottlenecks, future traffic increases that will result from trade liberalization will create a definite need for longer-term solutions to problems of transportation congestion barriers.

The prospect of a free trade agreement has generated unprecedented concern about environmental conditions in the border area. In particular, it is feared that U.S. manufacturing activities that have difficulty meeting U.S. pollution standards will move to Mexico in increasing numbers unless Mexican authorities enforce standards comparable to those in the United States. In principle this concern applies to location anywhere in Mexico, but in fact it is largely a border issue because this is where most foreign-controlled plants will locate to gain advantages of proximity to the United States.

In other words, asymmetry in environmental standards or enforcement of standards creates an asymmetric relationship in the border area with respect to pollution, which in turn reinforces the asymmetry of manufacturing location based on labor costs. On the other hand, the boundary is permeable with respect to many types of water and air pollution, so that residents of the U.S. side have an interest in what takes place on the Mexican side. However, differences in preferences and standards concerning the relative importance of environmental issues characterize not only the respective sides of the border, but also communities on the U.S. side. Relatively rich San Diego is much more concerned about environmental quality than the relatively poor border cities in Texas. Nevertheless, national pressures from environmental and labor organizations in the United States will likely result in more uniform standards and enforcement on both sides of the border, with the U.S. side assuming part of the cost of pollution abatement on the Mexican side. This still leaves open the question of how vital underground water in transborder aquifers will be apportioned between the two sides. Until this issue is resolved the permeability of the boudary will only encourage over-use of the scarce resource.

Finally, the presence of Hispanic populations on both sides of the boundary has encouraged strong transboundary social and cultural linkages; and informal transboundary cooperation at the local level has often served to temper the impacts of asymmetric economic relations as well political problems engendered in the distant national capitals, where border issues are frequently inadequately appreciated. While the border region is clearly influenced by the respective nations, in many respects it is a distinct entity. Thus, it reflects not only the obvious asymmetries between the United States and Mexico, but also represents a kind of laboratory where both sides exist in a symbiotic relationship in which mutual problems and concerns have given rise to mutual cooperation. The integrative function of the border area would no doubt be enhanced if local authorities were given greater responsibilities for initiating and implementing transboundary cooperation efforts.

REFERENCES

Alm, R. and B. Tomaso, **Dirty Water: U.S. Must Live with Border Pollution or Aid Mexico's Cleanup**, Transboundary Resources Report, 4(2), 1990, pp. 3-5

Applegate, H.G., and C.R. Bath, **Air Pollution in the El Paso - Ciudad Juárez Region**, Transboundary Resources Report, 3(1), 1989, pp. 1-2

Banco National de México, **Review of the Economic Situation of Mexico**, September, 1990.

Bath, C.R., Alternative Cooperative Arrangements for Managing Transboundary Air Resources along the Border, **Natural Resources Journal**, 18, 1978, pp. 181-199

Farquharson, M., Cleaning up the Border, **Business Mexico**, 1, 1991, pp. 34-36

Ganster, P. and A. Sweedler, **The United States-Mexican Border Region: Security and Interdependence**, United States-Mexico Border Statistics since 1900 (D. Lorey, ed.), UCLA Latin American Center, Los Angeles, 1990, pp. 419-441

Gruben, W.C., Mexican Maquiladora Growth: Does it Cost U.S. Jobs? **Federal Reserve Bank of Dallas Economic Review**, January, 1990, pp. 15-27

Hansen, N., Conflict Resolution and the Evolution of Cooperation in the U.S. Mexican Borderlands, **Journal of Borderlands Studies**, 1, 1986a, pp. 34-48

Hansen, N., The Nature and Significance of Transborder Cooperation in the Mexico - U.S. Borderlands: Some Empirical Evidence, **Journal of Borderlands Studies**, 1, 1986b, pp. 57-65

James, D.D., and J.T. Peach, Border Studies and Socioeconomic Issues of the Borderlands, Unpublished paper. New Mexico State University, Las Cruces, 1991.

Martinez, O.J., **Border Boom Town: Ciudad Juárez since 1848**, University of Texas Press, Austin, 1978.

Mexico Business Monthly, August, 1991a.

Mexico Business Monthly, October, 1991b.

Molina, O.J., and S.L. Cobb, The Impact of Maquiladora Investment on the Size Distribution of Income along the U.S.- Mexico Border, **Journal of Borderlands Studies**, 4, 1989, pp. 100-118

Mumme, S., **The Politics of Water Apportionment and Pollution Problems in United States-Mexico Relations**, Overseas Development Council, Washington DC, 1982.

Nijkamp, P., P. Rietveld, and I. Salomon, Barriers in Spatial Interactions and Communications: A Conceptual Exploration, **Annals of Regional Science**, 24, 1990, pp. 237-252.

Peach, J.T., **Demographic and Economic Change in Mexico's Northern Frontier**, New Mexico State University, Las Cruces, 1984.

Patrick, J.M., Maquiladoras and South Texas Border Economic Development. **Journal of Borderlands Studies**, 4, 1989, pp. 89-98

Shaiken, H., **Mexico in the Global Economy**, Center for U.S.- Mexican Studies, University of California, San Diego, 1990.

Sklair, L., **Assembling for Development: The Maquila Industry in Mexico and the United States**, Unwin Hyman, Boston, 1990.

Stoddard, E.R., **Functional Dimensions of Informal Border Networks**. Center for Inter American and Border Studies, El Paso, 1984.

Texas Comptroller of Public Accounts, Fiscal Notes, November, 1988.

104

Texas Comptroller of Public Accounts, Fiscal Notes, February, 1989.

Tomaso, B. and R. Alm, Economy vs. Ecology in Mexico's Drive for Growth Eclipses Concerns about Toxic Waste from Border Plants, **Transboundary Resources Report**, 4(1), 1990, pp. 1-3

U.S. Bureau of the Census, **Statistical Abstract of the United States: 1989**, U.S. Government Printing Office, Washington, D.C, 1989.

Urquidi, V., **A Mexican Perspective. U.S. Policies toward Mexico**, (R.D. Erb and S.R. Ross, eds.), American Enterprise Institute, Washington, D.C., 1979, pp. 20-30

Utton, A., Water Supply in the El Paso-Juarez Area, **Transboundary Resources Report**, 3(1), 1989, pp. 2-4

Zlatkovich, C., Transportation Impacts of U.S.- Mexico Free Trade, **Texas Business Review**, August, 1991.

CHAPTER 7

BARRIERS AND COMMUNICATIONS TECHNOLOGIES

IN A GLOBAL SOCIETY:

AN OVERVIEW AND A CASE STUDY

Ilan Salomon and Boaz Tsairi

1.   **Introduction**
      Globalization of production processes is a manifestation of the underlying basis for international trade. It evolves as a result of agents' identification of the comparative advantages of particular locations. Communications systems, through transport and telecommunications act as necessary facilitators of such processes. In the wake of the "information age", in which knowledge and information become major production factors and products, the impacts of New Information Technologies (NIT) on the organization of economic activities are attracting increasing interest (Wellenius, 1984; Parker, 1984; Giaoutzi and Nijkamp, 1989). While evidence on the potential role of NIT in the globalization of production is abundant (Masuda, 1980; Cole, 1986; Warf, 1989), there is relatively little knowledge about the actual flow of information through various channels of communications in the normal operations of a production process.
      Global production, beyond the exploitation of comparative advantages, also implies that barriers which usually exist between countries can be overcome at a cost lower than the benefits accrued from the trade of production factors. Barriers of various types and intensity act upon any spatial interaction. However, their impacts vary by type and by the channels used to traverse them.
      The objective of this paper is to examine the procedures which lie at the basis of global production. The daily operations of professionals and managers, using various modes of communicating and overcoming barriers to exploit comparative advantages are the building blocks of such international activities. In this paper, we employ a micro-level analysis of these operations. We examine how international cooperation in production takes place in the presence of multiple barriers, and how different communication channels, some transportation-based and others based on NIT, are used to cope with these barriers. A case study approach focusing on an Israeli firm and its Japanese clients is examined, within the framework of coping with communications barriers.
      The paper first presents the background, discussing the relationship between telecommunications and economic activity, the nature of barriers and the context of the case study. Then, the operating conventions of the Israeli-Japanese firms are

discussed, emphasizing their use of various communications channels. The concluding section presents the lessons learned from this case study with regard to technology's impacts on international production and barrier effects.

2.   Background

2.1   New information technologies, development and spatial interaction

The theory of international trade is based on the (often implicit) assumption that transportation infrastructure and services are available at a cost lower than that which may eliminate the comparative advantage of regions. The transition into the post-industrial or information economy (which is less dependent upon transportation of material goods), and the technological developments and proliferation of NIT require that we define transportation systems in a broader sense than in the past. In this paper, communications systems are defined as the infrastructure and services available to move people, information and goods from one location to another (Mokhtarian, 1990). Consequently, communications include both transportation and telecommunications. As telecommunications are nowadays inseparable from the terminal equipment that process, store and retrieve the information, we refer to NIT as a synonym to telecommunications.

The relationship between telecommunications and development has attracted interest over the last two decades. The technological advances of NIT, the growing importance of information in the economy and the assumed analogy to transportation systems are the main reasons for this interest. Numerous authors have suggested that investments in NIT infrastructure will bring about regional development (Wellenius, 1984). More recently, the role of NIT is seen as a facilitator of development rather than a cause (Nijkamp and Salomon, 1989). That is, for certain types of development, NIT infrastructure is a necessary, but not a sufficient condition for attracting economic activities.

The literature on NIT and development has generally focused on the impacts on developing countries (Clapp and Richardson, 1984; Inose, 1988; Akwule, 1991; Chowdary, 1988) or on less-favored regions of developed countries (Goddard and Gillespie, 1986). The conclusions usually tend to support the need for investments in NIT infrastructure. The economic value of telecommunications in developed regions received less attention. Implicitly, it may have been assumed that in developed regions the relationship between demand and supply of NIT are cyclical, so that none is a bottleneck for development.

NIT, as transportation, is part of the infrastructure for overcoming distance. In recent years, Aschauer (1989), Munnel (1990) and others have shown that such infrastructure has significant effects on productivity, when measured at a macro level.   The benefits realized through the "friction-reducing" function of transportation and telecommunications are accrued by the private sector, thus stimulating productivity increases.

However, there is no clear framework for explaining at the micro level (firm and household), how and why such infrastructure services affect development or productivity (Bell and Feitelson, 1991). This is particularly true in the broader perspective that takes into account not only traditional manufacturing industries, but post-industrial economies, and not only physical transport, but telecommunications as a spatial technology.

While the macro-level relationships between infrastructure, development and productivity have been noted, analysis at the micro level is lacking. A case-study approach is used to examine how NIT and transportation are employed by a particular organization which practices the relationship suggested in recent literature. Specifically, we investigate the operations and communications of a firm that operates from Israel in the Japanese market. To do so, the firm uses a variety of communications modes, which complement each other. The communications pattern of the firm, as well as the firm structure have evolved as a response to barriers which had to be overcome in this example of international trade. Although, due to commercial discretion, most of the information is given in qualitative terms, the analysis of communications flows between locations which a few years ago could not be conceived, does shed light into the role of telecommunications on economic activity and international trade.

Telecommunications, in contrast to transportation, can collapse distance, not just shrink it, to borrow on Abler's et al. (1975) terminology. However, as Gillespie and Williams (1988) indicate, the changing distances do not occur uniformly across space. That is, some areas are better served and hence "get closer" more than others. In fact, the global production may create a new form of core-periphery relationships, where an agent at a remote location, typified in some respects as a peripheral location to a particular market, can participate in that market (Gillespie and Williams, 1988). But, the core-periphery relationship implies, as will be shown in this case study, that the participation is not without a cost, even in the era of advanced NIT.

Economic activities generate demand for four types of movement:
a)   Goods (raw material, products or production equipment),
b)   People (as manual labor or as information, in the form of knowledge stored in their brains),
c)   Information in the form of hardcopies (books, reports, letters) delivered by mail and courier services, and
d)   Information in the form of electronic data.

The relative weight of each type of demand varies across organizations and may change over time. Therefore, the relative impact of technological advances in each transport/telecommunications technology is likely to have a different effect on inter- and intra-organizational interaction patters. For example, as in the case discussed below, while telecommunications have effectively reduced the distance between Japan and Israel to seconds, there are still no direct flights between the two countries. Thus, depending on the type of communications necessary for collaboration, a firm in Israel may be at a disadvantage compared to one in central Europe, which does have direct flights to Japan.

Emphasis on the development of telecommunications to entertain comparative advantages has been observed, for example, in the Caribbean (Demac and Morrison,

1989), and in Ireland (Wilson, 1991), where American corporations use low-wage labor for data-entry tasks, using international telecommunications facilities.

The effects of NIT on development are thus two-fold. On the one hand, they allow to exploit comparative advantages where, in the lack of NIT, these advantages did not exist due to prohibitive transportation costs. On the other hand, NIT facilitates productivity gains, as firms can act in wider markets, at lesser production costs.

Software production generates two major types of demand for transportation and telecommunications. At the local scale, the workers must reach a work location, using a variety of commuting modes. Once at a work-place, the worker relies primarily on the transfer of information primarily through electronically-based media. However, not all communication needs are met by the commuting trips and often face-to-face meetings are necessary. Indeed, it has been shown that high-tech industries, in contrast to some common notions about their footlooseness, do generate transportation demand for air travel of employees as well as other inputs and products (Mahmassani and Toft, 1985; Button 1988).

With a relatively high share of information demand amenable to telecommunications, software production is a likely candidate for a geographically dispersed process, where organizations located at wide distances from each other can collaborate in production. Areas with a comparative advantage in software production, namely human capital, can offer their services to organizations which have a gap in this field.

2.2　The nature of barriers

Barriers can be seen as discontinuities in the cost of traversing physical or administrative space (Nijkamp, Rietveld and Salomon, 1990). They can be physical, technological, economic, administrative (or political) or cultural. Barriers distort the geographical space as defined by distance or travel time. For example, a border control point increases the travel time between locations across the border and thus increases the cost of communicating face-to-face between these points.

Telecommunications systems are characterized by some barriers that differ from those typical in physical transport (Giaoutzi, 1990). For example, telecommunications channels, using satellite, microwave or physical cables are not affected by conventional national borders (although tariffs may reflect international barriers). However, from the users' perspective, there are also a number of barriers that warrant discussion.

In the present context, at least four types of barriers to telecommunications and travel may take effect:

Cost barriers While costs per se should not be considered a barrier, a discontinuity in a cost schedule, or the unequal distribution of costs can be seen as a barrier. Communications from Israel "locate" Japan at a greater distance than its actual position. While the physical distance to Japan is roughly equivalent to the distance from Israel to New-York, the former is effectively much farther away. As there are no direct flights between Tel-Aviv and the Far-east, flying time and fares are disproportionally greater than flights to the United States. Thus, from an Israeli perspective, collaboration with Japan is a priori at a disadvantage, when compared to interactions with other markets at similar distance.

The cost barrier also applies to telecommunications. The telephone call from Israel to Japan is more expensive than to the United States (6.97 NIS and 6.31 NIS per minute, in Feb. 1992, respectively), but the rates to the United States are based on Peak-Load-Pricing, which means that at off-peak the rate per minute is only 3.15 NIS. This reduced rate is not available to Japan. The availability of time-based rates does not reflect actual costs, but is an outcome of either demand or marketing considerations.

Barriers, as exemplified by the telephone rates, may not be symmetrical. As it is cheaper to call Israel from Japan than vice versa, the perceived barrier of calling acts differentially for parties at the two countries.

Time Zones The 7 (or 6 when daylight saving time is in effect) hour difference in time zones between Israel and Japan implies that in a normal workday of eight hours there are only one to two hours overlap. To have real-time communications, one of the parties need to bear the costs of diverting from the normal work schedule. Under normal conditions, one can assume that such coordination is not too problematic. Time zone differences do act as a barrier when close cooperation and frequent communications is necessary for a smooth production process.

Language barriers Howells (1987) has pointed to the limited success of British NIT industries in penetrating the French market. He attributed it, among others, to the language and cultural barriers. While English is increasingly becoming the international language of NIT, many end users need or want their own language to be used. Also, the difference in the level of mastering of a common language by professionals who have to work jointly on a project is another serious impediment to collaboration. While the use of professional interpreters can solve some of these problems, it still involves costs: monetary costs for employing interpreters as well as costs of mistakes in translation which may occur in the process.

Cultural barriers While very difficult to define, it is widely accepted that cultural barriers play an important role in hampering international cooperation. If these exist between western-European countries, as pointed out by Howells (1987), they are certainly more profound in the case of communications between western cultures and Japan, as noted by Nagai (1983) and Tung (1984). The cultural barriers may be divided into two. First are those which may be labelled as formal. These include the attitudes and norms associated with holidays, working hours, and so on. Being relatively institutionalized and known, they can be considered in advance and arrangements can be made to overcome their costs. More complicated are the less structured barriers of work style, modes of communications and the like. Here, as western business people may have learned through costly failures, the Japanese practices differ widely from those of the west.

2.3 Communications behavior: A conceptual framework

The daily operations of an organization, particularly those involved in international trade and global production, rely heavily on the efficient use of communications. The communications patterns which evolve in an organization are constantly adapted to new needs, changing policies, changing individuals and most notably, a changing technology.

Coping with barriers is an increasingly important issue for communications-intensive organizations. De Meyer (1991) has identified three major strategies employed by organizations to stimulate communications in global Research and Development (R&D) activities. Software production seems to fit well in this context. First, organizations seem to adjust their organizational structure to accommodate open communications flows. As collaboration and efficient communications among individuals is often a result of personal acquaintances, projects and people's assignment may be structured so as to facilitate the communications. Second, particular individuals assume or are assigned to serve in the role of gatekeepers for boundary spanning of the organization. These individuals are capable of obtaining and conveying information between facilities and their tasks are so defined. The third strategy is the efficient employment of telecommunications technologies, realizing that these tend to complement each other rather than serve as single independent channels.

In his empirical work, De Meyer identified six solutions which emanate from the three basic strategies:

1) efforts to increase socialization to enhance communications.
2) implementation of rules to increase formal communications.
3) assignment of boundary-spanning roles to particular individuals.
4) creating a communications management facility.
5) development of a network organization.
6) replacement of face-to-face communications by telecommunications.

This list is diverse enough to offer strategies for organizations to choose from and solve the particular communications problems they face.

In the case study described below, we have examined how some of these strategies were in fact employed by Company A.

3. Developing Projects across the Continent: A Case Study

3.1 The context

Company A is a software house based in Israel and producing solely for the Japanese corporate market. Israel seems to offer a comparative advantage in the area of software production. Some 0.856% of the employed labor force in 1989 were systems analysts and computer programmers (CBS, 1990). This compares with 0.72% of the US employed labor force (for 1986). Japan, as noted earlier, suffers from a shortage of software professionals.

In its present form Company A is active since early 1991. Its operation is based on two sister companies: Company A-Israel, and Tokyo-based Company A-

Japan. Company A specializes in programming in Japanese for major corporations in Japan. Thus, there is a basic problem of translation between Japanese and English, as the Israeli employees of the Company do not master Japanese.

Company A-Japan has initially served as a marketing front for the Israeli company. As the products are geared to major corporations and not to wide markets of consumers or small establishments, the marketing tasks are to a great extent a communications function, between the clients and the software house. Specifically, this means that the Japanese company generates and maintains all the contacts with the clients and serves as an intermediatory between the clients and the producers. This can be viewed as a case where multi-site corporations specialize in different functions of the production process. The Israeli site is the production location whereas the Japanese site serves the marketing functions, as well as, to a limited degree, the market research functions.

The relationship between the companies is schematically shown in Figure 1. Since the beginning of 1991, the company in Israel has a permanent Japanese team which serves mainly as a communications team, assuming the roles of both lingual and cultural translation. The activities of the company before 1991 were characterized by very severe communications problems with the Japanese corporations, problems that were largely overcome by the introduction of the Japanese team in Israel.

The analysis is based on interviews with the management and employees of Company A.

3.2   The mode of operations of company A

Japanese R&D is often a collaborative effort on behalf of a number of big corporations. The Ministry of International Trade and Industry (MITI) plays a primary role in initiating and funding such collaboration (Davidson, 1987; Teubal, 1991). The initiative for large scale projects in the Japanese computer industry originates from one or more of the big Japanese corporations. Discussions among the big corporations leads to agreements on the mode of collaboration and responsibilities of each participating organization. At this stage, the corporations agree on the allocation of tasks, financing, the division of profits and rights to the eventual product.

In the second stage, according to the ideal project development, each big corporation invites smaller companies to discuss the new project. To compete in the Japanese corporate market, a company must be invited by corporate initiative. Decisions about which smaller corporations will be involved in the project are based entirely on previous relationships with those smaller companies, and based on their assessment of their ability to perform. A specific part of the new project is discussed in detail with each smaller company. Company A-Japan, for instance, in the first discussions on a new project, was given detailed information about its expected share of the project, and asked to provide the best plan including such things as deliverables, financing, and a schedule. The discussions can take weeks, even months and take place only after the big corporation has chosen the small companies with which it will work on the project.

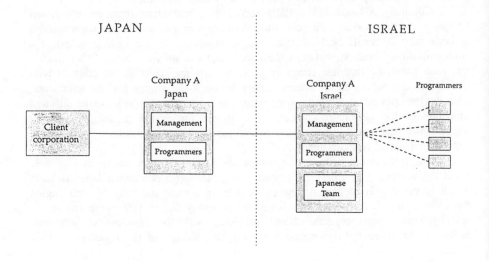

JAPAN

ISRAEL

Figure 1: The Initial Structure of Company A

Discussion between a big corporation and the small companies takes place in weekly meetings, at the headquarters of the host corporation. All of the small companies attend the same meeting, and each big corporation on the project holds its own weekly meetings. At the beginning of each weekly meeting answers are given to questions presented by the corporation to the small supplier, in the former weekly meeting. Answers are given by the smaller companies. Next, a progress report is given by each of the smaller corporations. After the progress reports, new sets of questions are raised to be answered at the meeting the following week. A meeting summary is presented at the end of the meeting. This summary includes a timetable, deliverables and the list of questions to be answered at the next meeting.

The importance of the temporal cycle must be recognized. It implies that the one week cycle routine imposes the work plan of the small companies, and if they are located away from the client (Tokyo), then the reliance on reliable telecommunications becomes more evident. Similarly, the cultural barrier with regard to holidays and work schedules may negatively affect the remote company from adhering to the rules set by the Japanese client.

At the weekly meetings, Company A-Japan is represented by her marketing manager. Company A-Israel does not attend. Company A-Japan acts as the spokesman for Company A-Israel. But Company A-Israel answers all the questions, gives all the solutions, and provides the timetable. The software in development by

Company A-Israel is transferred to Company A-Japan from Israel every few days and presented by Company A-Japan in the weekly meeting.

Company A-Israel starts working as soon as information is received from Company A-Japan. During the week the programmers of the client corporation examine the material presented by the small companies and prepare a set of questions. These questions may ask the small companies to adjust their work, provide explanations, and to debug their programming. These extra questions and requests must be resolved during the week, and before the weekly meeting.

Company A is seen by the Japanese corporation as a local software firm, one of many with which the corporation works. Company A-Japan serves as the front for this purpose. Company A-Israel is thus a branch of the front, differing from its Japanese competitors only in the communications costs.

3.3 Communications between Israel and Japan

In the normal mode of operations, Company A uses a variety of communication channels, as shown in Figure 2. Three types of information are exchanged, as shown in the figure: professional, managerial and hardware-based. The latter refers to intelligent machines, such as computers, printers etc. Each of the modes of communications that serve the company's needs exhibits certain advantages in terms of the type of information it can transmit, the quality of the communications, the speed, the costs and some other attributes. Thus, each mode is used for one or more particular purposes where it is perceived as the most efficient.

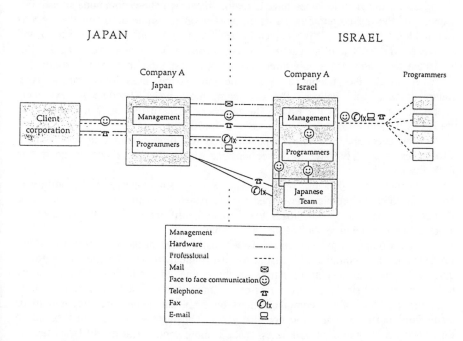

Figure 2: The communications network of Company A

Within Israel, Company A-Israel uses telephone services for primary communications and normal postal services for secondary communications. Electronic mail (E-mail) is occasionally used between Company A-Israel and employees who work outside the Jerusalem office or with sub-contractors within Israel.

FAX (facsimile) is used for a variety of purposes within Israel. The most important use is for programmers working away from the Jerusalem head office. They send a screen print of a trouble-shooting message that is displayed in Japanese to the Jerusalem head office. There, it is translated into English and returned as quickly as possible to minimize development delays.

Company A-Japan communicates one-way with Company A-Israel by courier to send off-the- shelf, bilingual (English/Japanese) Japanese software, which is not available in Israel. Company A-Japan also communicates one-way with Company A-Israel by air freight to send Japanese hardware and equipment needed for development of the Japanese software products. Before this material is sent, the Israeli team, in Israel, identifies what is needed. They use catalogues for the equipment and materials, and the advice of the collaborating Israel/Japanese teams in Tokyo for identifying, testing, and ordering Japanese software required in Israel.

Company A-Japan and Company A-Israel send information in both directions by FAX, telephone and modem. FAX is the most-frequently used communication mode. All meeting summaries, requirements, questions and progress reports are send in Japanese from Japan to Israel where they are translated into English.

International time zones have a major impact on these communications. For instance, if the big corporation wants an answer on the same day, and the FAX is sent at 11 a.m. in Japan, it is received in Israel at 4 or 5 a.m.. The Israeli team will not receive the FAX until at least 8 a.m. Israel time, when they arrive at work. For the Israeli team this means only three hours, not a whole day to provide a solution.

Although the telephone was supposed to be used only rarely as a communications tool between the two companies, it has become an extremely important supplement to the FAX. The telephone is used to clarify information in the FAXs, to add information and to assist in translation.

The telephone, providing a personalized real-time communications medium, also serves as a safety valve to reduce tensions when communications are unclear in FAX format.

E-mail, through a use of a modem, is the main tool used for exporting to Japan the software products developed by the Israeli team in Israel. In Tokyo, the Company A-Japan team downloads the E-mailed software to diskette and takes the diskette to the meeting as the weekly deliverable.

The Company in Japan and in Israel has invested in the very best and fastest FAX and modem equipment available to enable them to send lengthy messages as quickly as possible, keeping user time of phone lines to a minimum. The Company has set rules for using the three forms of communication, based on keeping costs to a minimum. Most of the communications by FAX and phone are supposed to be made from Japan to Israel, and not vice versa. The Japanese phone rates, based on time-of-day pricing and on bulk rates, make it more economical to call Israel then in the other direction, as Israel does not have scaled rates to Japan.

However, for many reasons the rules are often broken, as will be discussed below.

3.4 Barriers, communications problems and structural adjustments

When problems and delays occur, the pressure of the weekly deliverables and meetings on the small companies are dramatically increased. When outside circumstances prevent the small company from delivering to schedule, the resulting delays and problems have enormous impact on the relationship between Company A-Israel and Company A-Japan. The pressure is even greater when Company A-Japan fails to deliver on time.

For instance, the final deadline for a project was set as the end of July, 1991. In the weekly meeting in early June, two months before the deadline, everyone on the segment of the project in which Company A-Japan and Company A-Israel were involved realized that a basic mistake existed in the software, and that major reprogramming would be necessary. This would mean a six months delay. This put enormous pressure on the big corporation to which Company A-Japan reported. It also affected all other big and small corporations on the project.

The relationship between Company A-Japan and Company A-Israel was also dramatically affected. In the meeting of the second week of June, the client corporation ruled that the barrier of distance, or the non-monetary costs of (mis) communication were too high and it insisted that a team from Company A-Israel must come to work in Japan together with a team of programmers from the big corporation. This was first seen as a temporary solution emanating from the particular crisis.

Two programmers went from Israel to Japan to work in the Company A-Japan offices with the programmers from the big corporation. This new situation changed the relationship between Company A-Israel and the big corporation. For the first time, the Israeli programming team and the Japanese client's programming team worked together on the same program. The part of the Israeli team that remained in Israel continued to be involved. Debugging and program alteration was done in collaboration by the Israeli teams in each country.

The results of the crisis of June 1991 had long-term impacts on the character of communication between the two parts of Company A and the Japanese companies. New relationships and standards for working were established. The client corporation insisted that in Company A-Japan there would always be an Israeli programmer. As a result, the Company A-companies decided to rotate an Israeli programmer to Japan every three months. The resulting new structure is depicted in Figure 3.

The new structure opened new communications channels. The client corporation sent its programmers to work together with the tokyo-based Israeli programmer, in the same office. Thus, the face-to-face daily communications between the professional level counterparts substituted for the professional contacts between the Company A-Japan personnel and the clients. This direct contact at the professional level implies that the client has obtained greater control of Company A's work, as its programmers are almost insiders now to the professional work done

116

at Company A.

Other barriers also hampered the efficient operations of Company A. A mistake in international time zones can be made. An emergency, misunderstandings or need for speedy clarification of FAX messages may require Israel to call Japan. "Cultural misunderstandings" and confusions must be immediately clarified. For example, the holidays of complete rest, and the reserve army service which affect the schedule of the Israeli side must be repeatedly explained to Company A-Japan in order that they can convey the information to the client corporation. Although these special circumstances in Israel are understood in Japan, they are not readily accepted. This often makes repeated and emergency explanations essential.

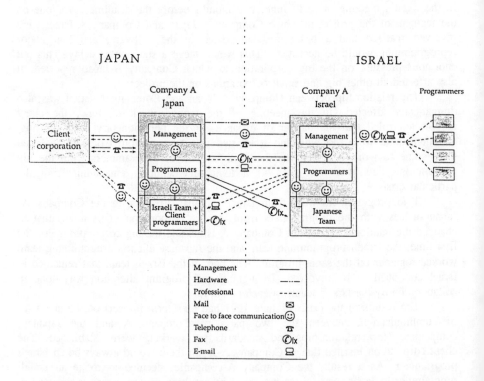

Figure 3: The Revised Organization and Communications Patterns of Company A

Although the weekly meetings impose a cyclical communications pattern, the actual turnaround of information within Company A is also subject to cultural barriers. The Japanese custom of never responding to a question before a complete answer is available is not easily accepted in Israel. Many extra communication contacts result from the Israelis' attempt to obtain even partial responses. For example, in some instances, especially when large projects, involving some big corporations are concerned, Company A-Israel will ask for information about the best way to do the project and will hear nothing for a year. When the answer arrives at Company A-Japan, it includes orders to provide deliverables immediately. Company A-Japan transfers this information to Company A-Israel, and Company A-Israel reacts inappropriately (in Japanese terms).

Another aspect of cultural nature was the fact that Japanese normally send employees for a year or more at a time to another country, with no provision for visits home nor for family to visit abroad. Israelis rarely stay away from home and family more than a few weeks at a time. Therefore the pressure on the Israeli programmer located for three months in Japan is compound. Tension results from the Japanese inability to understand why more than three months in Japan is not possible for the Israeli programmers, and from the Israeli inability to accept the Japanese attitude. However, the results of three months co-location is extremely positive for all as better understanding of cultural behaviors develops.

Over time, these barriers are decreasing as the Japanese and Israelis visit each others' countries and sites of operation. At this time, every Israeli team member has been in Japan at least once, and most of the Japanese team members have been in Israel at least once.

3.5   Communications adjustments

The experience gained by the company in coping with barriers has led to the development of a rather stable pattern of communications that employs a variety of channels, exploiting the relative advantage of each.

As shown in Figure 3, five different modes are used. Each mode serves one or more information transfer purposes (professional, managerial and hardware).

The major barrier, that of language, is overcome by the presence of native speakers Japanese, English and Hebrew at the two ends of the company's operations. These allow for the translation of written/verbal information into the richer face-to-face communications. The richness of the latter stems from the ability to augment it with non-verbal communications, as much as with transferring the flavor of the message, thus bridging over some aspects of the cultural barrier as well.

Because Company A-Japan is the marketing division, and Company A-Israel is the technical division, and the marketplace in Japan requires detailed information exchange between the companies, electronic communication is not entirely adequate. The management of both companies must meet at least three times a year in Japan to share information and develop plans. They must also regularly attend technical exhibitions to mutually acquire current information on the hardware and software markets, and they must meet with potential clients.

The Japanese managers of Company A-Japan must visit Israel at least once a year. This is essential to maintain and strengthen the bonds between the Japanese and Israeli companies, to improve understandings between the companies. A great deal of the time the Japanese manager spends in Israel is used to overcome the barriers between Japanese and Israeli cultures and corporate customs.

118

4. Conclusions

The operations of Company A prove that international cooperation across distance and culture is a viable option for software production, and possibly for other information-intensive economic activities. The use of multiple communication modes supports the claims raised in the literature about the globalization impacts of NIT. Beyond that general conclusion, there are a few lessons concerning the relationship between remote facilities, and between communications modes that should not be overlooked. These do not reverse the general conclusion about the viability of such operations, but qualify the circumstances under which NIT can affect international collaboration.

First, the communications system which serves the counterparts is a complex one. It includes both transportation-based elements (mail, courier, air freight, and most importantly, face-to-face meetings) and several NIT-based channels (telephone, E-mail and fax). All channels seem to complement each other rather than to substitute for each other.

Second, the presence of barriers affected the organizational structure of the company and the communications patterns within it and between the company and its clients. Organizational change was in fact suggested by De Meyer (1991). Communications problems resulted in cross-delegations of each company at the other's facility. These delegations have multiple roles. They serve as translators of both language and culture. In addition, the Israeli team in Tokyo was positioned there permanently, because of the clients' demand for direct professional contact with the Israeli site. It seems that at least in software production, there is a necessity for face-to-face communications among the professionals, in addition to on-going communications among managers.

One may conclude that to bridge cultural barriers, face-to-face communications is warranted. The personal communications between the Israeli teams in Tokyo and in Israel, and similarly, between the Japanese teams at both ends, are sufficiently efficient to overcome the variety of barriers. The nature of face-to-face communications, as can be learned from this case study, can be differentiated into submodes. Some face-to-face communications can overcome the constraints imposed by NIT, such as the lack of social presence, but these do not necessarily overcome cultural barriers. Other face-to-face communications are capable of overcoming cultural barriers. These seem to be successful if at both ends there are respective delegates of the other culture.

Acknowledgment:
The authors thank Eran Feitelson, Pat Mokhtarian, Peter Nijkamp and Eran Razin for their constructive comments to this paper. We also thank Tami Sofer for the graphic contribution. Partial Support for their paper was given by the Basic Research Foundation of the Israeli Academy of Science and Humanities.

REFERENCES

Abler, R., D. Jannelle, A. Philbrick and J. Sommer (eds), **Human Geography in a Shrinking World**, Duxbury, North Scituate, Ma., 1975.

Akwule, R. Telecommunications in Nigeria, **Telecommunications Policy**, June, 1991, pp. 241-247.

Aschauer, D., Is Public Expenditure Productive?, **Journal of Monetary Economics**, 23,2, 1989, pp. 177-200.

Bell, M., and E. Feitelson, US Economic Restructuring and Demand for Transportation Services, **Transportation Quarterly**, 45, 4, 1991, pp. 517-538.

Button, K., High Technology Companies: An Examination of Their Transport Needs, **Progress in Planning**, 29, 2, 1988, pp. 93-108.

Central Bureau of Statistics - Israel, **Labour Force Survey 1989**, Special Report No. 894, Jerusalem, 1990.

Chowdary, T.H., Telephones in Rural Areas: An Indian Experience", **Telematics and Informatics**, vol. 5, no.1, 1988, pp.

Clapp, J., and H. Richardson, Technological Change in Information Processing Industries and Regional Income Differentials in Developing Countries, **International Regional Science Review**, 9, 3, 1984, pp. 241-256.

Cole, S., The Global Impact of Information Technology, **World Development**, 14, 10-11, 1986, pp. 1277-1292.

Davidson, W., Japanese Telecommunications Policy: Directions and Old Dilemmas, **Telecommunications Policy**, 11,2, 1987, pp. 147-160.

Demac, D., and D. Morrison, US Caribbean Telecommunications: Making Great Strides in Development, **Telecommunications Policy**, 13,1, 1989, pp. 51-58.

De Meyer, A. Tech Talk: How Managers are Stimulating Global R&D Communication, **Sloan Management Review**, Spring, 1991, pp. 49-58.

Fischer M., R. Maggi, and C. Rammer, Context Specific Media Choice and Barriers to Communication in Universities, **The Annals of Regional Science**, 24, 4, 1990, pp. 253-270.

Giaoutzi, M., Spatial Barriers in Information and Communications Systems, **NETCOM**, 4, 1, 1990, pp. 84-101.

Giaoutzi, M., and P. Nijkamp, New Information Technologies and Spatial Transport Development, The Free University, Amsterdam, Research Memo 1989-47, 1989.

Gillespie, A. and H. Williams, Telecommunications and the Reconstruction of

Regional Comparative Advantage, **Environment and Planning A**, 20, 1988, pp. 1311-1321.

Goddard, J. and A. Gillespie, Advanced Telecommunications and Regional Economic Development, **The Geographical Journal**, 152, 3, 1986, pp. 383-397.

Howells, J. Developments in the Location, Technology and Industrial Organization of Computer Services: Some Trends and Research Issues, **Regional Studies**, 1, 6, 1987, pp. 493-504.

Inose, H., Information Technology in an International Perspective, **Information Technology: Social and Spatial Perspectives** (Orishimo I., Hewings J. and Nijkamp P., eds.), Springer Verlag, Berlin, 1988, pp. 66-70.

Mahmassani, H. and G. Toft, Transportation Requirements for High Technology Industrial Development, **Journal of Transportation Engineering**, 111, 5, 1985, pp. 473-484.

Masuda, Y., **The Information Society as Post Industrial Society**, World Future Society, Washington DC., 1980.

Mokhtarian, P. A Typology of Relationships between Telecommunications and Transportation, **Transportation Research A**, 24A, 3, 1990, pp. 231-244.

Munnel, A. Why has Productivity Declined? Productivity and Public Investment, **New England Economic Review**, (1990) 3-22.

Nagai, M. Cultural Lag and International Communications: The Case of Japan, **Information Economics and Policy**, 1, 1, 1989, pp. 69-74.

Nijkamp, P. and I. Salomon, Future Spatial Impacts of Telecommunications, **Transportation Planning and Technology**, 13, 1989, pp. 275-287.

Nijkamp, P., P. Rietveld and I. Salomon, Barriers in Spatial Interaction and Communications; A Conceptual Exploration, **The Annals of Regional Science**, 24, 1990, pp. 237-252.

Parker, E.B., Appropriate Telecommunications for Economic Development, **Telecommunications Policy**, 8,3, 1984, pp. 173-177.

Teubal, M., Technological Infrastructure in Japan: Implications for Israel, Jerusalem Institute for Israel Studies, Policy Background Papers, No. 1, 1991.

Tung, R., **Business Negotiations with the Japanese**, Lexington Books, Lexington, Ma., 1984.

US-OTA (Office of Technology Assessment, US Congress), Japanese Software: The Next Competitive Challenge, Washington DC, 1987.

Warf, B., Telecommunications and the Globalization of Financial Services, **The Professional Geographer**, 41,3, 1989, pp. 257-271.

Wellenius, B., On the Role of Telecommunications in Development, **Telecommunications Policy**, 8, 1, 1984, pp. 59-66.

Wilson, M., Offshore Relocation of Producer Services: The Irish Back Offices, Paper presented at the IGU Meeting, Miami, April, 1991.

Part B

CHANGING SPATIAL STRUCTURES AND TRANSPORTATION SYSTEMS

CHAPTER 8

CHANGING EUROPEAN TRANSPORT INFRASTRUCTURES

AND THEIR REGIONAL IMPLICATIONS

Roger W. Vickerman

1.   **Introduction**

There is an almost unprecedented change taking place in European transport infrastructure at the moment. Not since the heyday of railway development in the mid nineteenth century has such a degree of construction of major new links in the transport network of Europe been undertaken. Various reasons can be advanced for this. Pressures to curb public sector deficits have led to expenditure on public infrastructure in the recent past being reduced substantially below that necessary even to maintain existing networks in good working order. This has created a backlog of much needed investment. The growth in traffic and the concentration of population have led to increasing problems of congestion. New or improved technology has enabled major advances in high speed rail helping to create a demand for, in effect, a new travel mode. Increasing environmental concern has emphasised the advantages of rail for both passenger and freight traffic over both air and road. Finally, and probably of greatest importance, the move to a Single European Market for the European Community, its expansion to a wider European Economic Space including the EFTA countries, and the dramatic changes in Eastern Europe, have all contributed to the need for development of a coordinated Europe-wide transport network, uninterrupted by either physical or political barriers.

This paper aims to examine the nature of these barriers and the impacts of their removal. Too often such impacts are focussed on the regions close to the new infrastructures. Here I want to take a much wider view of the situation, tackling the question as to whether such changes will lead to greater concentration of economic activity and hence greater regional inequality in Europe or to greater dispersion and thus contribute to the greater economic cohesion sought. The paper has five main sections. First, we deal with the nature of the changes in question; secondly, we look at the different nature of different types of barrier and where they are to be found; thirdly we look at the development of European networks and how different networks interrelate; fourthly we look at the regional implications for new developments at the macro-scale across Europe and finally draw some policy implications for future needs. The paper concludes that much still needs to be done to remove institutional and financial barriers to the planning of European networks.

126

2. Europe's Changing Transport Infrastructure

The decades around the millennium will see an enormous change in the transport networks of Europe, principally because of the completion of a small number of critical links. Although often very short in length, these are of disproportionate cost and significance.

2.1 The Channel Tunnel

First, in both time and (at least perceived) significance is the Channel Tunnel. As well as the symbolic effect of providing a fixed link to Europe's most populated island, the Tunnel is likely to be the costliest single piece of infrastructure, at nearly £9 billion for 50 km, and probably unique as the only entirely privately financed project, without even government guarantees on the loans. It has particular significance by providing a connection between the British and continental rail networks for the first time and because it has brought into sharp relief the contrast between British and French approaches to both railway investment and regional planning as practised by "aménagement du territoire" (Holliday and Vickerman, 1990; Holliday et al, 1991).

2.2 Scandinavian links

Two further major projects involve maritime crossings, the Storebaelt link between Fyn and Sjaelland in Denmark and the Oresund crossing between Denmark and Sweden. The former will link the two halves of Denmark, Jylland and Fyn to the west (with 55% of the population) and Sjaelland - Lolland - Falster (with 45%) to the east (Madsen & Jensen-Butler, 1991). The Storebaelt crossing will provide both rail and road links at an original estimated cost of DKK 18 billion (about £1.6 billion). As with the Channel Tunnel, which has seen its estimated costs virtually double, these costs have increased and delays have put back the initial completion of the rail link from 1993 to 1996, with the road link to be finished by 1997. The Oresund crossing was agreed between Denmark and Sweden in late 1991 at an initial estimated cost of DKK 12 Billion, plus at least DKK 3 billion for associated infrastructure in Denmark, a start is hoped for during 1993. These two improvements to links within Scandinavia are complemented by a third proposal for a fixed link across the Fehmarnbelt on the direct route between Hamburg and Kobenhavn, although this has a much longer timescale with completion unlikely before 2004 at the earliest and may be dependent on substantial private finance to confirm German interest. A particular interest here is the changing accessibility of the different regions of Denmark through these three projects and the effects on service activity location in particular (Illeris and Jakobsen, 1991; Madsen and Jensen-Butler, 1991)

2.3 Alpine transits

The third group of mega-projects are the proposed improvements to Alpine crossings by the construction of base tunnels. There are three such proposed, the Lötschberg and Gotthard routes in Switzerland and the Brenner route between

Austria and Italy. The Swiss projects are part of the integrated Alp Transit plan for New Alpine Rail Axes which has been evolved over a long period with the objective of maintaining the share of rail in transit traffic through Switzerland under pressure from the EC to lift the severe weight limit of 28 tonnes and other restrictions on road transit traffic, but also contributing to regional policy considerations within Switzerland (Ratti, 1978; Berger, 1989). The plan for two new base tunnels at an estimated cost of SFR 15 billion (£6 billion) has been ratified, but needs to be confirmed in a referendum during 1992.

2.4 Peripheral infrastructure

All of these projects can be seen as part of the desire to achieve a greater integration of the geographically more peripheral parts of Europe which still constitute part of the economic core of developed Europe, the UK, Scandinavia and Italy. There are further projects which seek either to expand that economic core or to provide better links with more peripheral and less developed regions. These include links to Spain and within Spain and Portugal, a fixed link across the Straits of Messina to Sicily and improvements of transit routes through the Balkans to Greece and Turkey. Added to this, since 1989 has come the pressing need to improve east-west infrastructure. The transport infrastructure needs of German unification alone, to build new links, restore old ones and upgrade the decayed infrastructure of the new Länder, have been estimated at over DM 200 billion (£70 billion) (IFO, 1991).

2.5 A European high speed rail network

Thus far we have discussed essentially large, identifiably separate projects. In addition there is a substantial investment in both existing and new networks which, when taken together, constitute even larger projects, but which for various reasons are usually determined separately (Vickerman, 1991a). The obvious example of this is the European High Speed Rail Network with, at its core, the northern European network (Paris-Brussels-Köln-Amsterdam-London). The total network of new and upgraded lines has been estimated to cost of the order of 150 billion ECU. However, we should also remember the need for major road projects in certain parts of Europe to complete a basic European network, especially where rail investment cannot be justified, and a corresponding investment in infrastructure for air travel, principally runway and terminal capacity and air traffic control systems, both of which are at breaking point in the core regions of the EC.

2.6 Infrastructure and transport service

We have identified the main changes here as involving the physical infrastructure of transport systems. This is certainly the part which captures both the imagination and the cost, but more crucial for its economic impact is the level of service delivered. This too can involve substantial capital expenditure. High speed rail systems or highly utilised tunnel infrastructure requires major development of signalling and control systems. Improving the utilisation rate of congested motorways requires similar developments of adequate systems to assist drivers in making more efficient use of existing road space. For many of the most peripheral parts of Europe, the provision of physical infrastructure in the form of roads and railways will rarely be the most appropriate solution. For these regions, Ireland being the obvious example, access depends on mobile infrastructure in the form of planes and ferries.

3.   **Overcoming Barriers**
    We can summarise the discussion in the previous section by identifying the various infrastructure projects in terms of the type of barrier they are designed to overcome and their location.

3.1   **Types of barrier**
    There are three types of barrier being addressed by these projects:

*   **physical barriers** such as sea crossings or mountain ranges, which are the primary reason for the major projects. These barriers have been maintained to a large extent for reasons of technology and cost, but since they involve in many cases international links there are also political barriers which have prevented their earlier solution.
*   **political barriers**, even where there are no major physical barriers, the political fragmentation of Europe has hindered planning of the major infrastructure. The problems of planning the European high speed rail network testify to this, especially to secure compatible timing of the decisions. The gaps in the major motorway network also reflect the existence of political barriers.
*   **bottlenecks** exist on networks even where there are no physical or political barriers, simply because of the volume of traffic. The particularly significant bottlenecks are those associated with the need for traffic to pass through major metropolitan areas which may previously have been the principal destination for most national traffic, but now create problems for the increasingly international character of traffic in Europe. London and Paris are the obvious examples of this.

3.2   **Locational impacts of infrastructure**
    The key issue is to note that infrastructure has an impact well away from its immediate location, removing barriers at any particular place may thus have impacts over a widespread area (Vickerman, 1991b). We can locate these barriers in three principal situations in terms of their locational impact:

*   **peripheral infrastructure** is focussed on improving the accessibility of peripheral regions. It may be located either in the peripheral regions themselves, but increasingly it is recognised that the major problems facing peripheral regions are those of overcoming barriers in more central regions. Thus infrastructure such as the Channel Tunnel, Scandinavian links or Alpine tunnels, although connecting directly such core economic regions of Europe as London,

Kobenhavn or Milano, has important implications for the more peripheral regions of the UK and Ireland, the rest of Scandinavia or the Mezzogiorno.

* **core infrastructure** is that which is located in the core regions of Europe and is principally focussed on overcoming political or bottleneck barriers in integrating the major metropolitan centres of Europe. Although the Channel Tunnel falls partly into this category as well, indicating the way that a given piece of infrastructure has a multi-functional role, the completion of the northern European high speed rail network is the obvious example of this type of infrastructure.

* **metropolitan infrastructure**, falls within the core infrastructure, but is worth identifying as a separate category since it has a specific role. Whilst much core infrastructure has the purpose of integrating the metropolitan regions together, this may exclude more peripheral regions by denying them access to it because of the problems in getting through or round the major metropolitan bottlenecks. Thus the completion of orbital motorways or rail schemes such as the Paris Interconnexion, coupled with high speed rail links to major intercontinental airports will feature strongly here.

4.   Networks

Whilst it is major infrastructure projects which capture the imagination and, as the previous typology suggests, are critical in addressing some of the major concerns such as bottlenecks, it is the development of whole networks which is of the greatest long term significance. The development of European networks is now a major concern of the European Community, not just for the existing territory of the EC, but for its key links across other countries (Switzerland and Austria being the prime examples) and to other major economic partners. Identifying European networks is one thing, introducing practical measures to achieve these networks has been less easy. Attempts to introduce appropriate financial instruments have been frequently blocked at the Council of Ministers. The EC is reduced to having to use exhortation rather than concerted planning to achieve progress on networks (Vickerman, 1991a).

4.1   Levels of network

Three levels of network can be identified:

* **international networks** are those which carry the principal trade flows of the Community. These can be both extra- and intra-Community but together constitute a high level network of all the principal modes, air, rail, road and water (maritime and inland waterway). The characteristic of such networks is that flows are over long distances and that there may be some need for assembling traffic from a variety of origins to a variety of destinations along a trunk haul. International networks will therefore tend to link major metropolitan centres.

* **interregional networks** operate at a level below the international networks. Traditionally these would be thought of as being intra-national, linking either major metropolitan centres on the international networks to other centres or these lower order centres together. Increasingly, however, the removal of barriers will mean that regions will look to major centres in other states for access to the international network. Lower order centres in different states will see advantages in being linked directly rater than through, for example their national capitals. This process is aided by, for example, the reduction in regulatory control of airlines.

* **intraregional networks** operate at the lowest level and provide the links within a region. These too can be thought as having several levels, a principal regional infrastructure with secondary networks ad local networks. Whereas, international and interregional links will be primarily concerned with the trading potential of a region, intraregional links will be concerned more with the service potential and the efficient operation of labour markets within a region.

Although it is convenient to identify networks in this way, a given infrastructure may provide services relevant to more than one, even all three, networks. Most roads, for example, have access arrangements which cannot discriminate between different types of traffic. This may frequently cause problems of conflict. The M25 London Orbital Motorway, for example, was principally intended to serve an international and interregional function, taking traffic around and away from the congestion bottleneck of London. However, it has frequent access points, which also make it attractive to intraregional and local traffic, using it for short journeys. These have led to unexpectedly large generation of traffic and frequent congestion, thus imposing costs on its use for trade. Even where there is a charging system in operation it may be extremely difficult to achieve an efficient allocation of capacity to traffic according to the value it places on the use of the infrastructure. This in turn will create problems for efficient investment planning.

4.2   Interface between networks

One critical problem is achieving optimal interface between networks. Such interfaces involve both links between different levels of network within modes and between modes at different (or sometimes the same) levels of network. In the former case we have access between local roads and limited access (motorway) roads, connections between regional rail services and longer distance services, or between regional and international air services (including hub and spoke operations). It will be noted that this involves both infrastructure and the services on that infrastructure. In the latter category we can include such features as park ad ride, or the increasing development of airport rail links. It may be the case that this involves links between two high levels of network as well as the links between local access feeder services and high level networks. The linking of major airports to high speed rail networks, such as that at Paris-Charles de Gaulle, will involve two complementary high level international networks for which different modes are the more efficient for different links.

Interface between networks involves the creation of nodes. Between these nodes the links of the network form corridors of movement. Often links of several networks combine to form a major transport corridor as along major river valleys such as the Rhine or Rhône. Increasingly this may lead to multi-modal corridors across major physical barriers. The Channel Tunnel and major Alpine Tunnels are both rail links (for through passenger and freight rail services) and road links (for shuttle train or piggy-back traffic carried between the two terminals. Their efficacy as transport corridors depends on their adequate connectedness to each network. The identification of corridors and nodes is also a vital step in examining the regional impact of transport infrastructure. The key issues are the extent to which nodes develop around existing metropolitan (core) centres, how far corridors develop simply to link these, or to link more peripheral areas to the core, and what happens to those areas which are passed by (Ratti and Ferrari, 1991).

5.   Regional Implications

5.1   Infrastructure and regional development

The impact of transport infrastructure on economic development has been a long standing source of controversy (Straszheim, 1972; Gwilliam, 1979; Botham, 1982). The real difficulty arises because, although infrastructure is clearly an essential pre-requisite for development and the lack of infrastructure may act as a serious constraint on growth potential, the simple presence of the infrastructure does not of itself cause economic development without other factors also being present (Blum, 1982; Biehl, 1991). This is, at least partly, because production technology is not independent of location - firms in a location with poor transport can compensate for this by using less transport, or using transport differently in the production process. This explains why firms in less accessible locations do not have transport costs which are proportionately greater than those in the more accessible locations (Chisholm, 1987; Chisholm, 1992). It may also be the case that the main variation between good and poor locations is not firms' costs but their profits, which would explain why firms are typically interested in an improvement of transport infrastructure which enhances the productivity of other factors of production. This is particularly true if such infrastructure is provided as a public good.

Aside from the objective influence of transport provision on regional costs and competitiveness, transport provision may have a more subjective, and thus difficult to assess, impact. The ability of new transport systems to generate traffic above the predicted levels is well known - this applies to new roads providing good quality links which did not previously exist, to high speed rail links and even to upgraded services such as through electrification of rail lines or the introduction of new quality rolling stock. Places served by such improved services may gain a boost to their own image, to which the clamour for direct TGV services in France testifies (Plassard and Klein, 1990). Although it has to be recognised that this is not a universal finding and there are major new infrastructures which project a strong image, but which have had a minimal impact on either traffic flows or the local economy - the Humber Bridge is a classic case here.

Models of the impact of new infrastructure on regional economic development, especially in regions other than the immediate region, have not usually been able to capture these various dimensions adequately (Vickerman, 1992a).

5.2   Classifying regional impacts

Regional impacts of new infrastructure are best considered in three broad categories, bearing in mind the need to examine the impacts in both nearby and more distant regions to any particular infrastructure project.

* **Core-periphery impacts** consider the relative impacts on regions which form part of the current economic core of Europe and those which are more peripheral. It is important to recognise that core and periphery cannot just be defined on an aggregate basis according to geographical location or by use of simple economic potential measures. The main problem with potential measures is that they ascribe the calculated potential to a whole region, usually on the basis of the accessibility of the defined centroid of a region. This ignores the fact that much of a core region may have considerably poorer accessibility than a major node in a more peripheral region. The economic core of Europe is more likely to be a discontinuous set of the major metropolitan areas. This implies the need to calculate accessibility not just as accessibility along a network, but also involving accessibility to the network. Thus what is required for any new piece of infrastructure is a definition of what it does to both of these measures for different locations, defined at a geographically disaggregated level. It is relevant to consider what the change does to the definition of core and periphery as well as to the measure of potential for each category.

* **Corridor effects** consider, within the broad geographical definition of the region, the way that the new infrastructure affects relative accessibility between and within regions, by looking at accessibility to the network and hence whether a particular region is likely to suffer from the creation of a corridor. A corridor has the effect of channelling traffic through the region, possibly with some environmental and congestion costs imposed on the region, but without bringing substantial potential benefits to the region. Following our discussion of the core regions above, it is clear that one of the main incidences of corridor effects is likely to be in such regions. This helps to create the unevenness of economic development that is found in some of the more centrally located regions of the European Community. However, it is also clear that corridor effects could become a problem in more peripheral regions if there is an over-emphasis on the creation of major new infrastructures such as high speed rail to link major centres to the economic core. This could have the effect both of diverting traffic away from other peripheral areas to concentrate it on the new corridor and emphasising the metropolitan - non-metropolitan division in the peripheral region. The long-term effect is towards an economic core of a set of discontiguous metropolitan regions across Europe.

* **Shadow effects** are principally caused by the diversion of traffic away from traditional routes and modes. Again they may occur in central or peripheral regions. The importance of these effects is not just that they involve the exclusion of a region from a network, but that they may involve the additional problems of diverting traffic from an existing network. Thus ports will suffer from the creation of fixed links across maritime routes. This may involve both nearby ports and more distant ones if a new route is established, or the creation of fixed link causes a substantial switch in mode use. Thus,for example, on its own the Channel Tunnel may not divert a large proportion of traffic from the longer sea routes across the North Sea or Western Channel, since the time and cost savings will be minimal or non-existent. However, a substantial shift in the relative advantage of rail transport brought about by the Tunnel and other associated infrastructures, may cause a much more substantial shift.

The above discussion emphasises the need to distinguish impacts on accessibility both along networks and to networks. Regions may miss out by being peripheral and not connected at all, by seeing traffic collected in a corridor running through them, but to which they have no access, or by seeing traffic diverted to a new corridor which passes them by. All too frequently the concentration on peripheral problems for policy purposes has led to an excessive development of infrastructure which only addresses the first of these problems. Moreover, it fails to identify that even in the peripheral regions there may be corridor and shadow effects which will reduce the effectiveness of an infrastructure-led policy of regional development.

5.3 Transport effects and regional effects

This also highlights a conflict between regional considerations and transport effectiveness. For a transport system to work efficiently it needs to carry an optimal volume of traffic over a defined route. Road networks are reduced in their efficiency by the mix of traffic, and particularly the problems of joining and leaving traffic. High speed rail depends on a minimum number of stopping places. Each stop increases end to end times and unless there is a substantial enough intermediate market to warrant imposing the time penalty on longer distance travellers the loss of revenue from the marginal time elasticity of the latter will outweigh the additional revenue form the extra shorter-distance passengers. Additionally, there may be extra infrastructure or signalling costs incurred by having to cater for trains running at different speeds to serve different markets. Transport considerations thus favour the existing metropolitan regions which are the major traffic generators. If regional considerations are to play a part in the development of the infrastructure, this may require a revision to appraisal techniques. In particular it will make it more difficult to rely on the private sector to finance the developments of all but minimal links in a network.

6. Policy Needs

The discussion above has highlighted the potential conflicts which can arise from the development of infrastructure. The massive amount of infrastructure development currently underway in Europe suggests that the overall impact on the future pattern of regional development from changing accessibility at both the aggregate and more local levels could be substantial. This raises two principal questions, the appropriate level at which to coordinate infrastructure planning and how to ensure a consistent means of appraising and financing major infrastructure projects.

6.1 Levels of policy determination

Currently most infrastructure is planned and financed at a national (or lower) level in Europe. There has been an attempt to try and coordinate planning by defining principal European networks and providing EC funding for infrastructure improvements which have an impact on such networks in addition to the funding which is available through the ERDF for projects in designated assisted regions (Commission of the European Communities, 1989). Attempts to create a new financial instrument to assist the EC in building the European network have usually been blocked. The funds which were eventually approved in 1990 to assist in the major infrastructure programme are minimal in relation to the size of the investment needed (Vickerman, 1991a).

Since in many cases the principal traffic users will be national or local, this does not raise a problem. The specific nature of key international projects such as the Channel Tunnel and Oresund Crossing has meant that they could be coordinated on a bilateral basis. However, greater problems arise with both specific projects such as the major Alpine Tunnels, of which the major beneficiaries will be international transit traffic belonging to other countries, or the creation of a new network such as the Northern European high speed rail network, where the benefits require completion of a network which will have a variety of differing regional effects on the regions it connects or passes through.

6.2 Means of financing infrastructure

If there is an increasing inter-regional and international dimension to major infrastructure projects, at least in terms of the distribution of their impacts, there is also an increasing need for a fresh look at the means of financing such projects. As we have already noted above, it has proved difficult to produce even a small EC Infrastructure Fund to assist projects of major importance. It is of no use demonstrating that the planning of such projects needs to be undertaken at a supra-national level if that level is powerless to produce the finance for them. It is not clear that simply transferring the public sector responsibility to a supra-national authority such as the European Commission is the right answer. The authority has to be accountable to lower levels for the decision it takes, and to do this it has to have available an appraisal framework which is both transparent and acceptable to all levels providing the finance.

One way which has been attempted to get round this is to transfer the project to the private sector, allowing a private sector promoter to raise the money on international money markets, in the hope that the private sector will also be more efficient in managing the project. The obvious case of this is the Channel Tunnel, which is under purely private sector control, although other projects are being managed by the private sector under various forms of Build-Own-Operate-Transfer (BOOT) schemes. Such approaches are only likely to be possible where there is a sufficient opportunity to create a monopoly rent which makes the project attractive to private finance. Such attractiveness is defined, not so much in terms of the absolute level of the rate of return, but in the risk associated with that rate of return (Vickerman, 1992b). The private sector has not been prepared to accept the risks in such large scale projects which derive from uncertainties in construction costs, in traffic forecasts and (possibly of greatest importance) in the political environment.

A possible solution is through the creation of an independent Infrastructure Fund, which would have the responsibility of securing political agreement on projects, planning their execution and raising the finance from a variety of public and private sources, according to an agreed framework which would identify clearly the distribution both of benefits and of risks (Round Table of European Industrialists, 1988). Clearly such a solution would involve a transfer of considerable planning powers from all levels of government, but may be the only way of securing broad agreement. Only an independent decision making body can be in a position to treat the various interests of both transport users and regions affected in different ways in a consistent manner. Furthermore, only such an authority would be in a position to deal with the complementarities which arise between different projects in different parts of Europe to ensure a consistent treatment.

6.3   Final remark

What we have demonstrated in this paper is that despite the major changes in the European transport infrastructure which are in progress, and the removal of physical and political barriers to movement, there are still formidable barriers to the creation of a genuine European transport network. These are both institutional and financial. Without their solution and removal there will continue to be substantial barriers to movement which will have serious consequences for the process of economic cohesion in Europe. It is not clear whether the greater effects will be felt on more peripheral regions, from their inability to achive accessibility to major markets, or on the more central regions because of their being either stifled by congestion in metropolitan areas or by-passed by the traffic in other areas. It is, however, clear that there will be serious consequences for most regions in Europe.

136

REFERENCES

Berger, H-U., Long Term Developments in North-South Transport Demand and Infrastructural Needs, **European Transport in 1992 and Beyond** (H G Smit, ed), European Transport Planning Colloquium, Infotrans, Delft, 1989.

Biehl, D., The Role of Infrastructure in Regional Development, **Infrastructure and Regional Development** (R.W. Vickerman, ed), European Research in Regional Science, vol 1, Pion, London, 1991.

Blum, U., Effects of Transportation Investments on Regional Growth: a Theoretical and Empirical Analysis, **Papers of Regional Science Association**, 49, 1982, pp. 151-168

Botham, R., The Road Programme and Regional Development: the Problem of the Counter-Factual, **Transport, Location and Spatial Policy** (K.J. Button and D Gillingwater, eds.), Gower, Aldershot, 1982.

Chisholm, M., Regional Variations in Transport Costs in Britain with Special Reference to Scotland, **Transactions of the Institute of British Geographers**, 12, 1987, pp. 303-314

Chisholm, M., Britain, the European Community, and the Centralisation of Production: Theory and Evidence, Freight Movements, **Environment and Planning A**, 24, 1992.

Commission of the European Communities **Communication from the Commission to the Council regarding a Transport Infrastructure Policy: Concentration of Efforts and Means**, Document COM(89)238 final, Office for Official Publications, Luxembourg, 1992.

Gwilliam, K.M., Transport Infrastructure Investment and Regional Development, **Inflation, Development and Integration** (J.K. Bowers, ed), Leeds University Press, Leeds, 1979.

Holliday, I.M., G. Marcou, R.W. Vickerman, **The Channel Tunnel: Public Policy, Regional Development and European Integration**, Belhaven Press, London, 1991.

Holliday, I.M. and R.W. Vickerman, The Channel Tunnel and Regional Development: Policy Responses in Britain and France, **Regional Studies**, 24, 1990, pp. 455-466

IFO, **Ifo-Schnelldienst**, 28/91, 7 October, 1991.

Illeris, S., L. Jakobsen, The Effects of the Fixed Link across the Great Belt, **Infrastructure and Regional Development**, (R.W. Vickerman, ed.) European Research in Regional Science, vol 1, Pion, London, 1991.

Madsen, B., C. Jensen-Butler, The Regional Economic Effects of the Danish Great Belt Link and Related Traffic System Improvements, paper 31st European Congress of Regional Science Association, Lisbon, August, 1991.

Plassard, F., O. Klein, Le Réseau Ferroviaire à Grande Vitesse en France, paper Colloque on **Transports à Grande Vitesse, Développement Régional et Aménagement du Territoire**, Orléans, June, 1990.

Ratti, R., L'analyse Coûts-Bénéfices dans un Contexte Spatiale Différencié - Application au Cas des Projets de Tunnels Ferroviaires du Saint-Gothard et du Splugen, **Wirtschaft und Recht**, 30, 1978, pp. 309-324

Ratti, R., M. Ferrari, Les Grands Réseaux et l'Avenir des Zones Évincées, paper Colloque on **Les Nouvelles Trames de L'Espace: Villes, Régions, Réseaux**, Lyon, December, 1991.

Round Table of European Industrialists, **Need for Renewing Transport Infrastructure in Europe**, Brussels, 1988.

Straszheim, M., Researching the Role of Transport in Regional Development, **Land Economics**, 48, 1972, pp. 212-219

Vickerman, R.W., Transport Infrastructure in the European Community: New Developments, Regional Implications and Evaluation, **Infrastructure and Regional Development** (R.W. Vickerman, ed.), European Research in Regional Science, vol 1, Pion, London, 1991a.

Vickerman, R.W., Other Regions' Infrastructure in a Region's Development, **Infrastructure and Regional Development** (R.W. Vickerman, ed.), European Research in Regional Science, vol 1, Pion, London, 1991b.

Vickerman, R.W., Regional Science and New Transport Infrastructure, paper 4th World Congress, Regional Science Association International, Palma, Mallorca, May, 1992a.

Vickerman, R.W., Private Provision of Transport: Lessons from the Channel Tunnel, paper 6th World Congress on Transportation Research, Lyon, June, 1992b.

CHAPTER 9

BORDERS AS BARRIERS IN THE EUROPEAN

ROAD NETWORK: A CASE STUDY ON THE ACCESSIBILITY

OF URBAN AGGLOMERATIONS

Frank Bruinsma and Piet Rietveld[1]

1.   Introduction

The ongoing process of European integration causes an increasing competition between major urban agglomerations in Western Europe. The target of integration is the removal of all barriers to international trade, which includes among others the harmonisation of fiscal policies. An implication is that several of the policy instruments which national governments could use in the past to promote development of their major urban agglomerations are no longer applicable. The development of urban infrastructure is seen as one of the last opportunities of the national government to support their cities in the international competition. It is no surprise therefore to see that in a number of recent studies, urban infrastructure plays a role as a determinant of competiveness of urban regions (Biehl, 1986; NEI, 1987; DATAR, 1989; Cheshire, 1990; Bruinsma and Rietveld, 1991; Healey and Baker, 1991). In most of these studies, attention is focused on the intra-metropolitan infrastructure. However, the inter-metropolitan infrastructure will be equally important. The free market forces the cities to be outward oriented. Good connections in the international infrastructure networks will be a critical success factor in the distribution of economic activity in Europe.

It is generally recognized that national borders function as barriers in international interaction patterns. Research has shown that the crossing of national borders is more than just the physical crossing of an administrative barrier, which could lead to extra travel time, for instance as a consequence of customs formalities. A national border often can be understood as a non-physical barrier with an economic, political, cultural or language dimension (see Nijkamp et al., 1990a, 1990b).

This chapter is focussed on the relative position of urban agglomerations in the European road network and the impact of national borders as barriers in the international interaction patterns. In Section 2 the methodology used is described. In Section 3 some results of the accessibility of 42 urban agglomerations in Europe are presented when national border lines - which can be seen as non-physical barriers in international interaction patterns - are not under consideration. The effects of planned or possible future major improvements in the road infrastructure network on these accessibility patterns are studied in this section as well. In Section 4 an analysis is given of infrastructure densities in border regions and on the border line itself. In Section 5 we investigate the impact of borders on the accessibility patterns of the 42 European agglomerations described in Section 3. We have studied the effects of the decline of these border effects on the basis of assumptions on major political changes. In Section 6 the equity in accessibility is studied by analysing the average accessibility and the differences in accessibility among the agglomerations. Special attention is given to the changes caused by the improvements in the road network, the border effect and the reduction of the border effect by political changes. In Section 7 some concluding remarks are given.

2.   Methodology

The accessibility of each agglomeration is measured by the following simple gravity type formulation in which travel time is the main indicator:

$$A_i = \sum_j 1/T_{ij}^c$$

where:

A_i = accessibility of agglomeration i
T_{ij} = travel time from i to agglomeration j

The gravity parameter c is assumed to equal 1 (cf. Keeble et al., 1982). The total travel time T is measured in minutes and consists of three elements:

$$T = V + RT + I$$

where:

V   =   a penalty when ferries are used because one cannot depart at the moment most desired
RT =   real travel time while moving
I   =   check in and check out time of ferries

The penalty V is estimated as follows:

$$V = ¼ \ E/F$$

where E is the effective travel period during which one can depart - for instance between 06.00 hours and 18.00 hours - and F is the frequency of the connection. For example, if one would go at an arbitrary moment to the ferry, average waiting time would be half of the average time in between two departures (which equals ½ E/F). We suppose most travellers know their departure time, but we still give a penalty because travellers cannot leave at the moment they prefer. Therefore, we reduce the penalty from ½ (as would occur in the case of an arbitrary arrival at the ferry) to ¼ to express this inconvenience.

If interaction is supposed to depend on the size of the agglomerations with which an agglomeration interacts, then weighting can take place by using the population size of those agglomerations. This leads to the following formula, where P_j is the population of agglomeration j:

$$A_i = \sum_j P_j/T_{ij}^c$$

A weighting by population size makes it necessary to include the internal interaction in agglomeration i. The value of the share of the internal interaction in the total accessibility score of agglomeration i depends on two factors. The share is higher the larger the population size of agglomeration i and the share is lower the larger the number of connections with the agglomerations j located nearby.

To measure the interaction pattern for the road network, we selected the 42 agglomerations in Europe excluding the former U.S.S.R. with a population size of over 1 million. Data on travel time and frequencies between those agglomerations are obtained of the Thomas Cook European Timetable (ferries) and the Michelin Roadatlas of Europe. The data of the road network are converted from distance into travel time. For highways we used an average speed of 90 kilometres per hour, for roads of a lower quality this figure is 60. Within the urban agglomerations we used an average speed of 30 kilometres per hour (needed for the calculation of the internal interaction potential).

3. The Accessibility of European Agglomerations in the Road Infrastructure Network

To measure the accessibility of the 42 European agglomerations we start to make a distinction between on the one hand an index which is unweighted and on the other hand an index which is weighted for population size of the destination agglomerations. The index which is not weighted, for population size reflects only the spatial dimension of the location in the network, whereas the weighted index in which the internal interaction is included reflects a combination of the mass of the agglomeration itself and its external contacts.

In the situation where no weighting by population size has taken place the Central German cities score best, followed by the Benelux and Mid-England cities. The Mid-England cities are not centrally located in the European road system. They score high because here a relatively large number of cities is located close to each other. In the gravity model interaction over short distance is relatively high.

When weighting for population size takes place, Paris and London become dominant (Table 1, column 2 and Figure 1). This rising dominance is completely explained by the share of the internal interaction. For London and Paris the share of the internal interaction is (both in a relative and an absolute sense) rather large compared to its smaller competitors like the Ruhr-area and the Benelux cities. The scores of other large agglomerations also improve considerably.

We have formulated two future scenario's. In the first scenario all connections considered achieve highway quality (Table 1, column 3); in the second scenario, in addition to the improvement of the road network itself, the ferries are replaced by bridges and tunnels (Table 1, column 4).

The improvement of the road network leads to better scores for the East and South European cities and Stockholm. At the moment most of the roads in these regions are of a low quality. The relatively strong rise in the scores of the East European cities compared to the South European cities and Stockholm can be explained by the shorter distance of the East European cities to the centrally located agglomerations. In the gravity model a gain of 10 minutes travel time on a trip of one hour has a greater effect on accessibility than the same gain in travel time on a two hour trip.

If, in addition to the improvement of the road network itself, ferries are replaced by bridges and tunnels (the Channel Tunnel, links between Sweden - Denmark and Denmark - Germany), the impact on the accessibility index seems to be marginal. However, the individual index of, for instance, the English cities shows a relatively sharp rise. This rise in the individual score does not appear in the final index because also Paris (the reference city) profits from the improvement of the road network as well as from the Channel-tunnel.

	1	2	3	4		1	2	3	4
Düsseldorf	100	78	79	78	London	72	94	94	95
Essen	98	77	78	77	Vienna	71	60	62	61
Cologne	97	75	75	74	Prague	71	58	61	60
Brussels	87	70	70	70	Marseille	69	56	57	56
Rotterdam	85	69	69	69	Zagreb	67	54	57	55
Leeds	85	74	74	74	Budapest	66	61	64	62
Amsterdam	85	67	67	67	Rome	64	63	64	62
Frankfurt	84	70	70	69	Copenhagen	60	52	52	56
Manchester	84	71	71	71	Lodz	60	49	55	54
Liverpool	81	68	68	68	Belgrade	60	52	55	54
Milan	80	65	65	64	Barcelona	59	54	54	54
Turin	78	61	61	60	Naples	59	49	50	49
Munich	78	63	64	63	Warsaw	58	51	57	56
Zurich	78	63	63	62	Sofia	55	45	49	48
Birmingham	77	70	70	71	Dublin	52	43	43	43
Genoa	77	59	60	59	Madrid	51	58	60	59
Paris	76	100	100	100	Bucharest	51	50	54	53
Lyon	75	62	62	62	Stockholm	50	45	46	47
Newcastle	75	60	60	61	Istanbul	47	67	70	68
Hamburg	74	66	66	66	Lisbon	46	48	50	49
Berlin	72	74	75	74	Athens	44	52	55	54

1 = unweighted   2 = weighted   3 = road improvement   4 = road improvement/bridges/tunnels

Table 1: Accessibility of European cities by road traffic

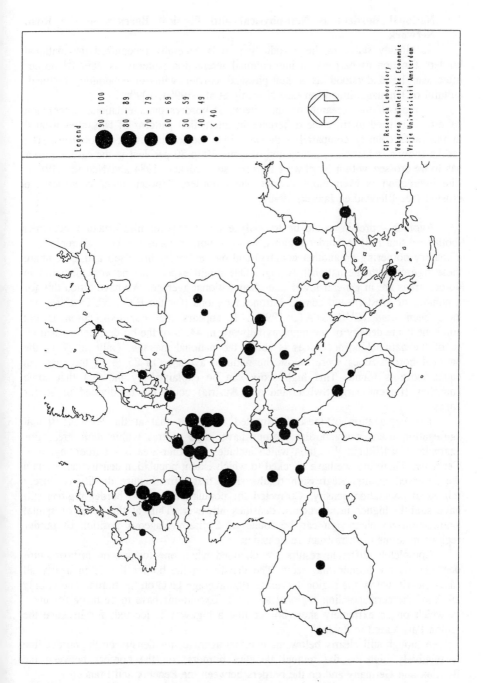

Figure 1: Accessibility for road traffic, weighted by population size

4. National Borders as Non-physical and Physical Barriers in the Road Network

As already stated in the introduction, it is generally recognized that national borders function as barriers in international interaction patterns. A national border often can be understood as a non-physical barrier with an economic, political, cultural or language dimension (see Nijkamp et al., 1990a, 1990b).

In most of the research on the effects of borders on international interaction patterns it is tried to trace the difference in interaction patterns of two cities located in the same country compared with two cities located in different countries. The results show a reduction in interaction of some 70 to 80 per cent in the case a border has to be crossed within Northwest Europe (see Bröcker, 1984 and Neusser, 1985). The interaction is even more disrupt when borders between other countries are crossed (see Rietveld en Jansen, 1990).

Another approach would be to analyze the density of infrastructure networks (both road and rail) in border regions, national border zones (contains all regions of a country bordering on another country) and on the border line itself and to compare these figures with the national average. One might expect that network densities in border areas are in general lower than their national average. We have tested this for a number of Western and central European regions (for the E.C., NUTS-II regions have been used (EUROSTAT, 1990)). It appears that our expectation is not confirmed: the density of the highway network in 44 % of the border regions and 49 % of the national border zones is above the national average. Only 26 % of the national border zones score below the national average. In 25 % of the cases an equal score is found. This high score can be explained by the fact that some countries (Luxembourg, Switzerland and Austria) could not be divided in border zones.

The explanation of these unexpected results is that at the level of spatial aggregation used, many border regions have large centres within their area. For example, North-Rhein Westfalia which includes the Ruhr-area is a border region in Germany. Therefore we have checked to which extent population density can explain the observed results. Regression results show that infrastructure density is closely related to population density. Corrected for population density, border regions still have slightly higher infrastructure densities however. Thus at this level of spatial aggregation no clear sign can be found of a disadvantageous position of border regions in terms of infrastructure densities.

Completely different results are obtained when one focuses on infrastructure densities on the border line itself. The density on the border line is in nearly all cases clearly below the regional average (the average level on the border line is only 29 % of the cerresponding regional average). Exceptions have to be made for areas in which on an extremely short border line a highway is located, for instance the region Pais Vasco in Spain.

Although still clearly below the national average, the density on the border line is relatively high on the mutual Benelux borders, on the borders between the Benelux and Germany and on the borders between the Benelux and France.

We conclude that, although the border regions are relatively well equipped with highway infrastructure, the density on the border line itself remains far below the national average. Thus it appears that the orientation of the well equipped border regions is focused on the national instead of the international economy.

Our conclusion is that national borders exert a barrier effect on international communication. In the case of road transport this barrier effect is due to both non-physical factors such as language differentials, and physical factors such as the low density of roads on border lines.

5. The Impact of National Borders on the Accessibility of European Agglomerations

It is interesting to investigate the impact of barrier effects on the accessibility measures as presented in Section 3. Barrier effects are taken into account by link-specific reduction factors which are used in the gravity model. The reduction factors for the different combinations of countries are given in Table 2. It is important to note that the domestic interaction flows are not reduced.

	E.C.-country	E.F.T.A.-country	East European country
E.C.-country	.250	.167	.125
E.F.T.A.-country	.167	.167	.125
East European country	.125	.125	.167

Table 2: Border related reduction factors for road transport

The results are striking compared to the situation without barriers (Table 3, column 1 and 2, Figures 1 and 2). London takes over the first position from Paris. The explanation is rather simple. Reduction factors are only used for international connections. The domestic connections, which are not reduced, are short distance connections. The use of a gravity model implies large interaction flows on those short distances. In our sample six English and seven German agglomerations are included. It is no wonder that they are all ranked within the first twenty. Only large agglomerations like Paris, Istanbul, Rome, Madrid and Athens are ranked in between them. Their high score heavily depends on the share of the internal interaction in the total score. The share of the internal interaction in their total score can be as high as 96 %, as is the case for Istanbul. Major losers are the smaller agglomerations in smaller countries which are rather centrally located, like Brussels, Amsterdam, Rotterdam, Zurich and Prague: their score largely depends on connections with foreign agglomerations.

We have next formulated four scenarios of future political developments which could decrease the barrier effects of national borders. In the first scenario we assume that in Europe after 1992 the cross-national interaction would be less

146

disturbed compared to the present situation. So the reduction factor of E.C.-countries changes from .250 to .333. In the second scenario, on top of this development within the E.C., we expect that the political transition in Eastern Europe leads to an easier access of those countries. So all relations with East European countries receive a reduction factor of .167. In the third scenario we analyze the changes when the E.F.T.A.-countries are welcomed in the E.C., While in the last scenario also Hungary becomes an E.C. member. In the last two scenario's the reduction factor changes from .167 to .333.

	1	2	3	4	5	6		1	2	3	4	5	6
Paris	100	97	1	-	-	-	Budapest	61	48	-1	1	-	4
London	94	100	-	-	-	-	Turin	61	49	1	1	-	-
Düsseldorf	78	69	1	-	1	-	Newcastle	60	61	-	-	-	-
Essen	77	68	1	-	-	1	Vienna	60	43	-	-	5	-
Cologne	75	64	1	-	1	-	Genoa	59	50	1	-	-	-
Berlin	74	71	1	-	-	-	Madrid	58	59	-	-	-	-
Leeds	74	77	-	-	-	-	Prague	58	38	-	1	-	-
Manchester	71	73	1	-	-	-	Marseille	56	47	2	-	-	-
Brussels	70	41	4	-	1	-	Barcelona	54	48	1	-	-	-
Birmingham	70	70	1	-	-	-	Zagreb	54	39	-1	1	-	-
Frankfurt	70	59	2	-	-	-	Copenhagen	52	42	1	-	1	-
Rotterdam	69	49	3	-	-	-	Athens	52	55	-	-	-	-
Liverpool	68	69	1	-	-	-	Belgrade	52	41	-	1	-1	-
Istanbul	67	73	-2	-	2	-	Warsaw	51	44	-	-	-	-
Amsterdam	67	47	3	-	-	-	Bucharest	50	45	-1	1	-	-
Hamburg	66	60	1	-	-	-	Naples	49	46	1	-	-	-
Milan	65	54	2	-	-	-	Lodz	49	39	-	1	-	-1
Rome	63	62	-	-	-	-	Lisbon	48	48	1	-	-	-
Munich	63	62	1	1	-	-	Sofia	45	35	-	-	-	-
Zurich	63	40	-1	-	7	-	Stockholm	45	41	-	-	3	-
Lyon	62	51	1	-	1	-	Dublin	43	36	1	-	-	-

1 = without border effect 3 = change due scenario 1 5 = difference between 3 - 2
2 = with border effect 4 = difference between scenario 2 to 1 6 = difference between 4 - 3

Table 3: Impact of borders as barriers in the road network on the accessibility of European cities

147

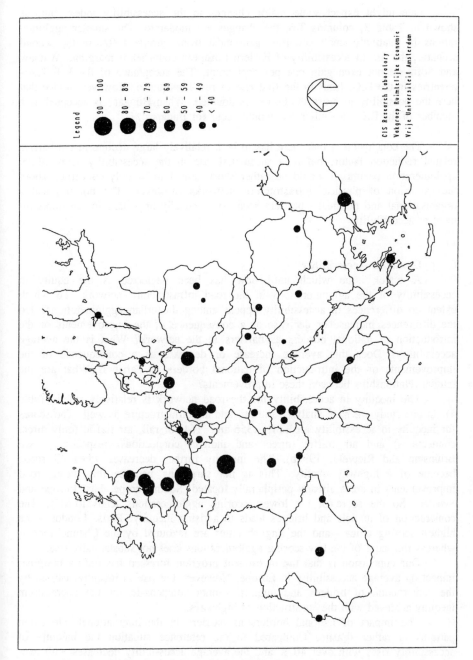

Figure 2: Impact of borders as barriers in the road network on the accessibility index of European cities

One might expect some major changes in the accessibility index, but, as shown in Table 3, columns 3-6, the changes are moderate. The smaller agglomerations in relatively small countries gain most from Europe 1992. In the second scenario, the rise in accessibility of Eastern European countries is marginal; Warsaw and Sofia do not even gain one per cent point. The acceptance of the E.F.T.A.-countries in the E.C. leads to the first rise of real importance. However, notice that here the possibility to cross the border is doubled. When Hungary is accepted as a member of the E.C., a similar rise would occur for Budapest.

The conclusion is that there has to be a relatively large decline in the barrier related reduction factor, before a substantial rise in the accessibility score of an agglomeration occurs. It would be rather short-sighted to be only concerned about the extension of physical infrastructure networks, however. The non-physical - organisational and political - barriers seem to be equally important for an improvement of accessibility.

6.   Equity in Accessibility

A major issue which until now has been neglected is the equity in accessibility of the agglomerations in the road infrastructure network. To which extent do differences in accessibility appear among the urban agglomerations? Do the differences increase or decrease as a consequence of the improvements or the introduction of national borders as barriers in the network? What is the average accessibility? Does this average increase or decrease as a consequence of the improvements or the introduction of national borders as barriers? What are the mutual relationships between these improvements?

The inequity in accessibility for the road network is relatively small (Table 4). In our study we have analysed the rail and air infrastructure as well. The scores for inequity in accessibility are .281, .356 and .164 for rail, air traffic (only direct connections) and air traffic (direct and indirect connections) respectively (see Bruinsma and Rietveld, 1992b). The inequity further decreases when all roads become of a highway quality. This is not surprising because this means road improvements in areas already peripherally located: South Europe, East Europe and Sweden. So the score of the lowest scoring agglomerations tends to rise. The construction of tunnels and bridges leads to a rising inequity. Paris, London - the highest scoring cities - and the English cities are favoured by the Channel-tunnel, whereas the score of the low scoring agglomerations does not substantially rise.

Our conclusion is that the investment program foreseen has only a marginal impact on average accessibility in Europe. However, the rise in inequity, caused by the construction of bridges and tunnels, cannot compensate for the decrease in inequity achieved with the construction of highways.

The impact of national borders as barriers in the international interaction patterns is rather drastic. Compared to the reference situation the inequity of accessibility rises with over 40 % and the average accessibility decreases with over 30 %. This shows once more the impact of non-physical barriers on the accessibility of urban agglomerations.

In Table 5 the results are presented when the barriers are reduced by political changes as formulated in section 5. A decrease of the barriers within the E.C. with one third (scenario 1) as a consequence of the common market only has a small impact on the average accessibility. The impact on the equity issue is negligible. The impact is rather meagre if one bears in mind that here the barriers of 30 out of the 42 agglomerations are concerned. The same could be said for scenario 2 where the barriers for the eight East-European agglomerations also decreases with one third. The coefficient of variation decreases because here the relative score of the lowest scoring agglomerations rises.

Scenario 3 concerns only the four EFTA-agglomerations whose barriers decrease from .167 to .333 (what means a doubling of the possibility to cross a border). The equity in accessibility increases in a relatively sharp way as does the average accessibility. The same pattern occurs when Budapest undergoes a similar decrease of barrier effect (scenario 4).

Keeping in mind the coefficient of variation before introducing the barrier effects (Table 4) one may conclude that the existence of non-physical barriers has strong impacts on the accessibility of cities.

	Actual	Highway	Bridge/tunnel	Barriers
Average score	212914	218698	222930	145251
Standard deviation	40843	38534	40150	39867
Coefficient of variation	.192	.176	.180	.274
Average accessibility	100	102.7	104.7	68.2

Table 4: Development average accessibility by road traffic

	Barriers	Scen. 1	Scen. 2	Scen. 3	Scen. 4
Average score	145251	149356	150237	150227	152829
Standard deviation	39867	40911	40467	40052	39977
Coefficient of variation	.274	.274	.269	.263	.262
Average accessibility	100	102.8	103.4	104.8	105.2

Table 5: Development average accessibility by road traffic, barriers included

7.   Concluding Remarks

The above numerical results depend on various assumptions about parameters, conventions used in measuring travel times and on the ways the scenarios have been formulated. We believe that the main patterns emerging are fairly robust.

The differences in accessibility of the European agglomerations by road are relatively small compared with the other transport modes. The improvement of the

150

road system in Eastern and Southern Europe is expected to contribute to improvements of relative accessibility of the cities there, which leads to a decrease in inequalities. The construction of bridges and tunnels lead to a rise of the accessibility of the already best accessible agglomerations. As a consequence, the inequity in accessibility grows.

Inequalities in accessibility are least pronounced in the road network when border effects are left out of consideration. In our study we also investigated the physical and non-physical aspects of borders. The infrastructure density in border regions is above the national level, but the infrastructure density on the border line itself is far below the national level. This makes it reasonable to assume that the border regions are oriented at the national instead of at the international economy. If national borders are seen as barriers in international interaction patterns and are integrated in the gravity model, the impact on the average accessibility and on the equity in accessibility is rather drastic. Especially the effects on the accessibility of the smaller cities in smaller countries are considerable.

This research project shows that attention should not only be paid to the extension of physical infrastructure networks, but that also non-physical aspects of networks should receive due attention in future studies and policies on infrastructure networks in Europe.

Notes

1. This study is based on Bruinsma and Rietveld (1992a) to which we refer for a more detailed account of data collection procedures and outcomes. The research project was funded by Urban Networks, The Netherlands.

REFERENCES

Biehl, D., c.s., **The Contribution of Infrastructure to Regional Development**, E.C., Brussels, 1986.

Bröcker, J., How do International Trade Barriers Affect Interregional Trade?, **Regional and Industrial Development**, (A.E. Anderson et al., eds.) North-Holland, Amsterdam, 1984, pp. 219-239.

Bruinsma, F.R., and P. Rietveld, **Infrastructuur en Stedelijke Ontwikkeling in Europa**, Stedelijke Netwerken, Werkstuk 27, Amsterdam, 1991.

Bruinsma, F.R., and P. Rietveld, **Stedelijke Agglomeraties in Europese Infrastructuurnetwerken**, Stedelijke Netwerken, Werkstuk 36, Amsterdam, 1992a.

Bruinsma, F.R., and P.Rietveld, **Urban Agglomerations in European Infrastructure Networks**, Free University, Amsterdam, 1992b.

Cheshire, P., Explaining the Recent Performance of the European Community Major Urban Regions, **Urban Studies**, Vol. 27, 1990, pp. 311-333.

Cook, T., **European Timetable**, Thomas Cook Publishing, London, 1991.

DATAR, **Les Villes Europeennes**, Maison de la Geographie, Montpellier, 1989.

Eurostat, **Regio's Statistisch Jaarboek 1989**, Luxembourg, 1990.

Healey and Baker, **European Real Estate Monitor 1990 Executive Summary**, Healey & Baker, London, 1991.

Keeble, D., P.L. Owens and C. Thompson, Regional Accessibility and Economic Potential in the European Community, **Regional Studies**, Vol 16, 1982, pp. 419-432.

Michelin, **Wegenatlas van Europa**, The Hamlyn Publishing Group Limited, London, 1988.

N.E.I., **Plaats en Functie van de Randstad in de Nederlandse Economie**, Nederlands Economisch Instituut, Rotterdam, 1987.

Neusser, H.G., Die Bedeutung von Hemmnisfaktoren für die Entwicklung des Verkehrsaufkommens, **DFVLR-Nachrichten**, Vol. 45, 1985, pp. 32-34.

Nijkamp, P., P. Rietveld and I. Salomon, Barriers in Spatial Interactions and Communications, **The Annals of Regional Science**, Vol. 24, 1990a, pp. 237-252.

Nijkamp, P., P. Rietveld and I. Salomon, Barrieres in Telecommunicatie, een Conceptuele Verkenning, **Tijdschrift voor Vervoerswetenschappen**, Vol. 26, 1990b, pp. 182-194.

Rietveld, P., and L. Janssen, Telephone Calls and Communication Barriers, **The Annals of Regional Science**, Vol. 24, 1990, pp. 307-318.

CHAPTER 10

EUROPEAN INTEGRATION AND THE ROLE OF

TRANSPORT RELATED BARRIERS AT NATIONAL BORDERS

Rico Maggi

1.   Introduction: New Borders and Economic Integration

Future freight transport in Europe will be confronted with important problems in terms of capacity of networks and quality of services. The reasons are manifold. The European integration is expected to bring about a rise in spatial interaction in general and hence amongst others an increase in the exchange of goods and thus freight transport. New production concepts, which can basically be summarised under the heading of just-in-time production (JIT), are another phenomenon which will increase demand for freight transport. On the other hand, the capacity of the networks is limited by various kinds of bottlenecks on all modes. This also seriously affects the quality of the services on these networks. Finally, freight transport, especially on road, is also struggling with attempts by environmental interest groups to reduce the volume of road traffic substantially. These problems have been reviewed in a recent report on missing networks in Europe (Nijkamp et al., 1990a).

Taking a closer look at the rationale behind the expected effects of integration, the following can be said. The economic impacts of the "open Europe" after 1992 are expected to arise in two domains, namely the exchange of goods and the mobility of production factors. In the case of goods and services, trade is expected to grow as a consequence of lower prices on the market site. These should come about through the vanishing borders which induce a fall in the non-tariff barriers to trade. Much in the same way as a trade union, an open Europe should promote internal trade. Bröcker (1988) has given recent empirical evidence on these effects for EEC and EFTA countries. Typically, his model of the Samuelson-Enke type includes transfer (or transport) prices and tariffs on which the trade union has an impact. In the context of an open Europe, both these elements will have to be discussed with regard to significant changes to be expected in future.

In the case of tariffs, the integration effects will mainly relate to non-tariff barriers. According to the Cecchini report (1989), the most important barrier in Europe (as seen by the business firms) are, in this order, administrative barriers, different norms and standards, and border related formalities. While regulations related to freight transport rank only on the sixth place, they are probably underestimated. If all the other, more important barriers fall, the rising demand for transport will increase congestion and hence put more stress on transport related bottlenecks. This is the major argument of this paper. Nonetheless, the harmonisation of laws within the EC will have an important effect. As Schmidtchen and Schmidt-Trenz (1990) correctly note, the extent of the market is limited by the extent of the law. Therefore, the effects will critically depend on the substitution of national law through EC laws which are simple and transparent. There are certain doubts as to whether EC law and jurisdiction will soon be transparent enough to meet the expectations.

Thus the transport related barriers are probably of more relevance than would be expected when reading the Cecchini report. It is often argued that the share of transport costs in the cif-prices is very low for most products. Hence, lowering transport cost related barriers in the sequel of integration is not expected to have important effects. But this argument neglects the relevance of user cost in transport. Not only in the case of passenger travel but also in freight transport, the frequent congestion problems on the transport networks together with the trend towards just-in-time production have led to important user costs related not only to the overall transport time but more specifically to the costs of non-reliability.

The "new borders, old barriers" issue must therefore be discussed in view of the remaining barriers on the transport networks in an open Europe. It has to be evaluated whether remaining barriers in terms of transport user cost will lower the potential trade effects of integration. Moreover, it has to be noted that Europe not only consists of the EC but also of some other countries which, in the case of Austria and Switzerland, have an important strategic location in terms of transport networks.

Apart from trade effects, European integration will increase the mobility of production factors. Higher factor mobility should result in a reorganisation of production processes and hence in a reallocation of activities. In this context, the presence of potential economies of scale and scope will lead to a higher specialisation of production and larger productive units which will lead to increased flows of material and goods. The extent to which this process will materialize depends again on the transport network. The potential mobility of materials and goods will influence the location decisions of firms. Hence, even if to a lesser extent than in the case of trade, the barriers in transport networks will influence factor mobility. Investors will carefully evaluate the possibilities to influence transport investments on a European scale (which is probably perceived by them as being much more difficult than on a national or local scale). In the case of labour mobility, wage differentials but also remaining differences in labour market and social policy will have an impact on migration which will redesign the European map of locational factors in the long run.

The question of interest is therefore, what the overall impacts of remaining barriers in the transport networks will be. In the next section, barrier problems in European transport networks on road and rail will be described. The expected effects of these barriers will then be discussed in some more detail in Section 3. Section 4 makes some arguments on the chances to reorganise transport networks in Europe in order to meet the expectations of an integrated economy.

2. Old Barriers on Road and Rail Transport Networks

According to Nijkamp et al. (1990b), barriers can be identified in spatial interaction phenomena in the form of discontinuities in the distance decay. On a microscale these discontinuities relate to obstacles in space which lead to a shift of supply and demand curves for interaction between regions on different sides of the obstacle (see e.g. Rietveld and Rossera, 1992). In the case of transport, trade barriers between two countries can induce such a shift in transport demand. The barriers on which this paper focuses are obstacles in the transport network itself arising at country borders. Hence they are supply side barriers which lead to discontinuities in the marginal cost of distance and, as a consequence, to cost jumps in the overall user cost of transport.

In a different context, missing networks in European transport and communication have been identified (ERT, 1990; Nijkamp et al., 1990a; Maggi et al, 1992). This section summarizes the most important findings of this study as far as they are related to borders as barriers in road and rail transport.

-Barriers in road haulage

The main problems related to road transport in Europe are congestion on major international traffic arteries and the problem of the Alpine barrier. Congestion is not typically a problem related to borders, though in some cases customs give rise to congestion. Rather, the problem is one of a general lack of capacity on the European road network. This is due to rising demand for transport in general but more specifically to the comparatively low user cost of road transport on the one hand and the difficulties to extend the network on the other. While in countries like Spain and France, new roads are extensively being built, the extension of the existing road network is not feasible in the medium term in many European countries. The general reluctance (due to the environmental impacts of motorised traffic and funding problems) to build new roads in these countries make it difficult to argue for the creation of a new road network.

A barrier problem that might be partly solved by the realisation of the open market is the waiting time at the customs. An informatisation of freight transport logistics would also allow for an improvement in transborder passages. The main problem will however, be the passage of frontiers between EC and non-EC countries. This concerns Switzerland, Austria, the republics of former Yugoslavia, Turkey as well as the Central and Eastern European countries. There is no reason to expect that the considerable time delays at some of these borders will diminish after 1992/1993.

Another problem related to the Alpine barrier is the Swiss 28 tons weight limit on trucks (as against a maximum weight of 40 tons in the EC). An abolition of this regulation may not even solve many problems in terms of the European network, as some of the European axes to and from the Swiss transit routes (e.g. the Rhine-valley motor way in Germany) would soon be congested if the Swiss barrier vanishes. In addition, expenditures for road maintenance would increase, while repair work will lead to congestion. This shows that when thinking in network terms it is important to consider the changes in flows brought about by changes in regulation. If a certain regulation serves as a regulator also in a network sense, its abolition may immediately give rise to new bottlenecks. The good thing about the Alpine barrier therefore is that it creates a pressure to find new solutions elsewhere. However, it is an instance which creates a transport related barrier at the Swiss border and leads to important traffic deviations. In 1984 the volume of trans-Alpine freight traffic amounted to 10.5 million tons. But only 1.5 million tons were transported on the shortest path through Switzerland. 6 million tons went through Austria and 3 million tons through France.

However, most of the barriers in road freight transport are not related to national borders. The most important barrier is certainly congestion on important European links. Proposals are made all over Europe to increase the efficiency of the road network through road pricing, technological instruments like route guidance and orbital truck fleet management or measures like the reorganisation of warehousing and retailing and empty truck space exchange boards (see Maggi et al., 1992). These measures will very probably not all be effective in 1993 and hence congestion problems and the ensuing barriers will continue to exist. Because the main barriers on the road network in Europe are not linked to the existing borders but to congestion, these barriers will not automatically vanish in 1993.

As one of the options discussed to relieve the congestion problems on road is combined road-rail transport, this issue will be discussed next. It will become clear that the problems of combined transport and of railway freight transport are closely interlinked.

- Barriers in combined transport

In view of the different problems with which road and rail transport are confronted (including the environmental opposition to road traffic) the issue of combined transport has become an important issue in recent discussions. Above all, the railway companies and the combined transport firms which are more or less closely linked to the railways push this "alternative". In February 1990 the European railways and the combined transport operators issued their "Brussels declaration" which presents a common strategy for the design, operation and marketing of combined transport.

A study by A.T. Kearney (1989) demonstrates that there are important problems limiting the capacity of this network which relate to factors like terminal capacity and loading profiles. The profiles for the individual railway networks vary significantly as can be seen in Figure 1.

It is evident that the cost barriers due to these capacity differences will arise at national borders. Concerning the terminal capacity, the situation is critical in Germany with only 4% of free capacity. Even in countries like France, the Netherlands and Austria 80% of the terminal capacity is used. This creates again barriers which are not linked to national borders.

In addition to these problems other factors hinder the performance of combined transport in Europe. These relate to organisational issues, logistics and technical coordination of the wagons and the loading techniques. In their Brussels declaration, the European railways and combined transport operators cite various other fields of action where combined transport so far is not competitive (CEC, 1989).

Even the realisation of a performing European combined transport network would only provide limited additional capacity. The study by A.T. Kearney (1989) foresees a tripling of combined transport by the end of the century with a doubling of the market share from 4% to 8%. Hence, a combined transport network will not be able to solve these problems in the short run. Important infrastructure investments, like new Alpine rail axes, investment in countries where the free profile of tunnels is limited (e.g. Italy) and the adaptation of the Spanish railway gauge to the normal European standard, will have to be solved before barriers in combined transport vanish.

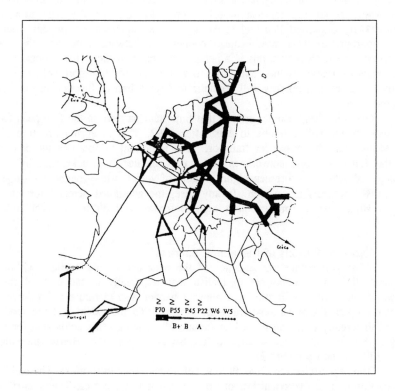

Figure 1: Maximum profiles for combined transport in Europe
Source : A.T. Kearney (1989)

- Barriers in rail freight transport

Much of what has been said on combined transport holds for freight transport on rail in general - there is not much to be added.

Most important in rail freight transport are organisational problems. The European railway companies are national companies. While the influence of the public authorities on the national railways has diminished and the companies have gained more freedom for market oriented operations, they are still left with a lot of problems related to their status which hinder the development of European networks. The problem of the separation of networks and operation remains to be solved. Moreover railways still take a national perspective on the planning of infrastructure with European impacts. The most striking example is provided by the network of European rapid trains with many national projects where the main European effort of integration consists in the mapping of the national networks. While the tendency to intensify coordination on a European level (e.g. on the combined transport issue) is to be welcomed, it probably has a structural defect. As a result, the inter-national framework is not the most appropriate one. Rather, for the realisation of a hierarchically organised hub and spoke system, an inter-regional model would be more appropriate. This would mean cooperation between hubs and the spokes connecting them. However, this is a perspective that is difficult for national railway companies to accept, if they still have to fulfill national transport policy goals. It follows that national borders will continue to have a barrier function in the case of rail transport.

Overall it has become obvious that important barriers in the European freight transport sector will continue to exist after 1992. This is even more true if one would also consider passenger transport. It is important to note that the congestion on the European road network is not mainly created by trucks, but by private vehicles. Whether the foreseen higher pricing of vehicle use throughout Europe will be realised remains to be seen. In any case, the additional demand for transport services in an open Europe is bound to be confronted with old barrier problems.

3.   Expected Impacts of Remaining Barriers

What will be the consequence of the existence of old barriers within new borders? It is most important to realise that, especially in the case of the rail network, the borders will still be a relevant barrier also in future in so far as they limit the operation of national transport systems. To the extent that the roads are priced differently (e.g. the French or Italian toll systems), this holds also for motor ways. The same is of course true for the Swiss weight limit. Hence, the situation can be illustrated by Figure 2.

The two circles represent Europe before and after integration. The solid lines divide Europe into five countries, one of which lies in the center. The country in the center is assumed not to be a member of the EC and, therefore, the arguments presented above on the national transport networks, lead to a situation, where after the realisation of an open Europe, the ancient borders remain a location of relevance in terms of discontinuities of user cost. These cost jumps are directly linked to problems of necessary transshipment, reliability, congestion, different tarification etc. The figure also wants to illustrate that even after the realisation of an open Europe the transport networks will not be integrated and as a consequence the borders will still represent barriers. This is illustrated in the figure by keeping the same style for the lines representing the national transport networks before and after integration.

To say that freight transport demand depends on price and quality of the services is not revolutionary. Nonetheless, one has the impression that in freight transport the interest of analysts is focused too heavily on monetary cost issues. While in passenger transport the relevance of user cost has been recognized and most studies on transport demand are done in view of generalised transport cost freight transport studies treat qualitative issues in a rather unorganised way. Typically, the different quality aspects like transport time, infrastructure capacity and standards of the vehicles are discussed separately. Here, the focus lies on the influence of barriers on the short term transport demand via the generalised cost of freight transport services in Europe (see also Maggi, 1991).

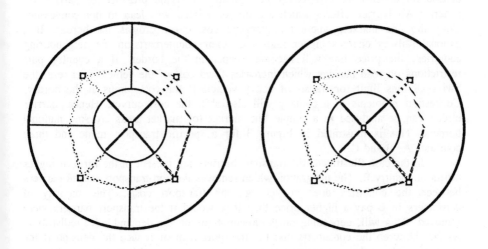

Figure 2: Borders and transport networks before and after 1992.

For the arguments that follow it is assumed that transport services are not provided by the firms under consideration but bought on the market. Hence, the impact of network characteristics on the transport cost as analysed e.g. by Caves et al. (1985) or Filippini and Maggi (1992) are not of interest. Moreover, the location of the firm and its customers are fixed in the short run. The same holds for warehouses owned by the firm. Hence, the choice to be considered implies mainly the choice of a transport mode and a shipping, warehousing policy. This complex decision on logistics has been modeled by McFadden et al. (1985). We will limit our discussion to the simple choice of a freight transport mode.

Let's consider firms which are producing the same good at locations i and selling their products at different locations j along a line market. The consumers are assumed to be equally distributed along the line and to consume one unit of the product from the firm with the lowest price as long as the price is below some reservation price, as is usual in Hotelling type models.

For a given transport mode the marginal cost to a firm located in i for selling its product in j, MC_j is equal to the sum of marginal production costs and marginal generalised transport cost:

$$MC_j = MC_i + D_{ij} \cdot ta + VT \cdot E(t_{ij})$$

where MC_i is marginal production cost at i (which for the moment is assumed to be constant), D_{ij} is the distance, ta is the transport tariff per unit of distance, VT is the goods-specific value of time and $E(t_{ij})$ is the expected travel time. Speed and reliability (punctuality) of the transport service and hence expected travel time depend on congestion, differences in regulation and the presence of barriers in general. All barrier effects which are border related will lead to non-convexities along the line market, where the marginal cost curve crosses the border. If a national railway charges higher rates than their counterparts in the neighbouring countries, the price line will become steeper at the border. If a country puts restrictions on road haulage which increases fixed cost of the vehicle fleet (e.g. the Swiss 28 tons limit for transit of heavy vehicles), the cost jumps at the border. Congestion problems in a country will also shift the cost curves. Hence, barrier effects can be analysed in a simple line market for market areas crossing national borders. This is illustrated in Figure 3 for a specific transport mode and three countries A, B and C.

In the case illustrated, the transport barriers are present in the form of higher tariffs in country B. The integration which removes the non-transport related barriers between the countries does not change the transport costs. The majority of consumers in B pay a higher price than they would if the transport barriers were removed. This will, depending on the assumptions on the demand side, redistribute welfare between the consumers and the transport firm or reduce the demand if the cif-price is above the reservation price for some consumers. Moreover, the situation of B in the center makes it practically impossible for a firm located in country A to compete in country C.

European integration does not only remove obstacles for goods, it also gives free mobility to persons and money. Hence production factors become more mobile. This may lead to mergers in the case of industries with increasing economies of scale. This is illustrated in Figure 4. Again, if the transport related barriers are not removed, mergers may not happen, or if they do the price will everywhere be higher than without these barriers.

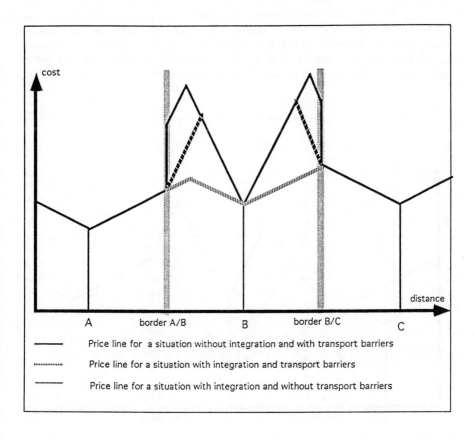

Figure 3: A spatial market with barriers at borders.

Overall, the impacts of the remaining transport barriers are the following: On a certain mode, they increase the marginal generalised transport costs, e.g. via congestion which will increase the expected transport time and hence the time cost. They will also increase monetary cost through detours and/or higher transport tariffs via monopolies in the national markets. Ceteris paribus this will lead to a reduction of the market size. In other words, the firm will sell its products on closer markets. It will also tend to reduce consumer welfare and increase profits of the national transport sectors. Moreover, if barriers are mode specific, the relative marginal costs will express differences in network quality and will lead to competitive advantages for modes with more performing and reliable networks. Given the evidence presented in the previous sections this will lead to a bias towards road

162

haulage. Through the value of time the network quality influences opportunity costs. Thus, the delivery time and reliability of a freight transport service have a direct impact on the opportunity cost of capital. The longer the time that the goods are under way, or the higher the risk that a good does not arrive in time, the higher the capital that cannot be used otherwise. This will bring an additional bias towards using more reliable modes in the case of high value goods.

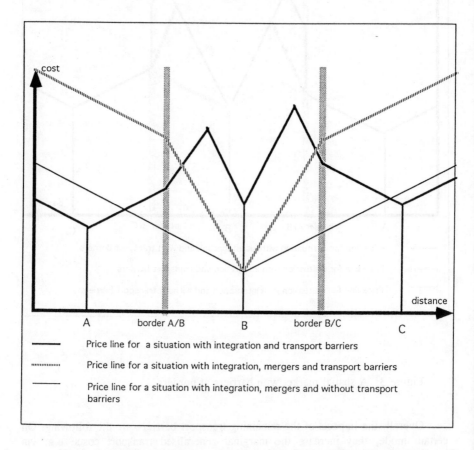

Figure 4: Transport barrier effects in the case of an industry with scale economies

Overall the short run impacts of barriers are a reduction of the size of market areas and a high use of the "least missing" networks. Dropping the assumption of constant marginal cost we can allow for economies of scale in production. Transport related barriers may then favour production at a suboptimal scale because of the relative small size of the market and the need to locate production close to the market. This last remark leads us to longer term reactions of firms to barriers. With highly performing networks the opening of European borders, i.e. the increased mobility of production factors will lead from a world of comparative advantages to one of economies of scale (and possibly scope). These can be realised through spatial centralisation of separable production processes. Barriers will prevent this transition to take place to the extent that the marginal generalised transport cost due to barriers is higher than the marginal cost savings from economies of scale.

4. Transport Policy Between European and Local Interests

In the situation just described the question is, why, in the framework of European integration transport related barrier problems are not solved in the same way as they are dealt with within nation-states. On the level of the latter, an important part of transport policy consists in relieving bottleneck situations. The main difference between nations and Europe is that in a local and national context, the actors are well identified and the rules of the game are clear and the coalitions formed. Therefore the demand for transport infrastructure will be met without big frictions. Also, the regulation on the national level has created important rents.

Transport bottlenecks at the border have a protectionist effect. Therefore, only competitive industries support the improvement of the transborder transport networks. The concern of the multinational firms and the competitive industries is for the "costs of non-Europe" (Cecchini, 1989) and more specifically the obstacles to European integration due to the absence of important links and layers in the transport and communication networks. Though the heavy regulation on road haulage in many countries will soon be abolished, and important plans for a rapid train system and a combined transport conceptions are put forward (CEC, 1989) there are important remaining obstacles which are partly related to the national borders. Therefore, big industries will address their regulatory demand to the European level. The problem with this policy level is, however, that it is not very powerful and relevant as compared to the national-one.

As to the households, they will probably experience an increase in welfare in the sequel of an improved efficiency of the European road transport system. However, these effects are not easily discernible and are not necessarily identified as being the outcome of improved transport conditions. On the other hand, environmental problems, which have a multitude of sources, are mainly identified by the households as being produced by the transport sector, and more specifically by cars. This has led to an important demand for an efficient environmental policy which reduces road traffic in many European countries. Traditionally, households will address their demand to the local or national policy level, rather than to the European one. By doing so, they can put the blame for the environmental damage that they help to produce on outsiders and ask for regulatory measures. One obvious object for such a regulation is (foreign) freight transport. This leads to policy measures like taxes on heavy vehicles, weight limits and the like (for the Swiss case, see Maggi, 1992). Thus, it is possible to make outsiders pay for environmental damages. In order to put this through, households have to address their policy demand to the local or national level, because otherwise no "foreigners" would exist.

Finally, the transport sector has learned to live well with national regulation. In the case of the railways, they behave as national monopolies and generally do not have a European scope in their activity. They are used to divide their market along the national borders and to (ab)use their monopoly power in the respective country. Similar arguments are valid for the road haulage sector. There, the national regulation is very often used to protect the national industry. While there are some improvements to be expected in the EC in future, countries of strategic importance in the European network like Austria and Switzerland are still outsiders. In Switzerland, the road haulage sector clearly favours the 28 tons weight limit which gives an important protection. Like in the case of industry, only the competitive transport companies have an interest in an opening of the markets.

It can be concluded that to solve the problem of the remaining transport barriers in Europe, the opposition of all those groups interested in keeping the existing regulations has to be overcome. This implies among else, that the competitive industries have to join forces with the competitive part of the transport sector. It also calls for a full internalisation of environmental externalities of transport so that the households need no longer worry about the amount of what they call unnecessary transport.

REFERENCES

Bretzke, W.-R., Auswirkungen der Just-in-time-Produktion auf das Dienstleistungsangebot der Verkehrswirtschaft, **Die Stellung der Verkehrswirtschaft im Rahmen moderner logistischer Denkweisen.** (Schriftenreihe der DVWG B121), Bergisch Gladbach, 1989.

Bröcker, J., International Trade and Economic Integration. A Partial Equilibrium Analysis, **Regional Science and Urban Economics**, Vol. 18, 1988, pp. 261-281.

Caves, D.W., L.R. Christensen, M.W. Tetheway, R.J. Windle, Network Effects and the Measurement of Returns to Scale and Density for US Railroads. **Analytical Studies in Transport Economics** (Andrew F. Daughety, ed.) Cambridge Cambridge University Press, 1985.

Cecchini, P., **The European Challenge 1992, The Benefits of the Single Market**, Gower, Aldershot, 1989.

Commission of the European Communities, **Council Resolution on the Trans-European Networks (presented by the Commission)**, COM (89) 643 final, Brussels, 18 December 1989.

European Roundtable of Industrialists, **Keeping Europe Mobile. A Report on Advanced Transport Systems Prepared for ERT**, Stockholm, 1987.

European Roundtable of Industrialists, **Missing Networks. A European Challenge**, Brussels, 1990.

165

Filippini, M., R. Maggi, The Cost Structure of the Swiss Private Railways. **International Journal of Transport Economics**, Vol. 19, 1992, pp. 307-327.

INRO-TNO/NEA, **Towards a Really Combined Transport**, Delft, 1990.

Kearny, AT., Gemeinschaft der Europäischen Bahnen, **Studie über die Perspektiven eines europäischen Netzes des kombinierten Verkehrs**, Abschlussbericht, 1989.

McFadden, D., C. Winston, A. Boersch-Suppan, Joint Estimation of Freight Transport Decisions under Nonrandom Sampling. **Analytical Studies in Transport Economics** (Andrew F. Daughety, ed.) Cambridge, Cambridge University Press, 1985.

Maggi, R., Some Speculations on Logistics and the Environment in European Transport Policy, **Transport Developments in an Integrating Europe** (H.G. Smit, ed.) Delft, European Transport Planning Colloquium Foundation, 1991.

Maggi, R., Swiss Transport Policy for Europe? Federalism and the Dominance of Local Issues, **Transportation Research A**, Vol. 26A, 1992, pp. 193-198

Maggi, R., P. Nijkamp, I. Masser, Missing Networks in European Transport and Communication, **Transport Reviews**, Vol. 12, 1992, pp. 311-321

Nijkamp, P., R. Maggi, I. Masser, J. Vleugel, **Missing Networks in Europe**, European Roundtable of Industrialists, Brussles, 1990a.

Nijkamp, P., P. Rietveld, I. Salomon, Barriers in Spatial Interactions and Communications, **The Annals of Regional Science**, vol. 24, 1990b, pp. 237-252.

Rietveld, P., and F. Rossera, Telecommunication Demand: The Role of Barriers. Paper presented at the International NECTAR Symposium, Amsterdam, 1991/1992.

Schmidtchen, D., and H.-J. Schmidt-Trenz, The Division of Labor is Limited by the Extent of the Law. A Constitutional Approach to Private Law, **Constitutional Poltical Economy**, Vol. 1, 1990, pp. 49-71.

CHAPTER 11

TRANSPORT NETWORKS:

BORDERS AND BARRIERS IN THE

HIGH SPEED RAIL NETWORK

Ulrich Blum

1. Introduction

In France, Germany, Spain and to a lesser degree in Italy and the Scandinavian countries national transportation policies have started to think in terms of high speed rail (HSR) systems. It was France which first put such a system into operation on a national level in Europe and proved that it was economically feasible in terms of passenger volume and changes in modal split in favour of the train. Many years before, Japan had already proven that such a venture could be implemented and run on a privately financed basis.

In Germany the federal transportation budget for the first time earmarks more money to rail than to road, a clear break in tradition, and most of this goes into completely new tracks or improved old tracks in an attempt to expand high-speed Inter City Express (ICE) service to become competitive against the car and the plane, but also to fill missing links in the process of European and German unification.

On the European level we find similar developments. Among the major problems of an European HSR policy is the prevalent undersupply of links which is the result of:
- geo- and topographical barriers: the Alps, the Channel or the Baltic Sea;
- political competition and technical differences: border crossings, crossings to non-EC member states, differences in track gauge, clearances or electricity supply;
- economic reasons: the demand in certain areas is not sufficiently large to economically justify the construction of new links.

It would extremely oversimplify the issue to only accuse the "Common Transport Policy" (CTP) of the European Community to have failed to appreciate the importance of railways as a means of moving freight and people; only overcongestion on roads and in the sky lead to a political reassessment. As, additionally, national governments also considered the development of their national industry standards as a means of an industrial policy, international cooperation was severely hampered from the start.

The opening of the East, especially the unification of Germany, and the near completion of the Channel tunnel also necessitate some additional planning on the many corridors emerging in Europe. Not only does the role of cities like Berlin, Warsaw, Prague or Budapest need to be culturally and economically reassessed; the Mediterranean basin and its access to the North and the West will lead to a reorientation of trasportation flows and the formulation of new transportation policies, especially with respect to the new growth regions of the "blue banana". The introduction of common carriage may trigger additional national investment into railroad infrastructure, as it allows the less developed nations of Europe to offer high-quality service through the operational import of advanced rolling stock. In fact, it should include those countries which, by their inferior road transportation infrastructure, have a productivity advance in their train system.

This paper inquires the role of the competition process in the transportation sector with respect to the spatial and the regional-sectoral structure of the economy. In doing so, we want to answer some of the following questions:

(1) What are the political and economic underpinnings of the HSR-euphoria in Europe which produce the necessary political momentum to accelerate HSR development?
  - We believe that the answers to this question are economic and political, as economies of scale and scope in industry and in transport systems encourage new alternatives.

(2) What are the political and economic constraints in implementing a HSR system? We may identify at least the following levels:
  - Firstly, infrastructure and rolling stock are not sufficiently standardized.
  - Secondly, European transportation integration is hampered through different norms and standards as well as incompatible organizational and financial structures.
  - Finally, **local** environmental concerns arise from the building of high-speed links and the complementary additional infrastructure or the re-tooling of existing ones.

(3) Is it possible to develop a model of spatial competition in this domain which explicitly accounts for the redistributional opportunities in space?
  - Train stations offer central goods (mobility) for which demand is limited to a certain area because of access costs.
  - Transportation links restructure space.
  - The demand for mobility differs according to distance and purpose; quality, especially speed, has different impacts on the resulting segments.

2. Competition and High Speed Railway Development

2.1 Optimal hierarchies for train service

Trips differ by purposes and length. This leads to different elasticities, spatial distances and hierarchies. The underling economic structure relates to the model of monopolistic competition introduced by Loesch (1940): for a given market size optimal transportation technologies are used; consequently, the envelope of all average transportation cost functions have increasing returns to scale, as each consecutive average cost function has a minimum at a lower price. The spatial demand curve is obtained by integrating f.o.b. demand over the market area. The maximum size is obtained at the point where the two curves intersect. Once the size of the region is reduced, the spatial demand curve bends inwards and the smallest zero-profit market is reached, if the demand curve is tangential to the envelope of average cost curves (see Figure 1).

Consequently, we can depict a hierarchical transportation system with overlapping or shared infrastructures as an economically efficient configuration with:
(1) mass transit systems at the lowest level;
(2) regional feeders of different types at the intermediate level;
(3) HSR systems with a national or European scope at the highest level.

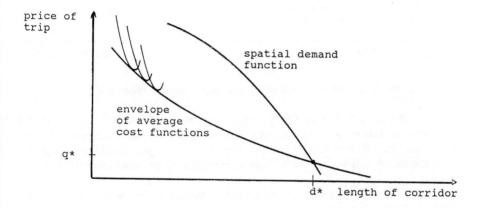

Figure 1: Spatial demand and optimal transportation area.

2.2 A topology of competition for high speed railway systems

What types of competition have to be distinguished to model the spatial competition for HSR systems?
- Firstly, regions may form alliances in order to create attractive corridor areas, if they think that they may benefit from this new system. Competition may emerge between different regional alliances.
- Secondly, for given corridors, cities will compete for an access, i.e., a railway station, to an HSR system.

It is obvious that areas not served by an HSR system are not very interested in its implementation. An increase in the number of stops is not efficient and is contradictory to service quality. The situation may depicted by the following graph that we adapted from the concept of efficient oligopolistic competition (Kantzenbach, 1967) (see Figure 2).

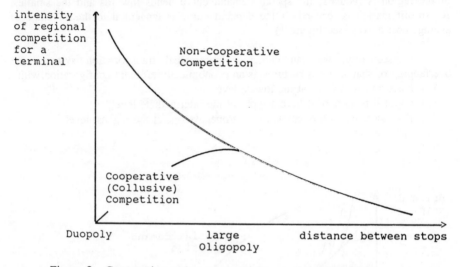

Figure 2: Cooperative and non-cooperative spatial competition.

If the distance is sufficiently large, the intensity of competition will be low and two terminals become economically feasible. The more the distance shrinks, the more locations will compete for stops. If they are extremely close and non-cooperative, competition will be cut-throat. This is portrayed by potential competition in the graphic.

A collusive settlement of two or more spatially close competitors leads to a level of effective competition and could imply that:
- passage will only be granted if trains stop in an overlapping way always at either place, or that
- the location not directly served gets compensation, e.g. a high-speed access.

2.3 Competition and common carriage
It may be efficient to allow or even to encourage operative competition within different levels of the hierarchy by separating service from infrastructure and allowing common carriage. Then the sunk costs of the network would no longer deter a contestant, if the incumbent threatens him with fierce competition.

2.4 Cooperation and competition : the modal aspect
Once corridors and stations have been established, organizational competition of the following types will emerge:
- competition between models alongside the corridor;

- competition for feeder services;
- competition among carriers in a shared HSR infrastructure in case of common carriage.

This may encourage train stations to develop into train ports, i.e., to become more similar to medium-sized airports.

3. Some Recent German Experience: ICE Lines Nuernberg-Erfurt and Stuttgart-Dresden

3.1 Scope of the problem

The unification of Germany did not only lead to a redefinition of what is a central location in Germany, but will also change opportunities because of the new transportation infrastructures that are being planned. North-Bavaria presently has two links to Saxony and Thuringia, one from Nuernberg via Jena to Berlin and another from Nuernberg or Regensburg via Hof, Chemnitz (with a link via Leipzig to Berlin) to Dresden. The present Master Plan for Germany has put emphasis on building a new link from Munich to Berlin; the proposal to improve the existing link from Nuernberg to Dresden has been studied extensively (Blum and Mandel, 1991), but will not be implemented in the near future.

Transportation demand in the corridor in question has been estimated; it suggests that additional capacities are needed. Based on the assumption of a full integration of East Germany into the EC, and on the levelling out of income differences between the Western and the Eastern provinces of Germany, the flows given in the Figure 3 were forecasted.

Total long-distance rail traffic between the southern and the western parts of Germany on the one hand and the eastern part on the other hand, i.e. traffic between what was the old Federal Republic and the old GDR, will amount to roughly 43 million passenger trips in the year 2010.

The corridor under investigation here would attract some 12 mln passengers by the year 2010. This excludes trips originating in this corridor and ending outside of it or vice versa as well as transit trips. This value of 12 mln trips would rise by roughly 3.5 mln trips, once the service is brought to HSR standards. Then newly induced traffic might increase the total by another 3 mln passengers.

Given the decision to only build one new link between Munich and Berlin, two alternative regional coalitions emerged: the Nuernberg-Erfurt and the Regensburg-Leipzig coalitions. Until today, a final decision has not been taken, but the first corridor proposal seems more attractive in terms of costs and demand and would be consistent with a later retooling of the link between Nuernberg and Dresden.

Presently, a fierce debate is going on which stops should be realized at the level of the ICE (with a speed of 250 km/h and above) which should stop at intervals of 100 km and more, and the high-speed InterRegio (IR) which has a speed requirement of 200 km/h and stops every 30 km. On the first level of hierarchy, the ICE, Nuernberg and Erfurt are sure stops; as they are nearly 200 km apart, the question has been raised, which other city in between should be included. Some cities along the track will only get access to a low level regional feeder service and have heavily objected against sacrificing part of their inner cities for additional tracks alongside the old ones and against the noise problem, to support a system which is of no apparent use to them.

The debate is also going on, how to integrate the HSR system (ICE, IR) with other modes; especially stations in city cores may generate huge volumes of trips and overburden the existing infrastructure. This implies that either new train stations have to be built at more favourable locations or old ones have to be retooled to remove this barrier of modal access.

Figure 3: The East-West corridor in North-Bavaria and transportation demand for rail service

As a consequence it has been proposed to solve the problem with an integrated approach by defining alternative options of corridors, stops and modal access; for one of the major cities in Upper Franconia, the cities of Coburg and Lichtenfels, this looks as follows (Blum, 1992) (see Table 1)

| | Corridor I | | Corridor II | Corridor I |
	Variant 1	Variant 2	Variant 3	Variant 4
ICE tracks	through Coburg	east of Coburg	through Lichten-fels	east of Coburg
ICE station	none	none	none	new station north-east of Coburg
IR tracks	through Coburg on new tracks	through Coburg and Lichtenfels on old tracks	through Lichten-fels	east of Coburg
IR station	main station of Coburg	main station of Coburg and Lich-tenfels	main station of Lichten-fels	new station north-east of Coburg
city train system	separately for both cities	separately for both cities	separately for both cities	connecting city train between Coburg and Lichtenfels

Table 1: Alternative options for an access to the HSR system

Initially, variants 1 and 3 were proposed (the two others will not be discussed here, as they were excluded at an early stage of the planning process, because the Thuringian mountains pose too many problems as natural barriers). Both pass through the cities cores, either of Coburg or Lichtenfels; the environmental impacts are severe, especially as it foreseen that up to 200 high-speed freight trains (InterCargoExpess) will use this link by the year 2010 in addition to a daily load of some high-speed passenger trains.

In the beginning of the planning process, both cities as representatives of corridor proposals were heavily competing for the new tracks; they both considered this investment favourable for their locational potential (variants 1 and 3). This faded, once they realized that the existing train stations would only be used by the regional high-speed train InterRegio as the demand potential of each city and its environment would not justify another stop and, consequently, would imply prolongation of travel time.

A solution which would put the high-speed ICE out of the city by circumventing Corburg is not satisfactory, as the InterRegio would then use the old tracks that link both cities (variant 2); even though this would mean that both cities have the IR access, travel time from Nuernberg to Erfurt would increase from 1 hour for the ICE to 1 hour 30 minutes for the IR and make it less attractive (at both ends one would still have to change trains to get onto the ICE).

Both train stations are also ill-prepared for the high-speed age in which train stations must have some of the properties of airports. Even if the slower IR service became a success, the capacity of other modes to serve the stations would be insufficient.

A solution was then proposed which is presently under investigation: it suggests to built a completely new station along the eastern track at a point were it intersects with one of the old city train tracks, close to missing links and supply a city service between all the regional agglomerations, thus doubling the demand potential and making it interesting also for the ICE to stop in Upper Franconia.

- - - - - - - Existing InterCity and InterCityExpress Links
———— Projected InterCityExpress Links

Figure 4: Alternatives for high-speed service in North-Bavaria

4.   **Conclusions**

We conclude that it is necessary to explicitly take into account regional aspects, if a HSR system is to be implemented. This implies that the decision space is increased and more information, especially on the regional level, needs to be gathered. As a consequence, a compromise can be developed that is supported by all formerly opposing parties which is also satisfactory from an environmental point of view.

It is extremely important to properly take into account the political environment with respect to a rivalry among regions and cities. Environmental considerations play their most important role on the regional level

REFERENCES

Blum, U., H. Hautzinger, P. Kessel, J. Kowalsky, H.-P. Kienzler, K. Kunzle, W. Rohling, W. Rothengatter, **Szenario zur Verkehrsentwicklung mit der DDR und Osteuropa**, Fieburg, Karlsruhe, 1990.

Blum, U., and B. Mandel, Leistungsfähige Hauptstrecke der DB Stuttgart-Nurnberg -Bayreuth-Hof-Dresden (Teilgutachten), 1991.

Blum, U., Coburg und der ICE, 1992, mineo.

Kantzenbach, E., **Die Funktionsfähigkeit des Wettbewerbs**, Vandenhoek & Rupprecht, Gottingen, 1967.

Loesch, A., **Die raumliche Ordnung der Wirtschaft**, Gustav Fischer Verlag, Stuttgart, 1962.

CHAPTER 12

BARRIERS AND MISSING NETWORKS

IN EUROPEAN INFRASTRUCTURE:

INLAND WATERWAYS AND COASTAL TRANSPORT

Maria Giaoutzi and Peter Nijkamp

1. **European Transport Policy Issues**

This paper will view the potential of European waterways from a general European policy perspective. The way in which governments can influence international transport are numerous (see Nijkamp et al., 1991). In most countries it is still the national government which provides - directly or indirectly - the major components of infrastructure, such as ports, airports, glassfibre networks, railway tracks, etc. Despite deregulation, the provision of and participation in infrastructure itself gives power, because - through its very location or capacity - infrastructure can influence the magnitude of a country's trade. This is also the background of the current competitive efforts among European mainports.

The power to charge for the use of the national transport or communications infrastructure offers a further device by which a government may attempt to influence trade and hence transport.

Apart from more direct measures and institutional arrangements which also serve to influence the costs of international transport (and thus violate the principle of laissez faire), governments may also intervene, again in numerous different ways, to protect their own domestic transport industries from external competition. For instance, cabotage is in particular often viewed in the same way as the "dumping" of goods in a market and is the subject of particularly severe restrictions in many European countries.

An important question in this context is what the limits of deregulation are in the light of the European economic integration with its ambitious goal of one common market after 1993. Clearly, it has to be admitted as well that some level of regulation always seems to be necessary (particularly in view of coordination and economic principles). In this framework, it is interesting to observe that the initial impetus for deregulation - or ultra-free competition, as it is perhaps better called - is in the meantime beginning to be questioned.

It is noteworthy that national intervention in the international transport market which is occurring up till now has two distinct effects. Firstly, many national policies are adopted to alleviate some short term problems, or are an attempt to gain some commercial advantage. In general, they bring forth responses from trading partners or from alternative, national suppliers. The long term effect is often a

178

reduction in the efficiency of the international economy. If the policies are all designed to protect local industry or domestic transport suppliers, then this means that almost inevitably the cost of transport is pushed artificially high and overall production is kept below its maximum potential. If the policies involve transport subsidies (e.g., to aid exporting firms), then the long term impact is equally damaging, because the overall cost of transport is too low, meaning that those which are normally deemed inefficient because of their exorbitant transport needs, now become competitive with their more economically efficient rivals.

Second, unfavourable distributional impacts on less developed regions occur in an even more pronounced way when one realizes that most tightening up of national policy occurs when the economy is in recession. The same holds for less developed border areas (or sectors within them) in the European context.

In terms of substance of policy concerns, an extremely important question nowadays appears to be the role and impact of deregulation (or of complete self-regulation) in transport and telecommunications policy. The policy views about and the evaluation of this "hot" policy issue cannot be placed under one common denominator, but broadly speaking, most international agencies agree on the usefulness of deregulation (if managed at least with tact), but certainly not at any cost or applied to any policy area; it should rather be seen as an - often useful - means, not as a (final) objective. In view of related trends such as privatisation, decentralisation etc. it may be supposed that for instance, (inter)national railways would function better when freed from state control. It has also been stressed by various agencies that deregulation is not a limitless policy instrument. In any case it should be functional, but its implementation turns out to be extremely difficult in policy areas where it is badly needed. In the context of planning and policy making, a critical self-review and an integrated incremental approach in which a flexible updating and upgrading of global plans seems to be more important than ever before, is an appropriate policy direction which is gradually taking place in various countries.

Another concern of policy makers is related to financial aspects. The financial burden of large scale investments is often hard to bear for one country. New possibilities for financing (infrastructure) projects with a border crossing character are: private financing, public/private partnerships (as can be illustrated by the Channel Tunnel project), and guaranteed state contracts (with a duration of 15 years or more as proposed by the Belgian government). In any case, the potential profits of international cooperation are by far not exploited to their full extent at the moment.

One achievement of competitive performance levels would need **coherent European** - rather than a sectoral or nationalistic - view. Only in this context a sound financing and environmental approach to infrastructure can be reached. Such a European view is also necessary to cope with the phenomenon of missing networks in a pluriform European society.

In the same vein the problem of **technological standardisation** has to be seen. Standardisation does not only pertain to hardware (like voltage systems in railways), but also to software (e.g., information systems for international customs procedures) and orgware (e.g., common carriage on European rails).

Finally, of strategic importance for commodity transport is also a further development of **multi-modal transport solutions** (such as piggy-back systems and containerisation).

In the light of the previous observations, the following policy concerns can be mentioned in the European transportation scene.

First, transportation plans usually are of long duration so that there is a large amount of built-in **uncertainties** regarding economic, demographic and technological factors. The identification of sources of uncertainty and finding ways to include them in transportation policy design, is far from being a well developed area, with grave consequences for the successful implementation of many transportation projects. Furthermore, some of these uncertainties involve benefits and cost to future generations. Therefore, ways should be devised to introduce directly inter-generational comparisons into transportation policy analysis.

Secondly, as the economies of most European countries are moving further towards heavy reliance on free market mechanisms, the question of **market sustainability** of transportation plans becomes a crucial one. Thus, it is possible to devise an optimal transport plan which in the medium and longer-run would not endure market forces and, consequently, would be unsustainable. As with uncertainty, market sustainability analysis is, at present, not an integral component of transportation policy analysis, though it undoubtedly should be so.

A third, and related problem, is that of the degree of **market contestability.** That is, it seems that the idea of deregulation of transport industries, such as air and bus, is gaining more and more ground among policy-makers. However, transportation markets are also prone to markets imperfections due to the existence of factors like scale and scope economies which, in turn, may cause deregulated transport markets to evolve into undesirable market forms like the domination of large-size monopolies. The theoretical answer, given to this problem, is to argue that such markets will be contestable in the sense that market forces will inhibit monopolistic firms from bringing about market distortions, in terms of prices and outputs. Suffice it to say that, currently, very little is known on how contestable transport markets indeed are functioning and how to incorporate this issue into transportation policy analysis. Public ownership of transport services and facilities vs. franchising, is a major example of a policy alternative which can result from such an analysis.

Fourth, policy analysis of transportation markets (or modes or systems) is commonly carried out in isolation of other markets (or modes). However, the **connectivity** of transport systems should be the focus of the analysis because of its importance to consumers and because the relative advantage of specific transport systems may emerge only when linked to other systems. In fact, finding ways to make transport systems more compatible with each other should be a major objective of policy analysis.

The previous remarks hold for all transport modes in Europe, including inland waterways and coastal transport. To provide a proper analytical scene, we will in the next section first discuss critical success factors of infrastructure.

2.   **Network Barriers: an Analysis via the Pentagon Prism**
      The removal of trade barriers in the European economy has brought to light
the existence of network barriers impeding international commodity, person and
information flows. Such barriers may be of two types:

- missing links: local barriers in infrastructure hampering an efficient throughflow
  of commodities, people or information; such barriers have been extensively dealt
  with by the ERT (1988).
- missing networks: the absence of strategic layers or components of Europe's
  transport and communications infrastructure, be it material or immaterial in
  nature; thus the term "missing networks" applies to the poor performance - in
  terms of convenience, speed, comfort, flexibility, reliability, costs, safety or social
  costs - of European infrastructure (see ERT, 1991).

      It should be added that networks connecting nodes in a spatial system are
often multi-modal in nature. If certain physical modes (e.g., railways) are missing,
we have a clear case of a missing network. But it may also happen that a certain
mode is present, but that its potential is not used up to its full capacity (e.g.,
because of organizational barriers, lack of technical standardisation etc.). This is
also a case of missing networks. And finally it may happen that connections between
different modes (i.e., vertical links between different network layers) are absent.
This situation of bad connectivity (e.g., lack of a telematics system for a truck fleet)
is also an example of a missing network.

      In a recent report by NECTAR (1990) it has been argued that the demand for
network services in Europe is rapidly increasing in recent years. At the same time a
lack of capacity and malfunctioning in almost all components of European networks
can be observed. The government response to such drastic changes has been
unsatisfactory so far, and nowadays the European economy is facing a severe
problem not only of "missing links", but even of "missing networks" as a whole.
This would require a rigorous European response in view of the long-term socio-
economic interest of Europe. But instead of systemic solutions most policy-makers
have taken resort to piece-meal, partial and uni-modal transport solutions, without
keeping an eye on the needs of the European network economy.
      As mentioned already, interest in the European scale of networks has not yet
been very significant, as transport policy and planning is seldom performed at this
scale. National frontiers have always provided a clear physical barrier between
countries despite growing transport demand. Intra-European transport infrastructure
networks have not followed this trend and show nowadays various bottlenecks in
terms of missing links and missing networks. The Internal Market between the
twelve members of the European community has put the focus of European
politicians and industry on issues of socio-economic harmonization in order to
remove distortions to free competition between industries in its member states, and
increasing consideration is now given to transportation.
      The major difference between a (more or less) nationalistic and a European
approach to infrastructure planning can best be described in terms of its economic

effects. Nationalistic infrastructure planning means focusing on the way in which national infrastructure building companies, vehicle producers and transportation companies are given a competitive advantage at the cost of their foreign counterparts. As other countries will use the same tactics, in most cases however, all parties will be losers in this way, since efficient economics of scale are not reached and large sums of public investments are lost; one of the reasons being that external competitors (e.g., Far Eastern or American companies) - while having large home markets - may outperform European companies.

Thus the existence of missing networks in Europe means the existence of missing economic development potential, as will be illustrated below for various transport modes.

A look at the European transport and communications map teaches us the existence of serious missing networks in freight transportation, both in terms of capacity as well as of quality of road and rail networks and goods terminals. This evidence calls for new proposals regarding combined freight terminals, a proliferation of EDI (electronic data interchange) and satellite-based orbital truck fleet management, and new forms of cooperation between transporters in goods distribution.

In air transport major problems relate to lack of runways, transfer and air corridor capacity, and inefficient pre- and post-transport facilities. Policies should focus on a new European network of improved and standardized air traffic management (ATC) systems and a concentration of the large number of air traffic centres.

European high-speed trains present a new challenge of Europe. The lack of a European standard train (e.g. TGV next to ICE) with uniform technical and organizational needs and transport potentials, and its insufficient compatibility with conventional trains (leading to the need for enormous investments in both track and trains) may become a serious stumbling block for its potential. Both track planning and financing problems have led to serious disconcert in Europe, leading to slackening of the pace of investments and actual building and thereby inducing nationalistic thinking. There is a need for a European-oriented high-speed train network (for passenger and goods), which overcomes the problems of national monopolies.

Separating carriage and infrastructure on rail is the key idea of European common carriage. The negative effects of natural monopolies in transportation are however manifest everywhere. A good illustration is provided by the existence of twelve national railway companies in the European community. This calls for a new solution, where for instance the efficient organization may be laid in the hands of a new institution, a European Carriage Organization, whose (low-level) intervention should resolve the needs for transport between major central places in Europe (including Eastern Europe).

Next, in European telecommunication, the basic network that is missing at this moment, is a network for fast and reliable transmission of data throughout Europe. Instead, we have seen a number of small scale pilot projects and lack of investment in (standardized) hard ware and soft ware. Next to substitution of physical transport for non-physical transport, the use of telecom facilities for traffic guidance may be a good option for extending the capacity and quality of other transport networks.

Finally, European inland waterways show also various missing networks, as a large part of this network cannot be used efficiently, because of geographical conditions and lack of investments in maintenance and new building. Nevertheless, inland waterways together with new forms of efficient coastal transport may certainly have some potential. In some countries there is a revival of container transportation between ships and road vehicles, leading to a need for intermodal freight terminals. Compatibility between the various modes of transport is therefore strongly needed. State regulation (including large subsidization programs to preserve national employment) may also lead to distortions of competition. Furthermore, in a European setting there is a need to improve informatization in this sector.

Thus we find many missing networks in Europe which act as barriers for development. There are many reasons for the existence of such missing networks:

- **political:** emphasis on local benefits rather than on European advantages, or an orientation toward simple short-term, but less strategic solutions.
- **nationalistic:** emphasis on protection of domestic activities (e.g., via toll systems, landing rights), or an orientation towards sectoral (rather than macro) interests (e.g., in freight transport).
- **economic:** lack of a financing structure for risky new network investments, or lack of a sound user charging policy.
- **institutional:** unsatisfactory coordination between different modes, or orientation towards specific interests rather than overall economies.
- **technical:** lack of standardization (especially in an international setting) or lack of penetration of new or existing technologies.
- **social:** existence of conflicts between different objectives or groups, which prevent a more coherent network configuration.
- **behavioural:** rigidity of attitudes and behaviour, which hampers an adjustment to new conditions.

This illustrative list of considerations clarifies the existence and continuation of missing networks in Europe's infrastructure.

In the past, solutions to infrastructure barriers (including missing networks) were mainly seen as having only one or two dimensions, viz. the hard ware (physical infrastructure) and the fin ware (funding) dimension. A number of failures in developing infrastructure projects points to the importance of dealing with these problems in a more sophisticated and comprehensive way. In the abovementioned NECTAR study, it has been argued that proper solutions should take account of the following dimensions:

1)   hard ware (physical infrastructure)
2)   soft ware (logistics and informatics)
3)   org ware (institutional and organizational setting)
4)   fin ware (financial arrangements/funding)
5)   eco ware (environmental and safety effects).

These five critical success factors for appropriate network design and implementation can be represented as a pentagon (see Figure 3). It should be noted, that the pentagon model not only applies to links and uni-modal networks, but in particular to multi-modal network systems in which synergy is a sine qua non. We will briefly elaborate on the elements of this pentagon.

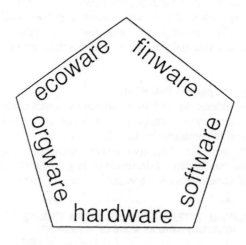

Figure 1:   The Pentagon Prism

When focusing on hard ware, we see the emergence of modern technology (e.g., new materials technology, new information technology) penetrating the transport sector at a rapid pace. This has dramatically increased its potential. The acceptance of advanced hard ware is however found to be hampered by a lack of European uniformity and standardization.

Sophisticated soft ware systems are nowadays available in Europe and they are in principle able to enhance the performance of the transport sector. Co-ordination and harmonization of soft ware is however far from sufficient in Europe to warrant a rapid progress in Europe's network systems.

Transport is a multi-modal, multi-actor and multi-national activity, which needs both competition and flexible regulation (orgware). The European scene shows many rigid and fragmented decision and planning structures/institutions, which form a severe obstacle to a progressive European space-economy.

Improvement of the European transport and communication networks is often hindered by a severe lack of coordinated European financing initiatives/institutions (fin ware) in both private and public spheres.

There is a growing environmental (eco ware) concern in Europe and transport is increasingly regarded as one of the major sources of social costs of environmental

184

pollution. It is necessary that a market orientation towards environmental quality is pursued, focused on technology, infrastructure design and vehicle use.

It should also be noted that the development of a European infrastructure network takes shape via a double-tier system. On the one hand, the European network economy requires efficient transnational transport and communications connections focusing on long-distance corridors (roads, railways, airline connections, waterways, telecommunications). On the other hand, the nodes of the European network are formed by large metropolitan centres (e.g., Milan, Paris, London, the Dutch Randstad) and these nodes also require a proper and efficient mix of all transport modes. Thus missing networks may also refer to both international infrastructure combinations and interwoven metropolitan infrastructures.

3. Waterways: Neglected Potential

Waterways belong to the most forgotten components of Europe's infrastructure. This is once more surprising, as the volume of transport via waterways (inland, coastal, sea) is considerable (see Figure 2).

This sector however, has also severe problems. Apart from the lack of transport speed and the outdated infrastructure (e.g., sluices), there is also a serious barrier in terms of standardisation (especially in case of trans-shipment).

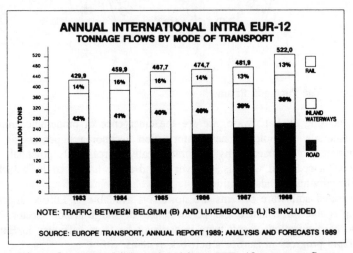

Figure 2: Annual international intra EUR-12 transport flows

Thus waterways may offer a good case study for testing the above mentioned pentagon prism. They also offer much potential in view of the emerging importance of intermodal transport, the absence of limits to capacity, and the new role of East-Europe (Amber et al., 1985; Seidel, 1988; Simons and Wansink, 1990).

The important role of waterways infrastructure was also recognized in a recent report of the Group Transport 2000 Plus (1991), which claimed that intermodal sea transport (i.e., containers by sea, road, rail, inland waterways) is by far the more effective and progressive system of transport. This group also emphasized the very low environmental costs involved in this type of transport. Furthermore, in their report coastal transport was advocated as an important complement and a vigorous improvement of existing transport systems (e.g., for long-haul routes).

The relative environmental burden of waterway transport vis-à-vis road and rail is illustrated in Figure 3.

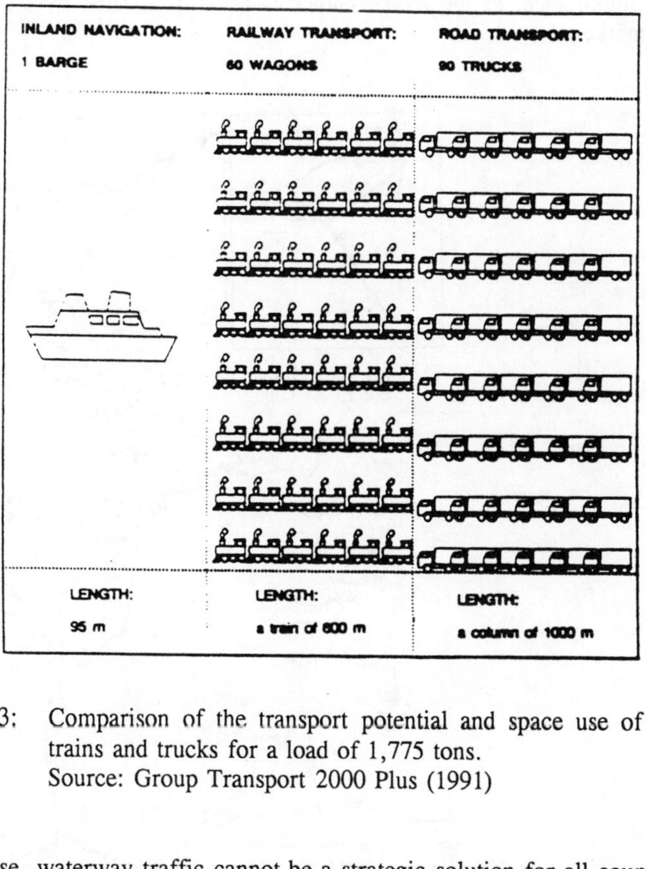

Figure 3: Comparison of the transport potential and space use of barges, trains and trucks for a load of 1,775 tons.
Source: Group Transport 2000 Plus (1991)

Of course, waterway traffic cannot be a strategic solution for all countries, as it is highly dependent on specific geo-nautical conditions. Major axes may offer in this respect a huge potential, such as the Rhine and the Rhine-Main-Danube Canal. It should be emphasized however, that the connectivity of inland waterways, viz. the network connections with other inland waterways, the compatibility with respect to coastal and sea transport (e.g. standardized containerisation) and the linkages with other transport modes at transhipment points (e.g., ro-ro techniques), is a critical success factor. Thus both vessel technology and waterway systems design are of utmost importance for a proper competitive functioning of waterway transport. An

186

example of a failure in policy leading to barrier and missing networks in this context can be found in Winkelmans (1988), who presents the French case where segmented investments in inland waterways have failed to generate a benefit because of the isolated character of most of these modernised waterway sections (so-called "culs-de-sac"). This is illustrated in Figure 4.

The latter examples make clear that a system split - rather than a modal split - is critical for the use of various transport modes. Thus connectivity of a network which ensures flexibility, reliability, accessibility and cost-effectiveness are of decisive importance, as the modal choice is actually dictated by the client (i.e., a buyer's market).

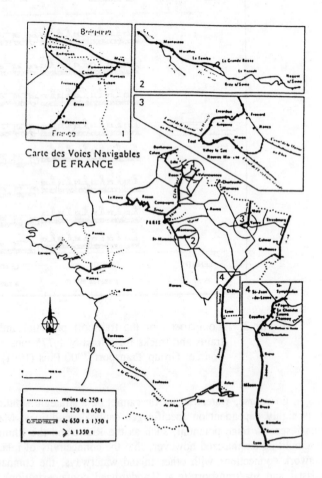

Figure 4: Inland waterways in France: example of an incomplete (ineffective) network

4.   **Missing Networks in Coastal Transport and Inland Waterways in Europe**
    Missing networks manifest themselves in various modes and in various
configurations for both inland waterways and coastel transport:

(i)   **Inland waterways**

    Using the Pentagon model, a cross-national comparative analysis (see
Giaoutzi, 1990) shows the following results.
At the **hard ware** level, the following barriers appear:
    (a)   a lack of standardization and network integration (e.g., lack of standar-
            dized vessels in transit areas).
    (b)   a lack of infrastructure in nodes connected to other transport networks
            (combined transport) (see transshipment and cargo handling).

At the **soft ware** level, problems are mainly related to barriers regarding handling
and storage operations in the ports.

Org ware bottlenecks can be found in:
    (a)   the fact that the different parts of the network are state regulated or
            monopolized with different sets of rules and norms for modes of trans-
            port, type of cargo, type of investment etc.
    (b)   the lack of an intermodal uniform approach at the European level giving
            responsibilities for organizational issues to individuals (shipper-forwar-
            der-receiver) rather than to governments.
    (c)   the split of the network between East and West.
    (d)   the fact that waterways have been used as defence networks in almost
            very country which implies that bridges, dams, etc. have been adjusted
            to meet the likely needs of a war situation. As a result, parts of this net-
            work can hardly cope with the increasing demand, while others have a
            far higher capacity than will ever be required.

Fin ware bottlenecks are stemming mainly from the segmented initiatives for
infrastructure development left in the hands of local actors (lack of integration).

The **eco ware** barriers include:
    (a)   the use of sea or river water to clean ship tanks illegally and dumping a
            mixture of water, oil and detergents in the environment, instead of using
            more expensive port facilities.
    (b)   the use of environmentally dangerous paints for ship bodies.
    (c)   numerous cases of wrecked vessels having lost all or part of their
            (dangerous) freight, due to a mixture of bad weather, the use of old and
            unsafe (single-chamber) vessels, badly trained crews taking too high
            risks, and collisions with other ships.

(ii)   **Coastal transport**

Coastal transport consists of a number of overlapping networks in the shipping sector. There is no particular problem at the hard ware and the soft ware level. There are however severe bottlenecks, in particular at the fin ware level stemming from the subsidization of vessels as an unemployment buffer, and indirect support for the metal industry and the shipbuilding (e.g., machinery and equipment) industry.

5.   Suggested Improvements

The reason for presenting the shipping sector as a number of separate networks is that integration in one of the networks implies a certain restructuring in the rest of the transport system. The following structural solutions and policies are needed here.

(i)   **Inland waterways**

As far as **inland waterways** are concerned, solutions should focus on:
- the **org ware** level:
  (a)   Integration: the harmonization of the regulations where geonautical conditions allow for waterway transport.
  (b)   Coordination: this will be reached by making the different parts of the transport network as a whole compatible, including multimodal solutions. Subdue the system to certain international (commercial) treaties for shipowners, cargo and liabilities, with chapters (partial treaties) on bulk cargo, liquid, container, chemical dangerous transport etc.
  (c)   Harmonization of labour regulations. This should also be reflected in a standard list of types of cargo to be transported, types of vessels, and standard rules of transport accepted by all parties involved (e.g., air draught, waiting time, width of vessels, speed, oil pollution control systems etc.). There have already been certain steps by the European Community towards better organization and development of waterways infrastructure. Standardization, harmonization and unification issues will be dealt with at the economic, legal, organizational and techni-cal/technological level. Org ware aspects though should enjoy high priority in order to avoid severe problems in other aspects of the network development.

- the **fin ware** level:
  (a)   Certain resources required for co-ordination and organization should be found via well regulated taxation systems. Available funds from the European Community should also be utilized.

- the **soft ware** level:
    (a) Pilot projects for integrated solutions should also be pursued via the European Community funding.

- the **eco ware** level:
    (a) Certain rules similar to the MARPOL (the international treaty to prevent marine pollution) should also apply to environmentally dangerous transport behaviour in the inland waterway network and to harmonization of regulations for environmental protection among the various parties involved in the network. They should also include a ban on unsafe ships.

(ii) **Coastal transport**

Coastal transport as such is going to profit even more from the improvement of the inland waterway system. Some problems will appear as a result of the improvements in Mediterranean transport (1000-3000 grwt) which mainly (80 %) serves the Mediterranean basin. One likely impact for coastal transport will be a slight increase in the average tonnage.

To improve **combined transport** the following measures are needed:
- at the **hard ware** level:
    (a) improvement of the hard ware equipment on board the vessels
    (b) development of new technologies for the transportation of semi-processed products.

- concerning **org ware:**
    (a) improvement of the status of competition between land and sea transport
    (b) integration of transport processes and more particularly of short distance transport, cabotage and land transport
    (c) less restrictions on cabotage
    (d) less transit constraints
    (e) improvement of the port efficiency especially concerning infrastructure and management issues
    (f) development of European standards for the above.

- concerning **soft ware:**
    (a) informatization of maritime procedures
    (b) improvement of statistics in the sector.

- at the **eco ware** level:
    (a) European standards and legal instruments to efficiently prosecute coastal polluters.

Technical standardization of **hard ware** and **soft ware** is needed in most sectors (given the need to achieve a long term transport policy performance by

190

increasing transport capacity, speed, reliability and safety, and by reducing transport costs) and effective **environmental** policy strategies (less accidents, more efficient transport etc).

The debate concerning changing cargo and vehicle standards should incorporate the efficiency and costs of transport, the costs of new investments and sunk costs, and the potentials for combined transportation (see Figure 5). This means that standard dimensions for cargo should serve the transportation needs of all modes. The Eureka-context might be considered as a useful scheme to implement these ideas.

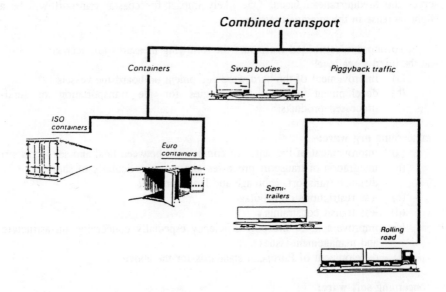

Figure 5:   Integrated standardized intermodal transport
Source :   De Leijer & Tanja (1989)

6. Policy Conclusions

Existing natural barriers seem to impede the development of a European unitarian vision of the latter mode (inland waterways), while issues of strong competition between harbours within the European region have failed to develop the idea that they are part of a European network. In view of the above problems, the European Community should be engaged in an effort to develop the inland waterways network.

Investment in inland waterways (including sluices) and coastal transport systems is necessary to establish a European waterway network for mass transportation as well as for the growing container transport. The proposed and more or less environmentally-induced shift from road to rail transportation is likely to highlight strong capacity constraints in the railway network. Although water transportation has a lower environmental impact than road transportation, building new waterways however, has also a strong negative impact on the environment. An extension of the waterways network and a restructuring of existing facilities should however be considered as a useful option.

In the context of our analysis we have dealt with two different types of networks: inland waterways and coastal transport.

From the large number of bottlenecks in this field we may mention - inter alia - lack of standardization and network integration (e.g., lack of standardized vessels in transit areas); lack of harmonization of regulations (cabotage) - also because national regulation is used to support national firms -; lack of investment and planning of new networks or upgrading existing ones; lack of investments in fleet modernization (also because of environmental reasons); lack of compatibility between barges, cargo specifications, train terminals and port facilities (necessary for multi-modal transport).

And if new infrastructure is eventually being built - as is currently the case with the Rhine-Main-Danube Canal - both planning and investment periods are very long.

To solve missing networks, policy makers should especially concentrate on (transnational) plans for main transport axes connecting at least Europe's major industrial areas with each other. Firms in each industrial area should be able to choose between road, rail and water as means of transport. Integration and harmonization of national policies and regulation (cabotage, labour, etc.), and standardization of hard ware and soft ware should also be favoured. Informatization is also called for to ensure Just-In-Time transportation. Thus competitiveness and connectivity are necessary ingredients of a contestable market for waterway transport.

REFERENCES

Amber, J., D.J.B. Shaw and L. Symons (eds.), **Soviet and East European Transport Problems**, Croom Helm, London, 1985.

192

ERT, **Missing Links**, Brussels, 1988.

ERT, **Missing Networks: A European Challenge**, Brussels, 1991.

Giaoutzi, M., **Missing Networks in Europe: Shipping**, Dept of Geography, National Technical University, Athens, 1990.

Group Transport 2000 Plus, **Transport in a Fast Changing Europe**, DG VII, European Commission, Brussels, 1991.

Leijer, H.F.W.J. de and P.T. Tanja, Gecombineerd Vervoer in Technologisch en Organisatorisch Perspectief: Potenties, Knelpunten en Oplossingsrichtingen, Notitie Sectorstudie Transport en Logistiek, WRR-project Technologie, Overheid en Samenleving, INTRO-TNO, 89/LOG/476, Delft, December, 1989 (mimeo).

NECTAR, **Missing Networks in Europe**, ERT Report, Brussels, 1990.

Nijkamp, P., S. Reichman and M. Wegener (eds.), **Euromobile**, Avebury, Aldershot, UK, 1991.

Seidel, H.P., **Das Technische Konzept des Main-Donau-Kanals**, Rhein-Main-Donau AG, Sonderdruck aus Thyssen Technische Berichte, Heft 2/88 - Verkehrstechnik -, Thyssen AG, Corp. Advertising Dept., Düsseldorf, 1988.

Simons, J.G.W., De Europese Vervoersintegratie: Nieuwste Ontwikkeling Eind 1989, Free University, Amsterdam, January 1990.

Simons, J.G.W. and H.P. Wansink, Freight Transport and Planning, Report Chamber of Commerce, Rotterdam, May 1990.

Winkelmans, W., Maintenance and Renewal of Infrastructures: Inland Waterways, **Resources for Tomorrow's Transport** (Proceedings 11th International Symposium on Theory and Practice in Transport Economics), ECMT, Brussels, September 1988, pp. 129-157.

CHAPTER 13

EUROPEAN AIRLINE NETWORKS IN THE NINETIES

Jaap de Wit

1. Introduction

Compared to surface transport modes the most striking characteristics of air transport are its network flexibility and adaptability. The simple fact, that links in an airline network do not exist physically but only operationally, implies that not infrastructure costs but other factors like aircraft technology and market regulation are the decisive factors in airline network shaping. For example, the deregulation of the US domestic market resulted in drastic network changes and a complete restructuring of the US airline industry.

In the meantime air transport in the EC is also moving towards a more and more deregulated internal market. In such a less regulatory environment European airlines will restructure their networks as well. There are however important differences between the US and European situation, which will certainly lead to a another response in the European airline networks.

2. Network Structure in the US

Before the enactment of the Airline Deregulation Act (ADA) in 1978 US domestic airlines mainly operated in linear networks, hedge hopping on routes between the more densely populated east and west coasts, and on north-south routes in the west and east coast regions.

This network configuration partly resulted from the federal regulation of airmail service. Since the twenties the Postmaster General of the US Post Office established a nation wide route network for airmail services, paralleling the existing transcontinental railroads. Bad weather conditions as well as frequent mechanical trouble made such a backup system on the ground indispensable in those days.

The succeeding regulatory agency for airline services, the Civil Aeronautics Board (CAB), applied the same regulatory principle the Postmaster General already used, i.e. restricting competition on the same routes. Well known regulatory doctrines like "fighting the danger of unfair and destructive competition", were the CAB's basic motives. At the same time this policy, realized through the CAB's route awards, protected the "natural" service areas of different types of carriers, segregating the long haul trunk carriers from the short haul local carriers (Pickrell, 1991).

The ADA ended the grandfathered route authority of the happy few airlines. From now on every applicant, "fit, willing and able" was granted authority to serve any route requested.

By allowing market forces to play a more important role in the air transport system a fundamental restructuring of the US domestic airline networks started. Although there were already symptoms of rudimentary hub-and-spoke networks in the pre-deregulation stage (Allegheny at Pittsburgh and Delta as well as Eastern at Atlanta), the route award policy of the CAB had prevented the development of complete hub-and-spoke systems until then. After deregulation the airlines started to restructure and expand their networks around the original major route junction points, developing these points into on-line connecting hubs. The major carriers also integrated the smaller routes of the regional airlines in their hub-and-spoke networks by making joint marketing agreements. These agreements usually imply code sharing, to suggest on-line transfers at the hub. Display priority of competing flights in Computer Reservation Systems (CRSs) can be manipulated in this way to influence consumer's choice.

As a consequence of these network changes different types of hub airports have developed in the last decade (Doganis and Dennis, 1989):
- hourglass hubs, like Chicago, St.Louis and Dallas, through which strongly directional, mostly transcontinental flights are funnelled;
- hinterland hubs, like Dayton and Charlotte, both developed by Piedmont, providing on-line connections between short distance routes to secondary cities and long distance routes to primary cities;
- a number of international gateways at the east and west coast, like New York JFK, Los Angeles and Miami, kept the same function after deregulation: primarily providing international services. On-line connections between these gateways and domestic points beyond are limited, because fifth freedom rights are not available to foreign carriers in the US domestic market. These gateways, used by foreign as well as domestic carriers, are not dominated by a single carrier.

In the post-deregulation period the domestic continent-wide network of each US major carrier ultimately consolidated around more than one hub. Each of these multi-hub systems contains one or more primary hubs as well as a number of secondary ones (Table 1).

3.   Economies of Hub-and-Spoke Networks
The rapid and drastic network restructuring has been influenced by different and unexpected factors (Kahn, 1988b). Because in the traditional opinion (White, 1979) economies of scale are limited in the airline industry, there were no reasons at the cost side to expect strong network expansions and industry consolidation after deregulation.

Nevertheless, at the marketing side several interacting drives to network expansion appeared to be active in hub-and-spoke systems. First of all, this type of network creates important economies of scope. The non-linear relation between the number of spokes, n, and the number of city pair markets served in a hub-and-spoke system, $n(n-1)/2$ (Doganis, 1991) provides a fast growing market coverage. A hub-and-spoke system offers more products, i.e. transport services in more city pair markets, than a linear network with the same fleet and frequencies. The larger the hub-and-spoke system the more striking the difference in connectivity and market coverage.

airport	airport size in 1000 seats per per week	dominant carrier's market share % of total seats supplied				
		AA	UA	DL	US	NW
Chicago	2180	40	44			
Dallas	1806	61		31		
Atlanta	1008			58		
San Francisco	1088		39			
Denver	911		44			
Detroit	745					71
Minneapolis	686					80
Pittsburgh	652				84	
Philadelphia	644				45	
Charlotte	617				93	
Salt Lake City	438			81		
Cincinnati	421			83		
Baltimore	412				67	
Washington	387		61			
Raleigh Durham	384	73				
Memphis	333					67
Nashville	319	63				

* Airports supplying less than 300.000 seats in a week have been ignored.

Table 1: Multi-hub systems of US megacarriers in 1990 *
Source : a summer week of the **ABC guide 1990**

By routing passengers for different city pairs via an intermediate hub and combining these transfer passengers with the passengers originating from and terminating at the hub itself the volume of travel can be increased significantly. The economies of higher route density are evident. Larger aircraft can be operated with lower operating costs per seatkilometre while maintaining the same frequency level.

The other way round, frequencies can be intensified by maintaining the same aircraft size. In that way hub-and-spoke networks include important marketing economies. The fact is that an airline with a higher than average frequency share in a city pair market usually obtains a greater than proportional market share, following the well known S-shaped relationship between these two variables (Renard, 1970) [1].

The development of new marketing tools like frequent-flyer programmes (FFPs) and computer reservation systems (CRSs) have further extended the marketing economies of hub-and-spoke systems. The larger the network, the faster frequent-flyer bonuses can be accumulated. Moreover, the larger the network, the more destinations are available and the more attractive these bonuses are to the traveller. The growth of FFPs underlines the importance of this marketing tool to create brand loyalty. An additional advantage of FFPs are the priceless databases on more than 27 million consumers these programmes now yield (Table 2)

	1981	1985	1990
cumulative miles earned (bil.)	86	430	855
cumulative unused miles (bil.)	62	310	650
individual members (mil.)	1.8	7.4	27.1
total memberships (mil.)	2.0	16.6	81.0
programmes per member	1.1	2.6	4.6

Table 2: US growth of frequent flyer programmes
Source : Airline Business, Oct. 1991.

Also the development of advanced CRSs in interaction with network size led to new marketing economies, which were only recently limited by a more diversified ownership of CRSs. Until then travel agents assigned a greater reliability of booking information to the system owning airline. This system bias is called the "halo effect" (SRI, 1990), rendering extra CRS-bookings to the system owning airline. Another bias in CRSs is the screen display bias [2]. The larger the airline network the more possibilities are available to influence the screen display order. The already mentioned code sharing agreements between megacarriers and regionals for example result in a higher screen priority than interline connections.

When hub-and-spoke networks develop into multi-hub systems these network economies are supplemented by additional economies. First, average handling costs at spoke stations can be reduced by serving alternately different hubs in a network. Furthermore the US Congressional Budget Office (1988) indicates important improvements in the utilization of aircraft and crew, when a single hub network develops into a multi-hub system.

4.   Industry Structure

The fundamental changes in the industry structure more or less reflect the consolidation of the networks. In the second half of the eighties the number of major carriers reduced to a few megacarriers. In the meantime this concentration process is still continuing, as the bankruptcy of PanAm as well as the actual number of chapter

11 carriers underline. Probably within a short time five megacarriers will dominate more than 90% of US domestic market.

The reduction in the number of major carriers has been further stimulated by the following conditions:

- CRS-owning airlines have been able to use real time information on booking patterns in specific city pair markets to refine yield management programmes and fare policies. By selectively offering discount fares for a limited number of seats the competition of new low cost carriers was countered. Most of these new entrants therefore did not survive.
- Repeatedly substantial mergers and take-overs have been used to acquire network size, especially in the second half of the eighties.

The merger control policy, at that time in the hands of the Department of Transport (DoT), was rather permissive: never a merger request was denied in that period. To explain this permissive DoT policy references have been made (Shepherd, 1988) to the contestability theory of (Baumol, 1982)[3]. Anyway, in its evaluation of the airline deregulation the US Department of Transport DoT (1990) definitely rejects the contestability of domestic airline market.

5. International Network Expansion from the US

Together with the deregulation of the domestic market the US international aviation policy remarkably changed. In the period of 1977-1980 the US started to renegotiate a series of bilateral air service agreements to liberalize international air traffic as well. The trendsetter for the new US bilaterals was the 1978 US-Netherlands agreement (Doganis,1991). From now on in the new bilaterals between the US and European states[4] items emerged like more flexible route access (multiple designation of carriers), reduced government intervention in scheduled tariffs (double disapproval), less or no capacity and frequency restrictions, full traffic rights for points beyond in Europe (old fifth freedom rights supplemented by new break-of-gauge rights).

In the period of 1978-1985 the US realized a certain degree of deregulation on international routes to and from the US, especially in the North Atlantic and Pacific markets.

In the second half of the eighties the US domestic megacarriers started to operate international services to Europe. Contrary to the traditional US flag carriers' international routes from the east- and west coast gateways, the European services of the new megacarriers are mainly operated from their own hubs. This new network expansion of the megas introduced a new dimension to the economies of scope. The substantial domestic feed is now also utilized to develop international services. CRS system bias is now also felt by foreign carriers. For example, display priority was manipulated by using a single flight number for an international flight including change of aircraft at the domestic hub.

The economies of their hub-and-spoke networks provide the new megas with a competitive advantage over the traditional US flag carriers, which are missing sufficient domestic feeder networks. This resulted in the recent bankruptcy of PanAm after the take-over of its main North Atlantic routes to London Heathrow by

American and United, and its routes to Frankfurt by Delta.

Also the network advantages of the US megas over European airlines on the North Atlantic routes are evident. The European carriers do not have direct access to the domestic routes in the US. Not even the 1992 "open skies" agreement between the USA and the Netherlands opens the oppertunity to a Dutch carrier to compete on US domestic routes. Their European feeder networks are rather limited. On the contrary, the US megas can easily penetrate the European market. Fifth freedom rights and break of gauge rights even gives the US megas the opportunity to develop their own European hub-and-spoke systems. These new competitive factors will certainly influence the structure of the European airline networks.

The growth of the US megas' international share in total revenue passenger-kilometres (RPKs) (Table 3) is accelerating. Partly this is a substitution of the US flag carriers' market share to the megas and partly an extension of international operations. Anyhow, more and more international services are transformed into spokes within the US multi-hub systems.

	total RPKs in 1990 (millions)	international share (%) 1988	1990
American	123.924	14	19
United	122.219	18	29
Delta	94.919	10	14
Northwest	83.999	41	n.a.
Continental	63.042	22	26
USair	57.211	4	3
TWA	55.596	39	42
PanAm	49.985	78	76

Table 3:   The international share of US megas operations
Sources: IATA-WATS '91, DoT (1990)

To penetrate the European market two different network strategies can be recognized:
- Summer 1992 schedules show 13 direct daily American Airlines-services from Chicago to European destinations, operated by smaller long range B767 twin-jets. This means that American is simply extending the number of spokes from its domestic hubs in the US.
- On the contrary United operates nine daily European services from London Heathrow in 1992 by short/medium haul B727 aircraft as well as six B747 flights to US gateways. In other words, United is developing a new offshore hub outside the US, utilizing break of gauge rights from Heathrow.
- Delta is more or less following both strategies: in 1992 12 European destinations

have direct daily services by 767's to the Atlanta-hub of Delta. Delta is also developing Frankfurt as its off shore hub in Europe, daily connecting nine US destinations with eight European destinations, utilizing break of gauge rights.

The viability of these different network strategies still have to be proved. At first sight the intercontinental flights of American with a single on-line transfer seem to be more promising than the United flights with a double on-line transfer at both sides of the ocean. This double-hub concept at least requires high quality standards of the hub-airports involved to be competitive.

The competition between US megas and European majors however is not only determined by the economies of network size and structure. Network characteristics are also involved in other important competitive factors like labour productivity and yield. Labour productivity differences between airlines require wage levels to be included, because especially in Europe airline wages are primarily based on widely varying national standards. For example, the average wage level of BA in 1990 was $37,953, while Swissair paid $62,668. Therefore available tonkm's (ATKs) are not expressed per employee but per 1$ labour input costs.

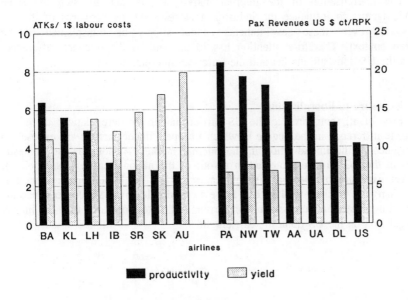

Figure 1: Productivity and yield
Source : ICAO and IATA Statistics 1990

As far as data are available, an inverse relationship between yield and productivity can be discerned (Figure 1). This partly reflects an important network characteristic, viz. average stage length. Ceteris paribus the greater the stage length, the higher labour productivity and the lower the yield. This corresponds with the geographical products of European carriers (Table 4). Of course productivity and yield also strongly depend on the regulatory regime and the resulting competition. This explains the fundamental differences in yield and productivity levels between European and US carriers.

In summary, for the first time European major carriers are confronted with the competitive power of US megas. This power has been built up in a deregulated domestic market by exploiting the economies of network structure and at the same time improving labour productivity and reducing fare levels.

To cope with these developments European carriers will have to develop network strategies in Europe, which generate similar economies as the US carriers did. At the same time price competition in a liberalized market will certainly lead to a downward pressure on fares. This development especially makes high yield/low productivity carriers in Europe vulnerable.

6.   European Network Developments: the Differences

The liberalisation of the internal market admits step by step the same economic factors to influence the industry, that reshaped the networks of the US carriers. However, these developments cannot simply be transplanted to the European context. Therefore attention has to be paid to the relevant differences between the US domestic market and the European internal market.

6.1   Exposure to liberalisation

First of all, compared to the US carriers under the deregulation, there is a remarkable difference in the degree to which Europe's major carriers are exposed to the influence of the liberalisation in the internal market. As long as the domestic markets in the EC will be protected in favour of the national carriers (see below), the direct exposure of the majority of major carriers in the European market is smaller than 25% of their total RPKs (Table 4, third column). As a consequence the liberalisation impact on European major carriers will take more time than the impact of deregulation on the US domestic carriers did.

	total RPKs in 1990 (millions)	domestic share (%)	European share (%)	total European (%)
BA	66.795	6	15	21
AF*	51.693	35	12	47
LH	41.903	7	19	26
KL	26.390	-	10	10
IB	22.112	22	30	52
AZ	19.126	10	25	35
SK	16.516	20	35	55
OA	7.764	15	35	50
SN	7.572	-	22	22
TP	6.836	11	36	47
EI	4.191	2	41	43

* AF also includes UTA and Air Inter

Table 4: The geographical products of some EC carriers in 1990
Source : AEA Yearbook 1991

6.2 Merger barriers and regulatory restrictions

Although the internal market is a fact now, it is not for air transport. Although restrictions on market access, tariffs and capacity control are eliminated, route access is not, as far as domestic routes are involved. The full implementation of cabotage will take a few years more. The first step now is the so-called "consecutive" cabotage, in 1997 to be followed by "stand alone" cabotage. This means that carriers serving large home markets, like the French and Spanish (see Table 4) have the advantage of reduced competition inside these markets[5]. These restrictions will further postpone network adaptation in the internal market.

Also consolidation in the EC will meet some barriers as far as transnational mergers are involved. The KLM-BA merger negotiations demonstrated the problem of nationally obtained traffic rights. As long as the external competence of the EC in bilateral negotiations with third countries has not been developed, the national traffic rights of both states in third countries outside the EC are not a simple addition sum for a new transnational airline. Third countries outside the EC will undoubtedly start to question their bilateral agreements with both states. This problem is even more complex in the possible merger of KLM and the European Quality Alliance, since non EC carriers are now involved as well.

Another issue in transnational mergers is the public ownership of most national airlines in Europe. In the US all carriers were privately owned, when deregulation started. These carriers did not have the backing of financial state aid in case of financial weakness. Bankcruptcies and take-overs of weak carriers actually were an important factor in the US consolidation, but these factors are not obvious in the European airline industry. Privatisation in Europe will take more time (Table

5). In the meantime state aid becomes an item more carefully supervised by the EC Commission.

privatised		minority stake	
BA	100%	KLM	38%
Icelandair	100%	Swiss Air	20%
majority stake		publicly owned	
Lufthansa	59%	Air France Group	99%
Sabena	64%	Aer Lingus	100%
SAS group	50%	Iberia	100%
Alitalia	85%	Olympic Airways	100%
Austrian	52%	TAP	100%

Table 5: Government stakes in European Airlines.
Source : Airline Business, Febr. 1992.

Since the end of 1990 the Commission is also qualified to test the admissibility of airline mergers with a "Community-dimension"[6]. If this new merger control policy develops in a less permissive direction compared to the antitrust policy of DoT in the eighties, an extra barrier for further concentration in Europe can arise. The Scylla for this merger control policy certainly will be the intensifying competition of the US megas in Europe, which needs the respons of a more consolidated industry, whereas the Charybdis becomes the decreasing competition in the city pair markets of merging European airlines.

Also modern marketing tools like CRSs and FFPs will have a much more restricted influence on industry consolidation. The carrier-specific CRSs of the US megas were powerful tools in the marketing of their new networks, but recently a more diversified ownership of these systems has been accepted. These CRSs with diversified ownership were introduced in Europe, i.e. Galileo and Amadeus. Consequently, from the beginning the "halo" effect has been absent in the European market. Moreover, screen display bias is further restricted in the European systems by the ECAC- and EC-codes of conduct on CRS which are going further than US-rules. In the end the impact of CRSs on network developments and industry consolidation in Europe will be significantly smaller.

FFPs of European carriers are still in their infancy, but will become an important factor in a liberalized internal market. The impact of this marketing tool is already experienced by the European carriers on the North Atlantic routes, where US megas heavily depend on their mileage programmes to create brand loyalty. In 1991 BA was the first European carrier to introduce an FFP, followed by KLM. Lufthansa and Swissair were the next.

All in all, as far as the impact of European liberalisation is involved, several developments indicate that the consolidation of the European airline industry will take much more time than the US industry demonstrated after deregulation. However, this conclusion is not to be mistaken. The competition of the US megas in the European market may accelerate this process unexpectedly.

6.3 Different networks at the start

Before discussing European network developments themselves, it has to be underlined that the network configurations of the US carriers were fundamentally different from those of the European airlines, when deregulation started. US major carriers already operated continent-wide linear route systems with rudimentary route junction points. These systems were transformed into mutually-competitive multi-hub systems.

Airline networks in Europe however have other characteristics mainly determined by the aeropolitical bilateralism in the past. Each national carrier operates a radial network from one central home base, the national airport. For lack of a significant national home market some smaller airlines developed a sixth freedom gateway on their home base, which provides optimal on-line connections between intercontinental and European flights and vice versa. Examples are KLM at Amsterdam, Swissair at Zurich and SAS at Copenhagen.

Although the resemblance of these radial networks to hub-and-spoke systems seems striking at first sight, as matter of fact it is not at all. Hubbing inside the internal market does not exist on European airports (De Wit and Veldhuis, 1991). A few airlines however intend to develop so-called Euro-hubs, like KLM on Schiphol and Sabena in cooperation with Air France on Brussels. Euro-hubs can be understood as hinterland hubs focusing on new regional connections. Daily operations on these regional destinations can only be justified by generating enough route density via the on-line connectivity at the hub. Connections between the Euro-hub and the main European airports already exist of course, but these connections will be transformed into spoke connections as well.

It can be concluded that at the beginning of the regulatory reform in Europe the national airline networks are radial, each dominating a limited territory. On the contrary at the beginning of the deregulation in the US, networks of the major carriers were linear and continent-wide, each competing with the other networks. This different starting position in an open internal market will deliver other network developments.

7. The Scope for Euro-hubs

Euro-hubbing will be one of first European network changes emerging in a liberalized environment. The scope for this type of hubbing however is limited, looking at the market conditions and the operational consequences.

Operationally the introduction of a hub means that the airport is transformed into a "traffic pump", accommodating alternating waves of incoming and outgoing flights. This process can only be implemented on airports with substantial excess capacity. Airport capacity in Europe however will become a major problem in the nineties (SRI International, 1990), limiting the number of available airports for these operations. Hubbing also requires accurate scheduling to guarantee minimum connecting times. In 1990 20% of European flights were delayed more than 15 minutes (AEA,1991), airport and air traffic control being important restraints. Therefore a Euro-hub will be a rather vulnerable system as long as these restraints are not removed (ECAC, 1990).

If an airline combines a Euro-hub with an intercontinental gateway function on its homebase, the reliability of the gateway function can be affected as well. Euro-hubbing requires European aircraft to overnight at the spoke stations in stead of overnighting at the homebase as usual for gateway operations. So departure times of connecting European flights for intercontinental passengers arriving early in the morning at the hub, can be influenced by delays incurred during the early morning flights from the spoke stations to the Euro-hub.

Beside these operational restraints also market characteristics are important for the scope of Euro-hubs. The European **market area** is less than half the US market area. European population is highly concentrated inside the well-known "banana" area, running from London to Milano. Contrary to this European situation the population density in the US is low in the centre and high in the coastal regions due to their major sities. This divergent spatial distributions of economic activities explains the difference in average stage length between European flights -768 km in 1990 (AEA,1991)- and US domestic flights -1038 km in 1990 (IATA, 1991)-. This means that transfer time at a Euro-hub is relatively longer than in the US in relation to total trip time. Also extra travel time caused by the diversion of indirect flights via a hub will be relatively more important. Therefore in Europe the compensation of higher frequencies through hub-and-spoke systems will be less effective, while the competition of direct flights will be more effective. These market conditions strongly limit the possibilities for Euro-hubbing.

Market size, being a vital condition for successful hubbing, is also restricted by other factors in Europe. Some 60% of the total passenger-kilometres performed within the EC were carried on **non-scheduled services** (Button and Swann, 1991). As long as the distinction between these inclusive tours charter operations and scheduled operations in Europe does not fade, this substantial market segment will not play a role in Euro-hubbing. However, in 1993 non-scheduled carriers are allowed to start charter operations in other EC-countries. This will be the first and probably the only opportunity to develop an hourglass hub in the centre of Europe to funnel substantial directional flows between the north and south of Europe[7].

A second factor restricting market size, is the **competition of ground transport modes** in Europe. This can be explained, partly by relatively small average route length of European flights, implying a modal split in favour of ground transport (ITA, 1991)[8], and partly by well developed road and rail systems in Europe.

This intermodal competition will be intensified by the expansion of high speed rail links in Europe. Because of the high infrastructure investment costs involved, these new rail links require substantial passenger flows. Therefore, only trunk routes of airlines can be affected severely, especially in the range of 250 to 1000 km as the crow flies. In this range air and rail will compete on high density routes because of the expected consumers' trade-off between travel costs and travel time (ITA, 1991). Below the 250 km range the train dominates the market as the faster and cheaper mode. Above the 1000 km the airplane will do, being three times faster on average while cost differences become negligible.

Developing a Euro-hub at an airport, which also provides direct access to the high speed rail network, requires the transformation of this thread into an opportunity by developing a new marketing concept of fully integrated air-rail transport services. Ticketing, fares, sales, reservation systems, promotion, baggage handling etc. are all involved in the complete integration of high speed rail spokes and air spokes in a multimodal Euro-hub system. The Lufthansa Airport Express is a first indication of these new intermodal integration.

8. The Scope for European Multi-hub Systems

In a liberalizing environment economies of network size will further stimulate the consolidation of the European airline industry. Already now consolidation on the national level has been completed. Nearly all independent airlines have been swallowed up by the national carriers. In the meantime strategic alliances between national carriers, whether or not supported by equity swaps, are made to deliver more network synergy in Europe. The next stage in this consolidation process gets a transnational dimension. Some national carriers will disappear, merge or become subsidiaries, reducing the number of independent major carriers in Europe to a handful of airlines.

This industry consolidation has different consequences for European networks than it had for US networks. The US consolidation mainly contributed to the development of continent-wide networks. In Europe industry consolidation mainly will contribute to the intra-regional concentration of neighbouring home markets. The resulting few multi-hub systems therefore are intra-regional too, each covering a part of the internal market. The anti-competitive dangers of this network structure are obvious.

In summary, beside the classic sixth freedom transfers a few European airlines will develop a new style of hubbing. Also ground transport facilities, especially high speed rail links, will be utilized as additional spokes and as supporting connections between hubs belonging to an intra-regional multi-hub system. The first example appears at the horizon. The Air France Group plus Sabena controls the airports Brussels, Paris CDG, Paris Orly and Lyon, each of them already now or in the near future interconnected by a high speed rail link. Also Lufthansa is developing a multi-hub system in the German market (Frankfurt, München, Dusseldorf, Köln/Bonn and Berlin) supported by rail connections of the Lufthansa Airport Express.

Looking at these network developments, the aims of EC-liberalisation - lower fares and more choices to the customer through more competition- can seriously be questioned.

Notes

1.   As long as bilateral air service agreements in international air transport contain conditions tomaintain a capacity balance, frequency competition is not involved. After the new liberal air service agreement between the Netherlands and the UK in 1984 was made, frequency competition for the first time emerged in European international services on the London-Amsterdam route. British Midland joined both flag carriers on this route and acquired a substantial market share by providing the same frequency level as the incumbents did, by using smaller aircraft.

2. Screen display bias is stimulated by the fact that 80% of CRS bookings are made from the first screen and 50% from the first three lines (Travel Business Monitor, April 1989).

3. This theory states that pricing behaviour needs not to be determined by the actual number of competitors in a contestable market, i.e. a market for which one can assume the absence of barriers to market entrance and exit. In that case the potential competition of new entrants already disciplines the pricing behaviour of the incumbents. That means, that under these conditions a merged airline cannot exercise more market power than two separate ones.

4. A few European states, notably France and Italy, resisted a too strong tendency towards deregulation.

5. The only way to fully penetrate the home market of another member state in 1993 is to form a new subsidiary having its principle place of business in that state.

6. The most important criterion is that total sales of both merger candidates exceeds 5 billion ECU.

7. Also Dutch touring car companies provide international long-haul services in Europe by using a location near the frontier as a hub between different domestic points and foreign holiday destinations.

8. The well-known S-shaped curve relating travel distance to the market share of the airplane versus other modes, shows a 20-30% airplane share for the average European flight distance. The private car however still keeps a 40-50% market share on this trip distance.

REFERENCES

Association of European Airlines, **Statistical Appendices to Yearbook - May 1991**, Brussels, AEA, 1991.

Baumol, W.J., Contestable markets: an Uprising in the Theory of Industry Structure, **The American Economic Review**, 72, 1982, pp. 1-15.

Button, K., and D. Swann, Aviation Policy in Europe, **Airline Deregulation, International Experiences** (K. Button, ed.), London, 1991, pp. 85-123.

Doganis, R., and N. Dennis, Lessons in Hubbing, **Airline Business**, March 1989, pp. 42-47.

Doganis, R., **Flying off Course**, 2d edition, London, Routledge, 1991.

European Civil Aviation Council, **Air Traffic Control in Europe, ECAC Strategy for the 1990's**, Paris, ECAC, 1990.

Institut du Transport Aérien, **Les Complémentarités Train/Avion en Europe**, Paris, ITA, 1991.

International Air Transport Association, **World Air Transport Statistics 1990**,

Number 35, WATS 6/91, Geneva, IATA, 1991.

Kahn, A.E., Airline Deregulation - a Mixed Bag, but a Clear Success Nevertheless, **Transportation Law Journal**, 16, 1988a, pp. 229-251.

Kahn, A.E., Surprises of Airline Deregulation, **American Economic Association Papers and Proceedings** vol 78, no. 2, May 1988, pp. 316-322.

Pavaux, J., The Lessons of US Airline Deregulation, **ITA magazine 54**, March/April 1989, pp. 3-11.

Pickrell, D., The Regulation and Deregulation of US Airlines, **Airline Deregulation; International Experiences** (K. Button, ed.), London, 1991, pp. 5-47.

Renard, G., **Competition in Air Transportation: An Econometric Approach**, Cambridge Mass, MIT, Thesis, 1970.

Shepherd, W.G., Competition, Contestability and Transport Mergers, **International Journal of Transport Economics**, vol XV, no. 2, June, 1988, pp. 113-128.

Stanford Research Institute (SRI), **Global Distribution Systems: Emerging Trends and Strategic Issues**, Croydon, SRI, 1989.

SRI International, **A European Planning Strategy for Air Traffic to the Year 2010**, a Study Prepared for IATA, Menlo park, SRI, 1990.

US Congressional Budget Office, **Policies for the Deregulated Airline Industry**, Washington DC, 1988.

US Department of Transport, **Secretary's Task Force on Competition in the U.S. Domestic Airline Industry, 10 volumes**, Washington DC, 1990.

White, L.J., Economics of Scale and the Question of "Natural Monopoly", **Journal of Air Law and Commerce**, vol 44, 1979, pp. 545-573.

Wit, J.G. de, and J.G. Veldhuis, Airport Connectivity in the U.S.A. and the E.C., **Colloquium Vervoersplanologisch Speurwerk** (P.T. Tanja, ed.), Delft, 1991, pp. 1321-1340.

CHAPTER 14

BORDERS AND BARRIERS IN

TELECOMMUNICATION SYSTEMS

Roberta Capello and Peter Nijkamp

1. **A Sector in Transition: High Potentialities with Low Adoption Rates**
    Our society is gradually but undoubtedly exhibiting the signs of a transition towards a network economy. The rapid rise of the service sector - not only for domestic but also for international activities - mirrors the fact that the western world is increasingly marked by a wide variety of communication and interaction patterns ranging from a local towards a global scale. This tendency is even reinforced by the emergence of the information sector, also denoted as the new information technology (NIT) sector or the information and communication technology (ICT) sector (Freeman et al., 1982; Giaoutzi and Nijkamp, 1988). The NIT (or ICT) sector has shaped the conditions for the current knowledge-based economies.
    The pioneering study of Machlup (1962), followed by Porat (1977), began to stress already the significance of a "knowledge based" economy in those years when Bell (1973) was signalling the emergence of service-dominated economies in our post-industrial society. From these early works, à series of theoretical and empirical analyses have emerged, strengthening the idea of a new development trajectory of an economy governed by different rules and actors and dependent upon different (information-oriented) strategic resources. Jonscher (1983), for example, sought to explain the emergence of the "Information Economy" through categorising economic activities into two classes, viz. "production tasks" (tasks associated with the manufacturing and delivery of products and services), and "information tasks" (tasks associated with the coordination and manipulation of production tasks). The major source of added-value appears to shift clearly from the production task to the information task.
    All these studies witness the emergence of an information economy, characterised by a growth and intensification of those activity indicators (such as investment and employment) associated with the collection, manipulation, storage and communication of information. Knowledge based and information-based activities are becoming important strategic resources upon which the competitiveness of firms and comparative advantages for regions increasingly depend (Gillespie et al., 1987). Thus, the economy is going through a period of transformation, signalled by the move from "capital-intensive" production systems to "information-intensive" production systems (Willinger and Zuscovitch, 1988), where information and knowledge are inextricably linked strategic resources for economic development.
    The emergence of the Information Economy is highly dependent upon the

widespread diffusion and adoption of new Information and Communications Technologies (ICTs), born from the interaction of computing and telecommunications, which give rise to new potentialities in the way of storing, manipulating, organising, visualising and transmitting information. Given this perspective, the telecommunications sector and its future development become critical for the understanding of future economic positions of countries and regions, and thereby of the competitiveness of national, regional and urban territorial and industrial systems in the 1990s. Thus, at first glance the ICT sector seems to be a promising sector with a high growth potential.

Paradoxically, empirical analyses on the adoption process of these technologies in the economy demonstrate a relatively low penetration rate. While there has been significant growth in the level of expenditure on ICTs, there remain open questions on the extent to which these technologies are being used and exploited. In other words, there remain uncertainties on the extent to which the new techno-economic paradigm can be said to have been secured.

The relatively limited diffusion of computer networks is demonstrated by both official statistical data and primary data. In the U.K., for example, OFTEL (Office of Telecommunications) publications indicate a rather limited use of private circuits, central to computer networks, achieving only 10% of British Telecom revenues in 1988. Furthermore, 90% of private circuits are analogue and these circuits represent 75% of private circuits revenues, 25% is derived from digital circuits. Moreover, 75% of all private circuits are within the same exchange area while the City of London is the main geographic market.

The relatively limited diffusion of computer networks is also demonstrated by a recent survey of organisations[1]. Whilst 40% of respondents used a computer network, and over 65% of these organisations had installed their computer networks since 1985, the broad diffusion of computer networks into the functional structure of organisations has remained relatively undeveloped (Table 1) (Capello and Williams, 1991). In effect computer networking has predominantly remained within the account function and the dominant network application has been the maintenance and analyisis of the basic accounts ledgers. This evidence is in line with official statistical data which shows that in 1984 65% of large administrative offices (establishments) supported a computer network (Ducatel, 1989). However, the 1989 survey of organisations has provided evidence of a growing technical infrastructure and increasing number of users. Thus, in 1982 69.4% of organisations had less than 10 users, whereas by 1989 only 23.6% of respondents had 10 users or less. This growth is also reflected in the number of users: only 5.9% of organisations in the survey had more than 100 users in 1982, whereas by 1989 28.1% of organisations had more than 100 users. A similar observation can be made regarding technical infrastructures: while only 13.1% of the organisations had 100% on line transactions in 1982, 28.3% had this possibility by 1989.

This situation which shows a rather limited use of advanced telecommunication networks and services is not only typical of the United Kingdom. In Europe, in general, the level of digital lines installed, representing the main physical infrastructure for the development of advanced services, is still very low (Table 2), although the situation varies considerably from country to country. Italy and Spain show very low levels of digital lines, and face a strong barrier effect on the development of advanced services.

Selected Applications	Finance	Marketing	Production	Purchasing	Distrib.
Data Processing	85%	47%	53%	54%	40%
Relational Data Base	30%	25%	21%	14%	12%
Electronic Mail	22%	16%	16%	9%	9%
Diarying	10%	9%	9%	5%	3%

Table1: Use of computer networked appliances in selected functions
Source: Taylor and Williams., Pict Survey (1989)

	A1	A2	A3	A4
USA	127.2	45.0	82.2	28.07%
Giappone	51.7	9.0	42.7	14.58%
Francia	25.8	15.6	10.2	3.48%
UK	23.4	5.5	17.9	6.11%
Germania Ovest	27.0	1.4	25.6	8.74%
Italia	20.0	2.2	17.8	6.08%
Spagna	10.5	0.7	9.8	3.35%
Svezia	6.1	1.8	4.3	1.47%
Ausralia	7.1	1.3	5.8	1.98%
Argentina	3.2	0.2	3.0	1.02%
Brasile	8.8	0.7	8.1	2.77%
Cecosiovacchia	2.1	0.1	2.0	0.68%
Cina	0.8	0.7	7.3	2.49%
Sudcorea	9.6	1.7	7.9	2.70%
India	3.5	0.3	3.2	1.09%
Indonesia	0.8	0.2	0.6	0.20%
Yugoslavia	3.1	0.2	2.9	0.99%
Malaysia	1.3	0.9	0.4	0.14%
Messico	4.3	0.7	3.6	1.23%
Rdt	1.8	0.2	1.6	0.55%
Taiwan	5.7	0.6	5.1	1.74%
Ungheria	0.8	0.1	0.7	0.24%
Ussr	30.3	0.2	30.1	10.28%
TOTALE	382.1	89.3	292.8	100.0%

Aree Geografiche

	A1	A2	A3	A4	
Europa Occident.	142.9	32.3	110.6	31.94%	
Nord America	140.6	50.3	90.3	26.08%	
America Latina	19.8	2.5	17.3	5.00%	
Africa/Medio Or.	9.5	2.7	6.8	1.96%	A1: Total Lines Installed
Asia/Pacifico	93.7	12.6	81.1	23.42%	A2: Total Digital Lines Installed
Europa Orientale	40.9	0.7	40.2	11.61%	A3: Potential of substitution
Totale	447.4	101.1	346.3	100.0%	A4: Potential of substitution

Table 2: Number of digital lines installed by geographical areas (1988)
Source : Zanfei (1990)

The empirical material provides prima facie evidence of the growing diffusion of ICTs but suggests also a complexity in the adoption of computer networks, both as public utilities and as intrafirm infrastructure. In this second case, difficulties are related to the integration into the activities and processes of organisations.

Thus there appears to be a **paradox** with, on the one hand, a growing awareness and focus upon the implications of a new techno-economic paradigm upon the behaviour and structure of organisations, and on the other hand, a pattern of adoption of new ICTs which suggests there are uncertainties and difficulties in translating these concepts into reality (Capello and Williams, 1992).

The aim of the present paper is to explain this paradox through the analysis of major elements that in diffusion processes of these technologies can turn into **barriers** to the widespread adoption of the new technologies. Moreover, some policy recommendations will be drawn, which may be useful in overcoming such adoption constraints in order to move realistically towards an "Information Economy".

2.   The Nature of Existing Barriers to the Development

Until recently, the telecommunications industry was rather restrictively defined as the area of production and distribution of voice and text communications, through the telephone and telex services (Pasini, 1959). Nowadays, this defintion is far too limited and insufficient to explain the characteristics of this rapidly changing industry. The radical technological innovations of the seventies and eighties have broadened the range of communications services and instruments, their technological transmission capacity and, moreover, have changed the role telecommunications services and infrastructures were playing in the economic system. The pervasive nature of the ICT sector has however also faced many barriers (OECD, 1988a and 1988b).

The nature of such barriers and bottlenecks is strictly linked to the profound changes taking place in the telecommunication sector. The drastic transition processes force actors - regardless whether they are users or suppliers - to adjust their behaviour to the new market rules, a development which has created problems at both the supply and the demand side.

Although technological forces are generally pinpointed as the major causes for modifications in the telecommunications sector, an approach to this transformation process focusing only on indigenous technological aspects would fail to conceptualise and describe properly the new characteristics of the telecommunications sector. At least four factors can be regarded as **prominent causes for the transformation** of the sector (Capello, 1991a):

- **technological dynamics**. Although it is not the unique reason for change, the technological revolution is certainly playing an important role in the development trajectories of the new sector. A host of product innovations takes place, from digitalisation of switching and transmission equipments to a broad range of new services which offer high transportation possibilities of data, voice, text and images;

- **institutional dynamics,** changing the market structure from a monopoly structure to a competitive market, imposing new "game rules", after decades of traditional static oligopoly (in manufacturing firms market) and monopoly regimes (in the service market);
- **market dynamics,** stemming from an increased awareness of users about the strategic importance of these infrastructures, and stimulated through customers' attempt to influence suppliers towards customised products and innovation, thus acting as "technological gatekeepers";
- **new economic relationships** characterising the telecommunications "filière", representing the matrix of economic relationships among manufacturing firms, and between suppliers, the operator and customers. The traditional oligopolistic rules which have historically governed manufacturing firms and their linkages with public operators have been substituted in the last decades by more competitive rules, by low national protective barriers and by greater competitive threats from firms belonging to previously separated sectors.

These profound changes provoke, paradoxically, on the one hand high technological potentialities but, on the other hand, bottlenecks and barriers to the development of high adoption rates. Barriers and bottlenecks arise at both the supply and the demand side.

Barriers in the telecommunications refer to all phenomena (economic, organisational, technological, cultural, political, etc..) that impede a smooth penetration, adoption and development of this ICT sector. This means that barriers can be interpreted as losses in (marginal) benefits accruing from the use or supply of telecommunication. To some extent barriers act as "negative production factors" decreasing the maximum possible productivity of conventional production factors (see Nijkamp and al., 1990). Barriers can be external to a certain information system (e.g., language barriers, physical bottlenecks) or internal (e.g., as a result of user externalities such as congestion). A good example of barriers in a telecommunication network can be found in a study by Klaassen, Wagenaar and Van der Weg (1972), who studied the implications of language barriers between the Flemish and the Walloons in Belgium by means of a spatial interaction model for telephone calls. More recent applications of the identification of barriers in international telecommunication networks can be found in Fischer et al. (1990), Giaoutzi and Stratigea (1990), Rietveld and Janssen (1990) and Rossera (1990).

From a **supply side perspective,** the profound changes mentioned above threaten the capacity of suppliers - both manufacturers and public operators - to deal with the rapid and increasing competition which quickly grows in front of the complex technological, institutional and market dynamics the sector is facing (Section 3).

From a **demand side perspective,** bottlenecks concern inter alia the complex nature of new technologies which require a high degree of interrelation with the organisational structure of firms to be secured. Moreover, the importance these technologies represent for achieving a competitive advantage for users, can turn into a threat imposed to users to adopt these technologies in a shorter time span and for new purposes (Section 4).

An accurate analysis of the bottlenecks to the development of this strategic sector is crucial for suggesting some policy recommendations in order to overcome the barriers to a quick and widespread development of telecommunication technological potentialities (Section 5).

3.   Barriers at the Supply Side

At the supply side, the major structural changes affecting the telecommunication market destroy the traditional economic rules governing the relationships among suppliers, public operators and the market. Increasing competition requires the development of different corporate strategies and different market approaches, that in some cases result to be a barrier for the development of market shares for traditional telecommunication suppliers. Thus manufacturing firms have to deal with two types of strategic issues:

a) an increasing competition, which may be difficult to face for technologically backward countries and regions;
b) a different nature of the market, which raises problems regarding appropriate policies to approach markets.

Both elements will be discussed in subsections 3.1 and 3.2, respectively.

3.1.   Barriers in the development of market shares

It is undoubtedly true that the level of competition has raised considerably in the telecommunications sector in the past decade and this change has had some deep supply implications. The reasons for this phenomenon stem from both **technological** and **institutional** changes, through which barriers to the development of national markets come about.

As far as the institutional side is concerned, major changes have been imposed by the EC through the publication of the Green Paper (1987) and of its further revisions, leading the system towards more liberalised market structures. The characteristics of these institutional changes reflects rather **narrow national trajectories** of the liberalisation process, despite the EC efforts to ensure a uniform process (Table 3). This non-uniformity in institutional behaviour at the European level has some drastic consequences for the national competitiveness of firms and thus for the national supply development. In fact, the existing differences in the national trajectories will become crucial - once liberalisation will be imposed in all countries -, when the specific innovative capacity of each single country is tested. Inevitably firms which have faced competition for a longer period will have more advantages in terms of marketing policies than those used to operate in an oligopolistic market.

Barriers in the development of market shares for firms with less liberalisation experience stem from:
- less consolidated market policies and consumer orientation, stemming from their shorter experience on the market and their weaker direct contacts with customers;

- lack of strategic efficiency-oriented mechanisms for a better harmonisation of telecommunication systems in an international economy;
- less consolidated product innovation policies, stemming from lower technological, scientific and organisational know-how.

The risk for firms still governed by monopoly rules is the loss of market shares, probably leaving the development of the sector in the hands of foreign firms.

The main changes in the manufacturing sector have taken place in the customer premises equipment sub-sector. The main problems in the protection of national markets can be summarised as:

- firstly, a major threat for many European firms is not caused by European competition itself, but by American and Japanese firms legally entering the European market. These firms represent a highly potential threat in terms of more advanced technical products and more ad-hoc marketing policies developed through years of experience in competitive markets (especially for the American case);
- secondly, even at a European level, competition favours countries with a stronger supply structure, created through years of extremely favourable telecommunications public policy. This is, for instance, the case with France, with a historically strong supporting public policy devoted to the creation of "national champions". The other extreme case is represented by Italy, which has always been reluctant to spend resources for developing strong national telecommunications supply, and has favoured other sectors in public policy. A concrete case of possible market losses by technologically backward firms is the British case. In fact, in front of Mercury competition, British Telecom changed its purchasing policies favouring Japanese and American technologically more advanced customer premises equipments, rather than national firms products, thus destroying British manufacturing firms (Charles et al., 1989; Williams and Gillespie, 1988).

Thus, the effects of internationalisation of customer premises equipments are profound, once radical technological differences among products exist. It is clear that barriers to the development of market shares for national firms stem from:
a)   the backward technological know-how;
b)   the backward policies to approach the market.

Even in the liberalised **provision of advanced services**, competition increases between firms belonging to previously separated sectors. While informatics firms are legitimated to offer their technical know-how in the provision of value added services, with a high software component, traditional manufacturing firms face a problem in developing their market shares in these sub areas because of the lack of technological know-how required ("infant industries").

Liberalisation in the domain of **public purchases** destroys the historical division of labour characterising the relationship between telecommunications manufacturing firms and public operators in most European Countries.

Thus, the extremely high R&D expenditures and investments required especially in the switching equipments market will act as entry barriers in this market, and liberalisation of public purchases pushes firms towards product specialisation in order to keep market shares under control and to achieve a "natural" division of labour in the market.

Minor negative effects on market shares provoked by foreigner competition will, on the contrary, affect the development of market shares for the public operators. The EC, in fact, clearly protects monopoly in the most profitable market area for public operators, namely the provision of network-based services.

Moreover, liberalisation of customer premises equipments may turn out to have positive effects on public operators business. By stimulating the use of services through low-pricing terminal equipments, traffic on public networks is consequently positively affected. This has been the case for the Italian videotex service, increasing considerably the number of subscribers after the abolishment of a monopoly on the too expensive terminal equipment.

Liberalisation of advanced services, which should help the development of these services on a broader base, meets obstacles because of the threat of the capacity resale phenomenon by the public operator, at least in the European monopolistic markets. The implementation of private networks through leased circuits can in fact lead to the illegal provision of network-based services on these networks, thus decreasing traffic on public infrastructures and generating economic losses to the legally protected network-based services market of public operators.

The concern about this phenomenon is related to both its highly geographical and quantitative diffusion and to the non-existence of control mechanisms for avoiding it. Although all European countries have witnessed the growing phenomenon of capacity resale on private networks, none of them has provided a legal efficient mechanism to keep the phenomenon under control. The most effective proposal to avoid this problem is concerned with the change of the present tariff structure of private leased circuits, based on leasing contracts. This tariff structure should turn out to be based on the volume of information transported, thus destroying economic advantages on which capacity resale rests. Objections to these changes are presented by business users, arguing that this solution would completely inhibit the use of private circuits, upon which the development of a networked economy is predicated.

3.2. Barriers to approach the market

There exists another source of barriers limiting the development of new telecommunication technologies from the supply side, viz. one related to the changing nature of ICTs markets.

Computer networks are far from being standard technologies and their exploitation for purposes of achieving higher economic performance is highly dependent on their integration into the organisational structure of each adopter (see Section 4). For this reason, these technologies have to be tailored to each adopter's need.

The markets for traditional telecommunication services (such as telephone and telex) are relatively homogeneous, and are characterised by standardised and mass produced outputs and the achievement of economies of scale playing an important role in defining competitiveness of individual firms. Technological knowledge required to produce such output is linked to the traditional background of telecommunications producers and suppliers. Thus competition may be based predominantly on price and quality factors, supported by traditional mass advertising and marketing policies designed to separate an individual producers' output from its competitors.

With respect to computer networks and their application the characteristics of the market are different from those of product markets, thus obliging suppliers to put in place different competitive strategies. Because the adoption of computer networks is dependent upon an interaction between the technology and the organisational structure, the marketing strategies need to be tailored to individual users.

In the light of the above observations, it is clear that barriers for the traditional manufacturing firms to develop appropriate policies stem from:
- first, their lack of experience in terms of marketing strategies based on customised policies for each adopters' characteristic, rather than mass advertising policies;
- secondly, and even more drastically, their lack of knowledge in the organisational sphere, which turns out to be of crucial importance to putting in place new ad hoc technologies.

Their weakness represents a possible chance given to the so-called "value-added resellers" to enter the market. The potentially strong positions in the market of these new entrants stem from their capacity to capture information from both the supply (for example, in terms of technological developments, and the demand side, for example in terms of the interaction between the technology and the organisational structure of individual customers). This market positioning allows intermediaries to integrate technological possibilities with the needs of users, generating from one side larger markets for computer networks and their applications, but from the other side market losses for traditional telecommunication firms.

4.   Barriers at the Demand Side

It is undoubtly true that some barriers to the development of these technologies exist also at the demand side; these are concerned with the complex nature of these new technologies, requiring ad-hoc learning processes to be used and exploited by both industrial and territorial systems. The adoption and widespread use of ICTs may require - and may in fact be dependent upon - organisational changes, and the relationship between technology and organisation undoubtly represents a barrier to the diffusion of these technologies.

From a users' perspective, in fact, the rapid increase in communications potentials embodied in the new communications technologies opens the way to the exploitation of competitive advantages on the basis of the achievement of more information and knowledge. Competitive advantages are now based on the capacities of new technologies to transmit, process, store and elaborate a greater volume of information (Gillespie and Hepworth, 1986). Thus, the higher technological potentialities present major opportunities for firms to achieve competitive advantages.

However, despite general beliefs, these opportunities are not provided by the simple adoption of these technologies, but by their innovative use. By **innovative use** we refer to the application of these technologies to produce new products, new processes, new transactional structures. The development of on-line services in the banking sector (e.g., points of sales, cash dispensers, home-banking, provided by the development of inter-banking computer networks systems) are a clear example of innovative use of these infrastructures. By the same token, process innovation can be generated through the use of these new infrastructures by enabling "islands of automation" (such as flexible manufacturing systems) to intercommunicate, either within a single site (Local Area Networks) or among a multitude of sites (Wide Area Networks). As a managerial innovation, computer networks operating over space through telecommunication channels have obviously greatly increased the ability of multi-site organisations to control and integrate their activities over space (Antonelli, 1988; Camagni and Rabellotti, 1988; Fornengo, 1988; Rullani and Zanfei, 1988).

The impact of ICTs upon business performance can be analysed in terms of increased efficiency, greater effectiveness and enhanced competitive advantage. Increased efficiency is achieved, for example, by reducing costs and maintaining existing output levels through the use of technology as a substitute for other inputs (e.g. clerical staff). Effectiveness is concerned with the capacity to deliver more and improved products within the existing resource base. Competitive advantage is obtained through the exploitation of ICTs to achieve more strategic information and to generate product, process and managerial innovations (Capello et al., 1990; Williams, 1987).

The innovative and strategic use of ICTs, generating positive effects on business performance, is strongly associated for its development to deep organisational changes. In fact, innovative use of these technologies implies the interrelation of technology and organisation as two unseparable variables (Mansell, 1990; Zeleny, 1985). Technologies in themselves appear as neutral devices, as a pool of opportunities available at a given cost and can be interpreted as some quasi-public goods. But what really matters - and what is not at all a public good - is the cultural and organisational capability of exploiting their potentialities, through a creative blend of technologies devices, organisational styles and business ideas.

Thus, the simple adoption of these technologies does not provide an immediate positive effect on corporate performances (Tolmie, 1987). The rather complex and relatively new technological possibilities embodied in computer networks have drastic implications for potential users, imposing profound changes in the organisational structure of a firm. Because of their capacity to support the transactional structure of a firm, these networks are inevitably able to reshape inter- and intra-corporate information flows with profound effects on the organisation (Bar et al., 1989; Ciborra, 1989; Williams, 1987).

To achieve higher economic performances through the use of computer networks, corporate users have to adjust their organisational structure to these new "routines" and organisational rules (Nelson and Winter, 1982). The development of modern networks is thus related to the capacity of firms to change their organisational routines, and to link the technological trajectories with organisational changes. It is thus very much the case that a high rigidity of attitudes and behaviour exists, which hampers an adjustment to new conditions and the exploitation of technologies to achieve higher economic performances.

A trade-off exists between the speed of technological development, the profitability obtained by the exploitation of new and advanced technologies, the organisational costs required to use them and the complexity of economic objectives achieved through the adoption of computer networks (Table 4).

The complexity of technological systems reflects ambitious economic objectives and requires profound organisational adjustments to new technologies and a long penetration speed of it. Consequently, we can expect a lower speed of diffusion for technologies implied to achieve more complex objectives, such as higher efficiency and effectiveness and, moreover, competitive advantages. These last objectives imply, in fact, a relevant capacity to use these systems to achieve innovative products and to adapt the organisation to new technology.

5. Policy Recommendations

The interpretation of barriers limiting the telecommunications sector development raises some crucial concerns about the most "appropriate policies" to be put in place. The notion of "appropriate policy" is concerned with the idea that telecommunications, and more in general ICTs, is increasingly regarded as an effective way to increase competitiveness of firms and competitive advantages for regions. Thus, appropriate policies are oriented towards overcoming barriers in order to avoid:
- a slow diffusion of modern infrastructures and advanced services over time and space;
- an increase of territorial (regional, national, international) asymmetries in the infrastructure endowment;
- an increase of discontinuities, in terms of "missing networks";
- an inability to exploit new infrastructures and applications for innovative uses, thus trying to achieve product and process innovations, and enhanced competitive advantages for firms, cities and regions;
- an increasing loss of competitive capacities of national suppliers.

The previous arguments suggest that "appropriate policies" regard different areas of application. The first and more general area is concerned with public policy, the second regards demand policy and, finally, the third is related to appropriate corporate strategies of telecommunications suppliers.

5.1. Public policies

The technological complexity and difficulty in the use of modern technologies suggest that the development of new communications technologies is a difficult process, while a smooth diffusion over time and space will require "public policy" stimuli.

The pattern of use of these computer networks suggests that the development trajectory of new technology is still in its infancy. Thus, inevitably, public policy support should create a pressure on those mechanisms that in diffusion processes generate accumulation rates through spin-off effects. Public policy should thus encourage computer networks development in areas with high potential demand density, e.g. central regions, where mechanisms such as network externalities could generate positive cumulative effects and, thus, where critical mass could be achieved in a shorter time.

Positive network externalities, in fact, arise because the total number of subscribers has an important effect on the user-value of each additional subscriber, and each additional connection has important effects on the user-value of the network of existing subscribers (Allen, 1989; Antonelli, 1989; Hayashi, 1992). This mechanism is more efficient when applied in central areas, where the user-value of the network of subscribers is higher.

Related to this idea is the assumption that most economically developed areas are legitimated to be "networked" first, in order to develop a cumulative process. A top-down public policy is thus suitable, implementing "information highways" between metropolitan areas. A bottom-up development policy, focusing on network development in local areas, risks to generate a development model with few possible inter-linkages among "islands of networks" and thus presenting a high risk of failure because of its local characteristic.

For instance, Italy witnesses the inadequacy of "bottom-up" policies in the telecommunications sector, with respect to many local projects stimulating geographically restricted advanced telecommunications networks. It is the case of the Sprint project in Prato (Tuscany) (Zanfei, 1986), or "Lombardia Cablata" in Lombardy, just to quote two of them, where local advanced networks were implemented and modern services offered, with the result of a complete failure in their use (Camagni and Capello, 1990; Capello, 1988 and 1989). Their failure is in part contingent upon the local development of these networks, which can rather be interpreted as "white elephants" instead of efficient projects generating real interest from the demand side.

A top-down approach is in this respect a more appropriate public policy to generate cumulative adoption processes. Nevertheless, to be efficient, these policies have to consider the geographical asymmetry in networks, which are created by following a top-down approach, only as a timing difference in investments among regions. These asymmetries must not turn into discontinuity, reflecting different investment intentions. In this case, in fact, discontinuity would become a structural difference between central and peripheral regions, these last being penalised by the lack of modern infrastructures, losing the possibility of achieving advantages typical of central locations, i.e. agglomeration economies, and thus the possibility of overcoming limits of a peripheral area.

By the same token, public policy should be concerned with the existence of "missing networks" at an international level. This concern should go far beyond the simple physical infrastructure, and should take into consideration a series of concerns in the form of critical success factors, as a recent study for the Round Table of Industrialists has pointed out (Maggi et al., 1991):
- hard ware (physical infrastructure)

- soft ware (logistic and informatics)
- org ware (institutional and organisational setting)
- fin ware (financial arrangements/funding)
- eco ware (environmental and safety effects)

In this study it was concluded that the telecommunications sector could perform much better. To improve the current situation in European telecommunications the following suggestions were made:
- the introduction of a base European telecom network including standard facilities, uniform rules and tariffs, and services;
- a separation of responsibility between regulators (government, policy) and operators implementation (org ware) is needed;
- avoidable barriers to entry should be minimised (org ware); the existence of monopoly should be avoided;
- since deliverable technologies are changing too fast, a sustainable basis for regulation is missing. Improving competition should then be the keyword (org ware);
- telecommunications prices should be cost-related (org ware);
- use the outcome of current ENS-applications (e.g. the European Nervous-system) in transportation, banking, environmental protection, health care, education (org ware, hard ware, soft ware, eco ware and fin ware) to develop European-wide applications.

These suggestions reflect a demand-side oriented policy, neglecting monopoly as a useful market structure in highly technologically dynamic sectors, and interpreting competition as a key force for rapid diffusion processes in an era of a networked economy.

5.2. Supply policies

Also at the supply level some policy considerations can be offered, regarding two aspects:
- policies related to corporate strategies to enter the market, in essence marketing policies;
- policies related to best corporate strategies to face increasing competition from other maunfacturing telecommunications firms, in essence strategic market policies.

The need for a strong interaction between technology and organisation brings into focus the changing nature of computer networks markets. The distinction between products and systems markets is important to overcome the limits of adoption due to the changing nature of ICTs markets.

With respect to computer networks and their applications the characteristics of their market are different to those of traditional telecommunications product markets, thus obliging suppliers to put in place different competitive strategies. Because the adoption of computer networks is dependent upon an interaction of organisation and technology, the marketing strategies need to be tailored to individual users, so that these technologies are essentially **customised products**.

The adoption process becomes a **bricolage** process, where new technological opportunities have to be linked to an efficient organisational structure in order to achieve a new "business idea" (Camagni and Capello, 1991; Capello and Williams, 1991).

This "bricolage" process allows intermediaries to integrate technological possibilities with the needs of users, generating larger markets for computer networks and their applications. This "bricolage" process can also be developed by manufacturing telecommunications suppliers through strategies of cooperation agreements with:
- some large organisational experts;
- some large firms users, strong in their learning processes;
- some experts in the field of software and integrated systems;
- some value added resellers, or experts in telematics applications.

In this way, complementary technological, organisational and strategic know-how can be exploited and most appropriate marketing policies developed.

Moreover, the development of new technologies is strictly linked to the structure of **power** in which these technologies are implemented. Because of their direct impact on transactional structure and, thus, on power relationships, computer networks are easier to be installed in hierarchical structures where the "division of power" is not disrupted. On the contrary, their development is particularly difficult when a transaction of bargaining relationships is involved. The case of the Sprint project in Prato is significant in this respect: here an attempt was made to substitute the traditional informal network of interpersonal relationships within the "local district" with a new telematics network, but different strategic intentions have not coalesced into a common purpose and unsolved power relationships among participants generated the failure of the project (Camagni, 1987; Camagni and Capello, 1989; Capello and Williams, 1991).

Another perspective is related to the supply policies, namely the strategic policies suppliers have to follow to face increasing competition in the market. Here it seems plausible that cooperation agreements, such as joint ventures and all kinds of equity agreements, should be developed between:
- telecommunications manufacturing suppliers. Firms supplying technologically backward products should develop agreements with advanced firms, in order to achieve two different purposes:
  a) to achieve better technical know-how in more restricted time;
  b) to share the market with a previously selected partner.
- telecommunications manufacturing firms and informatics firms, in the area of value added services, for the exploitation of complementary know-how;
- telecommunications manufacturing firms and experts in organisations, in the area of computer networks, for the exploitation of complementary know-how, necessary for supplying customised products.

5.3. Demand policies

As said already, the innovative use of advanced technologies provides major opportunities for users to achieve the highest economic benefits and advantages from these new technologies. However, the simple adoption of these technologies does not provide an immediate positive effect on corporate performances (Tolmie, 1987) and does not help in overcoming the barriers represented by the need to merge the technology with the organisational structure. In fact, because of their capacity to support the transactional structure of a firm, these networks are inevitably able to reshape inter- and intra-corporate information flows with profound effects on the organisation (Bar et al., 1989; Ciborra, 1989; Williams, 1987).

The best way for users to handle the complex interrelation between technology and organisation is the development of learning processes regarding (Camagni and Capello, 1991):

- technological potentialities of the new technologies;
- possible applications of these new technologies to solve corporate problems;
- possible integration of these technologies in the organisational structure.

These learning processes are the mechanisms to develop among users adoption processes of these new technologies, overcoming the rigidity of attitudes and behaviour associated with a transition phase, which hampers an adjustment to new conditions.

6.   Conclusions[2]

Major structural changes have affected the telecommunication sector in the last decades, which have profoundly modified the nature of the sector and its development trajectories.

In particular, in the last decade the academic debate has focused the attention on the emergence of an Information Economy, and has agreed on the development of the economy towards the fifth Kondratief cycle. However, empirical evidence suggests that the diffusion of these new communication technologies is fraught with difficulties and that still some efforts should be devoted to the understanding of the reasons and causes that hamper the "Information Economy" to become reality.

The paper has highlighted the reasons for this paradox and especially has underlined strategic policies from both the supply and the demand side, which should be able to overcome the still existing bottlenecks in the exploitation of the technological potentialities.

The problem of bottlenecks and barriers to the development of the ICT sector is a subject whose importance should be stressed more. The competitiveness of industrial and territorial systems in the next years is highly dependent on the exploitation of these technologies. Firms, regions and countries that will be able to understand this and thus to overcome bottlenecks and barriers in the development of the ICTs sector will also be the ones which will have the greatest probability to achieve a privileged position in the international economic competition of the 1990s.

Notes

1.   This project was financed by the ESRC and developed at the Centre for Urban and Regional Development Studies of the University of Newcastle, under the supervision of Prof. Howard Williams.

2.   Though the paper is the result of a common research work of the two authors, the first author has written sections 1, 3, 4 and 5, while sections 2 and 6 were jointly written.

REFERENCES

Allen, D., New Telecommunications Services, **Telecommunications Policy**, September, 1989, pp. 257-271.

Antonelli, C. (ed.), **New Information Technology and Industrial Change: the Italian Case**, Kluwer Academic Publisher Books, New York, 1988.

Antonelli, C., Induced Adoption and Externalities in the Regional Diffusion of Information Technology, **Regional Studies**, vol. 24.1, 1989, pp. 31-40.

Antonelli, C. (ed.), **The Economics of Information Networks**, North Holland, Amsterdam, 1992.

Bar, F., M. Borrus and B. Coriat, Information Networks and Competitive Advantages: the Issues for Government Policy and Corporate Strategy, OECD-BRIE Telecommunications User Project, Paris, 1989.

Bell, D., **The Coming of Post-Industrial Society**, Basic Books, New York, 1973.

Camagni, R., The Spatial Implications of Technological Diffusion and Economic Restructuring in Europe with Special Reference to the Italian case, Paper presented at the Expert Meeting on **Technological Developments and Urban Change**, Paris, 29-30 June, 1987.

Camagni, R. and R. Capello, Scenari di Sviluppo della Domanda di Sistemi di Telecomunicazione in Italia", **Finanza, Marketing e Produzione**, no.1, March, 1989, pp. 87-138.

Camagni, R. and R. Capello, Innovazione Tecnologica e Innovazione Organizzativa: la Telematica in Banca, **Quaderni di Informatica**, Bull Italia, no.2, 1990, pp. 13-27.

Camagni, R. and R. Capello, Le Caratteristiche delle Nuove Tecnologie e Loro Interazione con la Domanda, **Computer Networks: Mercati e Prospettive delle Tecnologie di Comunicazione** (R. Camagni, ed.), Etas Libri, Milan, 1991, pp. 4-45.

Camagni, R. and R. Rabellotti, L'innovazione Macro- Organizzativa nel Settore Tessile-Abbigliamento, **Sviluppo e Organizzazione**, n. 108, 1988, pp. 2-8.

Capello, R., La Domanda di Reti e Servizi di Telecomunicazione nell'Area Metropolitana Milanese: Vincoli e Strategie, **La Trasformazione Economica della Città** (R. Camagni and A. Predetti, eds.), IReR-Progetto Milano, Franco Angeli, Milan, 1988, pp. 309-321.

Capello, R., Telecommunications and the Spatial Organisation of Production, **Information Economy Series**, University of Newcastle, Newcastle upon Tyne, no. 10, 1989.

Capello, R., Dinamica Tecnologica e Dinamica Istituzionale: Verso Nuovi Comportamenti d'Impresa nel Settore delle Telecomunicazioni, **Economia e Politica Industriale**, no. 68, 1991a, pp. 261-277.

Capello, R., L'assetto Istituzionale nel Settore delle Telecomunicazioni, **Computer Networks: Mercati e Prospettive delle Tecnologie di Telecomunicazione** (R. Camagni, ed.), Etas Libri, Milan, 1991b, pp. 178-260.

Capello, R., D. Charles and H. Williams, Telecommunications: Services and Equipments, Research Study for AT&T Available from the Authors at Centre for Urban and Regional Development Studies, University of Newcastle, 1990.

Capello, R. and H. Williams, Computer Network Trajectories and Organisational Dynamics: a Cross-National Review (C. Antonelli, ed.), 1992, pp. 347-362.

Charles, D., P. Monk and E. Sciberras, **Technology and Competition in the International Telecommunications Industry**, Pinter Publisher, London, 1989.

Ciborra, C., **Le Tecnologie di Coordinamento**, Franco Angeli Editore, Milan, 1989.

Commission of the European Community, **Libro Verde sullo Sviluppo di un Mercato Comune dei Servizi e dei Terminali di Telecomunicazione**, Brussels, 1987.

Ducatel, K., Flexibility, Information and Emerging Special Division of Labour, Paper presented at the PICT National Conference, Brunel University, 17-19 May, 1989.

Fischer, M., R. Maggi and C. Rammer, Context Specific Media Choice and Barriers to Communication in Universities, **The Annals of Regional Science**, vol. 24, n. 4, 1990, pp. 253-270.

Fornengo, G., Manufacturing Networks: Telematics in the Automobile Industry (Antonelli, ed.), 1988, pp. 33-56.

Freeman, Ch., J. Clark and L. Soete, **Unemployment and Technical Innovations**, Frances Pinter, London, 1982.

Giaoutzi, M. and P. Nijkamp (eds.), **Informatics and Regional Development**, Gower, Aldershot, 1988.

Giaoutzi, M. and A. Strategea, Telephone Calls and Communication Barriers in Greece, National Technical University, Athens, mimeo, 1990.

Gillespie, A., J. Goddard, H. Hepworth and H. Williams, Information and Communication Technologies and Regional Development: an Information Economy Perspective, Paper presented for OECD ICCP Seminar on **Information and Telecommunications Technology for Regional Development**, Athens, 7-9 December, 1987.

Gillespie, A. and M. Hepworth, Telecommunications and Regional Development in the Information Society, **Newcastle Studies of the Information Economy**, no. 1, October, 1986.

226

Hayashi, K., From Network Externalities to Interconnection - The Changing Nature of Networks and Economy, **New Information Technology and Industrial Change** (C. Antonelli, ed.), 1992, pp. 195-216.

Klaassen, L., S. Wageneer and A. Weg van der, Measuring Phychological Distance between the Flemings and the Walloons, **Journal of Regional Science Association**, vol. 29, 1972, pp. 45-62.

Jonscher, C., Information Resources and Economic Productivity, **Information Economics and Policy**, vol. 1, 1983, pp. 13-35.

Machlup, F., **The Production and Distribution of Knowledge in the United States**, Princeton University Press, Princeton, 1962.

Maggi, R., I. Masser and P. Nijkamp, Missing Networks in Europe, **Transport Reviews**, vol. 12, 1991, pp. 311-321.

Mansell, R., Rethinking the Telecommunication Infrastructure: the New "Black Box", **Research Policy**, vol. 19, 1990, pp. 501-515.

Nelson, R. and G. Winter, **An Evolutionary Theory of Economic Change**, The Belknap Press of Harvard University Press, Cambridge, Massachusetts, 1982.

Nijkamp, P., P. Rietveld and I. Salomon, Barriers in Spatial Interactions and Communications. A Conceptual Exploration, **The Annals of Regional Science**, vol. 24, no. 4, 1990, pp. 237-252

OECD, **New Telecommunications Services: Videotex Development Strategies**, Paris, 1988a.

OECD, **The Telecommunications Industry: the Challenges of Structural Change**, Paris, 1988b.

Rietveld, P. and L. Janssen, Telephone Calls and Communication Barriers. The Case of the Netherlands, **The Annals of Regional Science**, vol.24, no.4, 1990, pp. 307-318.

Pasini, G., **Impianti Telefonici: Criteri di Progettazione Razionale nella Telefonia Moderna**, Hoepli Publisher, Milan, 1959.

Porat, M., **The Information Economy: Definition and Measurement**, Special Publications 77.22 (1), Office of Telecommunications, US Department of Commerce, Washington D.C., 1977.

Rossera, F., Discontinuities and Barriers in Communications. The Case of Swiss Communities of Different Languages, **The Annals of Regional Science**, vol. 24, no. 4, 1990, pp. 319-336.

Rullani, E. and A. Zanfei, Networks Between Manufacturing and Demand: Cases from Textile and Clothing Industry, **New Information Technology and Industrial Change** (C. Antonelli, ed.), 1988, pp. 57-96.

Tolmie, I., The Technological and Organisational Base of Computer Networks, Mimeo Available from the Author, Centre for Urban and Regional Development Studies, University of Newcastle, Newcastle upon Tyne, 1987.

Williams, H., The Use and Consequences of Information and Communications Technologies and Trade in Information Services, Mimeo Available from the Author, Centre for Urban and Regional Development Studies, University of Newcastle, Newcastle upon Tyne, 1987.

Williams, H. and A. Gillespie, A Small Firm Perspective on the Liberalisation of Telecommunications Services, **European Telecommunications Policy Research** (N. Garnham, ed.), Springfield Publisher, Amsterdam, 1988, pp. 183-202.

Willinger, C. and E. Zuscovitch, Towards the Economics of Information-Intensive Production Systems: the Case of Advanced Materials, **Technical Change and Economic Theory** (G. Dosi, C. Freeman, R. Nelson, G. Silverberg and L. Soete, eds.), Pinter Publisher, London, 1988, pp. 239-255.

Zanfei, A., I Vincoli alla Diffusione delle Tecnologie dell'Informazione in Alcune Esperienze di Applicazione della Telematica, **Economia e Politica Industriale**, no. 50, 1986, pp. 253-289.

Zanfei, A., **Complessità e Crescita Esterna nell'Industria delle Telecomunicazioni**, Franco Angeli, Milan, 1990.

Zeleny, M., La Gestione a Tecnologia Superiore e la Gestione della Tecnologia Superiore, **La Sfida della Complessità** (G. Bocchi, and M. Ceruti, ed.), Feltrinelli, Milan, 1985.

CHAPTER 15

ROAD TRANSPORT INFORMATICS

AND

ROAD TRANSPORT DEVELOPMENTS

David Banister

1.   Introduction

The main source of profit and power in the late twentieth century is knowledge and information, and conflicts are likely to occur over the distribution of and access to that knowledge. The control of knowledge is power. Even money is becoming less important and tangible as transactions are carried out electronically, only to be seen in a symbolic form on a screen. This global view of the shifts in power presented by Alvin Toffler (1991) will transcend all activities at all levels and will create a radically different society. It will also be instrumental in the current road transport revolution with the possibility of wired cities, wired highways and wired cars. The availability of knowledge and information will radically change road transport in at least four related ways.

In **production and distribution processes**, the production line methods introduced by Henry Ford at his Highland Park assembly plant in 1913 are now being extended. The conveyor belt now extends beyond the manufacturing system to the distribution system. Technology and information allows a complete service from the assembly of materials through the production of the car to the testing and distribution processes, and the delivery to the final consumer. These concepts do not just apply to the manufacture and distribution of vehicles, but to all commodities. Freight distribution systems have been restructured on regional and metropolitan warehousing depots, often at accessible motorway intersections. Road transport informatics (RTI) impact on all parts of freight transport operations as well as location decisions (Figure 1). With the trend in Europe towards longer distance trucking and the increased use of multimodal combinations of vehicles and carriers, integrated approaches to freight transport are essential to ensure the optimal use of information and the new flexibility in both production and distribution processes. The potential is available to develop a Europe-wide integrated freight transport network, but old barriers still remain, namely who should pay the costs of pollution, the increased resource costs caused by the growth in international road freight,and the compensation of individual member countries for transit traffic - "the territoriality issue".

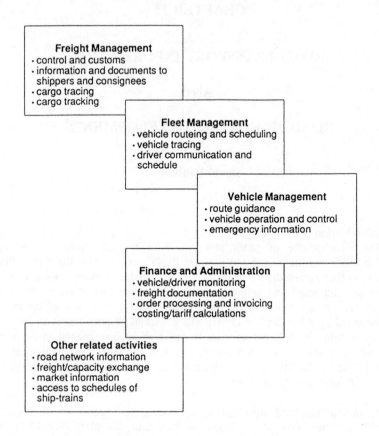

Figure 1: Information Technology Applications in Freight Transport
Source : Pangalos (1989)

Particular transit countries within the EC suffer from traffic generated at peripheral countries. These costs incurred by transit countries should be the responsibility of the road users and it is likely that a charge will be levied according to the distance travelled and the type of vehicle. However, such a charge is against the notion of a Single European Market and the liberalisation of the transport industry. RTI will be used to levy such a charge through automatic debiting and an intelligent tachometer could be used to record the trip history so that there would be no need to interrupt the journey (Hepworth and Ducatel, 1992). These user taxes are only likely to form a small part of total production and distribution costs, and so the impact on the location and competitiveness of industry will be limited.

The **movement of people** provides the second opportunity for RTI with the belief that technology can help delay the inevitable gridlock when the city comes to a complete stop through congestion. Traffic management schemes have been very effective in squeezing more capacity out of a given road network, and the expectation here is that technology through intelligent highways and smart cars can continue that process. Increased flexibility in work and leisure patterns together with the possibility of telecommuting have all provided the opportunity for change. Again, it should be noted that information and knowledge have both been instrumental in creating the conditions for this opportunity. However, each revolution in the past has resulted in increases in travel and average trip lengths, and there is no reason to expect a change as a result of the current revolution. As extra capacity is created, demand increases.

Road users will be affected in three different ways:

* Information services to the traveller which will allow decisions to be made on the basis of the best real time information. These services would apply equally to public transport services and to route guidance information given to the car driver.
* Control systems within the vehicle. By the year 2000, it is estimated that 10-15 percent of the costs of new cars will relate to RTI services (Lex Motoring, 1992).
* Control over the transport network, including demand management and traffic control systems.

RTI will also have considerable commercial applications through more efficient management of freight companies and public transport services.

The potential impact of RTI on growth in car ownership and use should not be underestimated. In all European countries over the last ten years there have been increases in car ownership, increases in trip lengths and increases in the numbers of trips made (Table 1). In thirteen OECD countries the growth in car traffic is greater than that for all traffic, but in the other three (Italy, Denmark and Sweden), the reverse is true. Similarly, in nine countries the growth in car ownership is greater than the growth in private road traffic, but in the other seven the reverse is true. Across all EC countries both car ownership and car traffic have increased at the same rate, namely 29 percent (1978-1988).

RTI may again cause similar increases in personal mobility, but its potential is much wider. Through the use of control systems it may be possible to produce vehicles which are suitable for both the elderly population and those who are too young to drive. A low powered fully automatic city vehicle could increase the market for small vehicles and travel, and allow teenagers as well as the over 75 age group greater independence. Such a development would both increase congestion in cities and reduce the demand for public transport, but it would make the car more accessible to more people. This is where equity has to be balanced against other policy objectives (Banister and Bayliss, 1991).

Country	All Traffic	Private Road Traffic	Increase in Car Ownership
Great Britain	30.0	37.8	34.4
FR of Germany	15.6	20.2	36.8
France	28.5	28.8	21.0
Italy	47.8	37.6	51.6
Japan	31.3	59.6	35.7
USA	15.8	16.2	18.2
Spain	9.1	11.6	55.9
Belgium	13.5	17.0	20.5
Denmark	22.8	19.7	16.2
Netherlands	35.8	40.1	21.5
Portugal	54.9	67.6	74.8
Austria	24.8	33.8	34.9
Finland	26.6	33.4	55.1
Norway	33.9	41.8	35.7
Sweden	22.1	21.2	20.1
Switzerland	12.8	15.0	27.9
Greece	-	-	81.3
Ireland	-	-	5.5

Table 1: Growth in Passenger Traffic 1978-1988

Source : Based on data from Transport Statistics (Department of Transport, 1990)

Notes : Figures give percentage increase in passenger kilometres travelled over the decade (1978-1988). Figures for Italy, FR of Germany, Belgium, Japan, USA, Norway, Switzerland are all estimated in the private road traffic column. Figures on car ownership increases are the percentage increase in cars owned per 1000 population (1978-1988).

The **infrastructure** is the key to an integrated Europe, and much of the existing transport infrastructure is over one hundred years old. A significant part of the motorway system is now over fifty years old. Very substantial investment is required to replace existing roads and construct new ones, and these links will help integrate peripheral areas as well as open up new markets in the old East European countries. Road investment will be complemented by the new European high speed rail network and telecommunications networks, including the new Value Added Networks (VANs) and the Local Area Networks (LANs). It is this combination of networks which will facilitate the most fundamental changes brought about by knowledge advances and information technology. These include:

* logistics planning
* electronic data interchange
* electronic route guidance
* emergency transport planning
* information systems
* databases for environmental monitoring

As a consequence, the **spatial imperative** will no longer apply as cities will become much looser spatial organisations, as the costs of urban centrality and high land prices will be balanced against the benefits of dispersal. The movement out of cities will continue with only front office functions remaining. Growth will be concentrated in corridors of good communications and at peripheral urban locations where it is cost effective to link in with both the transport and the information networks. Peripheral areas may still remain isolated and separate from the new infrastructure as access costs and capacity requirements may make the installation costs of the new networks uneconomic and the costs of using the system too high.

The most attractive locations in Europe will be those where the transport and information networks link in with other factors such as a skilled labour force, a high quality environment and the availability of low cost land. Interchanges may provide particularly suitable locations for logistical platforms. International airports and major motorway intersections could provide the sites of maximum accessibility which would minimise location and transport costs, and also be on the international information network.

Much of this introductory section has been speculative and set at the European level. There is no question that very significant changes are taking place on both the political and technological fronts in Europe, and RTI is likely to have a profound effect on road transport at all levels. However, the exact nature and scale of that impact is far from clear, and it seems that implementation of RTI will not be equal across all road transport sectors, but that it will be selective and take a considerable time for the full effects to become apparent. In the remaining parts of this chapter, the European RTI research programme is outlined together with reference to the parallel programmes in Japan and the USA. The focus then switches to the more detailed implementation level and the important economic, social and distributional issues which are raised, together with questions of the access to the information and the control of it.

2. RTI and Road Transport - The Vision

The scale of potential RTI impacts has been identified in the introduction and this futuristic vision was apparent in the original programme of DRIVE (Dedicated Road Infrastructure for Vehicle Safety in Europe) set up by the EC. However, more recently the concern has switched to market applications in the European research programme, and with the parallel programmes in Japan and the USA, there is now an unstoppable impetus for the application of RTI to road transport. The DRIVE programme is divided into seven areas of major operational interest, and particular attention in DRIVE II (1992-1994) will be given to the validation of research and development results achieved through pilot projects (Table 2).

As can be seen from this comprehensive list of projects, the potential range of applications is enormous and such a programme has been justified by the importance allocated to transport congestion, safety and technology in the development of EC research. Transport represents more than 6 percent of GNP with more than 10 percent of the average family budget being devoted to transport, and there is a strong expectation that with the growth in car traffic "bottlenecks will inevitably occur in land infrastructure in Europe" in the 1990's (CEC, 1991, p5).

These problems exacerbate the negative effects of road transport on human safety and the environment

* Every year in the Community around 55,000 people are killed on the roads, 1.7 million are injured and 150,000 permanently handicapped. The financial cost of this is estimated to be more than 50 billion ECU per year. The social cost in human misery and suffering cannot be measured.
* The cost of traffic in the Community is estimated to be around 500 billion ECU per year. A substantial part is due to congestion and poor routeing. In France alone in 1988 more than 400,000 km hours were spent in congestion. In the UK the Confederation of British Industry estimate that more than £15 billion (21 billion ECU) are lost each year in congestion.
* vehicle emissions contribute significantly towards the total of environmental pollution which is estimated to cost Europe between 5-10 billion ECU per year (Table 3).

Areas of Major Operational Interest	Applications
Demand Management	Area access control, area pricing, zone access control, zone pricing, parking control, parking pricing, road pricing at barriers, booked pricing, special points pricing, law enforcement, fares collection, parking management
Traffic and Travel Information	One way communication to vehicles, dialogue, route information, service information, pre trip information, traffic information, parking guidance, public transport information, fleet management, weather conditions, road conditions, pollution, traffic flow
Integrated Urban Traffic Management Integrated Inter-Urban Traffic Management	Coordinated junctions, integrated network control, tidal flow, tunnel control, specific road users, emergency services, traffic calming, parking management, route control, heavy goods vehicle control, traffic monitoring, congestion detection, incident detection, environmental monitoring, enforcement/policing
Driver Assistance and Cooperative Driving	Cruise control, anti collision control, intelligent manoeuvre control, cooperative intersection control, lane merging, medium range information
Freight and Fleet Management	Dynamic route planning and scheduling, fleet monitoring, vehicle dispatching, intermodal transport planning, transport order processing, consignment monitoring
Public Transport Management	Dynamic data on traffic conditions, information database on public transport schedules and networks, real-time information on vehicle locations, travel demand forecasting, scheduling software, in trip terminals, real-time information linked to traffic control centre, pre trip information, automatic debiting, fare collection and ticketing, public transport priority, real-time and static interchange information, real-time in car/in bus information, park and ride linked to route guidance

Table 2: EC DRIVE II Research Programme - the Seven Areas
Source : EC DRIVE II BATT Consortium (1992)

		Canada	USA	France	Western Germany	Italy	UK	Japan	North America	OECD Europe	OECD
ENERGY CONSUMPTION											
Total final energy consumption by the transport sector											
TOTAL	MTOE	42	482	40	49	32	43	66	523	254	868
of which: Air	%	11	15	9	10	5	15	4	15	11	13
Road	%	80	82	86	87	91	80	85	82	83	82
Rail	%	5	2	3	3	2	2	4	3	3	3
Diesel consumption											
by road transport	%change	447	191	233	112	279	86	210	203	172	191
Share of total	%	18	17	42	34	52	28	42	17	40	26
NOISE FROM ROAD TRAFFIC											
Population exposed to > 65 dB	Million	2	17	9	8	10	6	37	19	63	120
AIR POLLUTION											
Share of transport emissions in total emissions											
NO$_x$	%	61	41	76	65	52	49	44	43	60	49
CO	%	66	67	71	74	91	86	..	67	78	71
HC	%	37	33	60	53	87	32	..	33	50	39
SO$_x$	%	3	4	10	6	4	2	18	4	4	4

Table 3: Environmental Polution and the Use of Resources in Transport
Source : OECD (1991)

This is the level of the current challenge facing the EC, and if current trends are continued (Table 1), the demand for road traffic will increase by a further 34 percent over the next ten years. International road freight along the main corridors will increase by between 13-15 percent per year. The DRIVE programme attempts to improve road safety, maximise road transport efficiency and contribute to environmental improvements. It envisages a common European road transport environment in which drivers are better informed and "intelligent" vehicles communicate and cooperate with the road infrastructure itself (CEC, 1991, p.5). This **Integrated Road Transport Environment** (IRTE) will be achieved through pre competitive and collaborative research and development, the evaluation of systems, the harmonisation of European standards and common functional specifications, and the most appropriate strategy for implementation. The standardisation of systems is seen as being particularly important as this would reduce the costs of equipment and help in the development of a European market which would in turn increase international competitiveness. The DRIVE programme links in with other European research under the EUREKA framework (such as Prometheus and Carminat), EURET, IMPACT, COST, ESPRIT and RACE[1].

---

1. EUREKA : European Research Coordination Agency.
   Prometheus : Programme for a European Traffic System with Highest Efficiency and Unprecedented Safety.

In Japan, driver information systems have already been introduced into Tokyo with the primary aim of reducing traffic congestion. Each road user requires information about the destination, the actual traffic conditions on the selected route and alternative routes. An advanced traffic information systems needs to supply this information, and four experimental systems have been introduced (Kashima, 1989).

* The **bus location system** transmits data via a roadside unit to a central computer which then instructs the bus driver at what speed to run and also transmits the arrival time of the bus to each stop. The system was introduced in 1983 and has resulted in demand increases of up to 30 percent. The information on arrivals can also be obtained from the home and shops via local radio.
* **Automatic vehicle monitoring system (AVMS)** has been installed in taxis and trucks to monitor their position at any point in time. However, in Tokyo the density of beacons is not high and so the exact position of vehicles cannot be determined. The high costs of access to the system have resulted in only taxis participating fully. Installation has resulted in the number of vehicle trips increasing by 20 percent (Kashima, 1989).

The most important developments have taken place under the Comprehensive Automobile Control System (CACS) set up by the Ministry of International Trade and Industry (MITI) with a 7.3 billion Yen budget (45 million ECU: 1973-79) and a test site in South West Tokyo. Time savings between guided and non-guided cars were about 11 percent, and it was estimated that a system which covered all central Tokyo would give time savings valued at 80 billion Yen a year (500 million ECU).

Two systems were tested

* **Road automobile communication system (RACS)** uses road side communication units (beacons), in vehicle units and a systems centre. This system does not supply continuous communication services, but intermittent communication over very small distances. But it can provide a service to the whole nation using one radio frequency and it has already been introduced on a freeway network in Tokyo (1990).
* **Advanced mobile traffic information and communication system (AMTICS)** provides real-time traffic information collected by traffic counters and TV cameras, and this data is relayed to vehicles via a teleterminal system. The

---

Carminat	:	Provides for comprehensive in-çar information.
EURET	:	European Research in the field of Transport.
IMPACT	:	Information Market Policy Actions on Transport.
COST	:	Cooperation in the field of Scientific and Technical Research
ESPRIT	:	European Strategic Programme for Research and Development in Information Technology.
RACE	:	Research in Advanced Communications for Europe.

National Police Agency has installed 6200 traffic counters and 100 TV cameras to provide the information which is presented to drivers in the form of road maps. It requires each vehicle to be equipped with a standard digital road map database (Kawashima, 1990).

These systems are now being developed into full route guidance, but several unresolved questions still remain. It is unclear whether any system should be publicly or privately operated, who should pay for the installation of road side equipment, and the social acceptability of the technology (Tanaka, 1991).

In the USA, it is estimated that incident-induced congestion causes over half the total delays on urban freeways, and that this figure is likely to increase to 70 percent by 2005 (Khattak et al, 1991). The **Intelligent Vehicle Highway System (IVHS)** intends to use real-time information to guide drivers through the road network, and three linked programmes have been proposed (Chen, 1990).

* **Advanced traffic management systems (ATMS)** would include toll billing, incident detection and adaptive signal controls.
* **Advanced driver information systems (ADIS)** would cover vehicle location, vehicle navigation, information, route guidance and collision warning.
* **Automobile vehicle control systems (AVCS)** would be longer term and cover collision avoidance, speed/headway keeping, automatic highways and automatic guidance.

Chen (1990) concludes that the USA is behind Europe and Japan in both research and applications, and that progress in the USA is dependent upon the US Congress continuing to allocate a substantial budget for research.

Hepworth and Ducatel (1992) have neatly shown how the different groups of RTI technologies interrelate (Figure 2). Traffic management systems are at the centre of road transport innovation, but even with all the available technology there is no solution to congestion, even if electronic road pricing was extensively introduced in Europe. There are also unresolved questions of responsibilities and priorities as they relate to the control of passenger information systems, the form of regulation and accountability. The availability of information and the control of that information are two crucial determinants of power. It is likely that "infotactics" will be used to maintain that power (Toffler, 1991). The opportunity exists for greater control over cars and lorries through the use of RTI. On-board systems allow for the monitoring of vehicle performance and feedback to the driver. Traffic communication systems provide the link between the vehicle and the external traffic system. Finally, there are the driver support systems which give route planning and guidance information to the driver. All three aspects form the components of the "smart vehicle" (Hepworth and Ducatel, 1992).

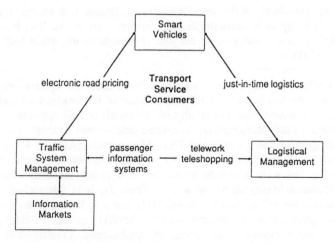

Figure 2:   The Road Transport Informatics Family
Source :   Hepworth and Ducatel (1992)

3.   RTI and Road Transport - the Reality

To many people the opportunities offered by RTI must seem very attractive, but this technologically led top down approach to the problems of traffic congestion and network inefficiencies must also realise its limitations. In isolation, RTI will not solve these problems, and at best it may help to alleviate some of the particular instances of congestion, if combined with other transport and land use policies. Bernard (1981) has identified three success factors in determining a technology's future market:

* technological superiority of the new substituting technology over the old
* life cycle cost advantage relative to the old technology
* size of the potential market assuming 100 percent substitution

The reality is less clear than the conditions set out above. The RTI technology is likely to exist in parallel with the old technology, its costs (at least in the short term) are likely to be considerably higher than existing technology, and market penetration will be limited (at least initially). Given these uncertainties, it is unclear whether RTI will actually have any impact, particularly where consumer choice is involved. Its greatest potential would be in systems about which the consumer does not know (eg car engine management systems) and in business activities where there might be clear competitive advantages in using the technology. In both of these applications the car industry and the private sector can be expected to take the lead. There may be a role for information services to develop as an industry in their own right. In twenty years time over 90 percent of the 190 million vehicles in Europe will have processors, communication and interface devices installed as standard. The EC is also concerned over the power of the USA which accounts for over two-thirds of the world's electronic databases. It wishes to develop a common EC industry to increase the existing market share of the UK, France and Germany which between them account for just 13 percent of the world total (Vogel and Rowlands, 1991).

The EC DRIVE Programme has defined seven areas for applications (Table 2) which can also be related to Figure 2 where some of the linkages are presented. In the management sectors there is considerable potential for RTI applications. This covers Integrated Urban Management, Integrated Inter-Urban Management, Public Transport Management and Freight and Fleet Management (Areas 3,4,7 and 6 in Table 2). In each case the decision to use RTI will be commercially driven whether the responsibility lies with a private enterprise or a public authority. Even with reference to Demand Management (Area 1 in Table 2), it is fairly clear that the public authority or the toll authority will use RTI. But it is here that such issues as the political acceptability of the implications of using RTI (eg road pricing) become important. In the remaining two areas of applications (Traffic and Travel Information and Driver Assistance and Cooperation), most uncertainty remains, as questions such as user response, the costs of the technology to the individual, and public acceptability arise. It is also unclear as to who should pay for the infrastructure and who should control access to the information. These two areas of RTI application form the focus of the remaining discussion in this chapter.

It may only be at the European level that such changes and decisions can be implemented, and this is reflected in DRIVE's aim of creating a pan-European network of "Information Centres" organised around distributed databases at the national, regional and local levels (CEC, 1991). These Centres form a key element in the Integrated Road Transport Environment (IRTE). It seems fundamental that the administration and control of the data should be in the public sector and this means that the funding will also come from taxation, with a possibility of charging for the information. Public sector control would allow the information to be comprehensive and it would allow equal access to the database. Private sector control would create difficulties in data acquisition, and could result in inequalities in data access unless there was a powerful regulatory control agency. New organisational structures are required in road transport to ensure equal access to information by all competitors, whether development takes place in the private or the public sector, or a combination of both.

One major unresolved issue is the nature of user response to RTI in road transport. As Bernard (1981) has stated, assumptions are often made about the level of market penetration and the substitution effects of one technology for another. With RTI, the diffusion process is likely to be slow in terms of the awareness of the technology, in terms of the turnover rates of the car stock (typically 8-10 years), and in terms of the rapid obsolescence and the high initial costs of new technology.

Consumer awareness of new technology in the car or of new public transport information systems is low. In a recent report on motoring in the UK (Lex Motoring, 1992), drivers were asked how much use they would make of each of a list of electronic systems installed in their cars (Table 4). The parking guidance system seemed most popular with 45 percent saying that they would make a "great deal of use" of such a feature and 32 percent saying that they would make a "fair amount of use". Responses to other types of RTI applications were less positive and similar percentages in each response category may indicate that some difficulty was experienced in differentiating between the options. Most surprising was the finding that car telephones were not perceived as a benefit and that few people would make any use of it at all. The fact that a cost constraint was not included in any of the questions means that the figures given are maximum ones.

RTI in transport is unlikely to appeal to all drivers equally, and ironically some of the main advantages result from all drivers not receiving the same information. For example, the competitive advantage of route guidance systems is to allow some users privileged information so that their journey times can be reduced. If all drivers had the same information the alternative route being suggested would be less attractive. The marketing of RTI should therefore be aimed at increasing consumer awareness of the opportunities offered by different RTI systems and in identifying potential market segments. Access to technology will lead to greater inequalities in society as not all people will have the knowledge or the ability to use it. Information becomes crucial as does the presentation of the technology to the potential user. Access to these networks is expensive at the individual level and at the company level. Toffler (1991) calls this information divide "as deep as the Grand Canyon" (p 366).

The conceptualisation of responses to RTI is based in traditional transport analysis. It is hypothesised that the individual will make more or less trips, change modes, change destinations, change routes, consolidate trips or reschedule them. These behavioural responses are typical and can be incorporated in conventional demand analysis. However, there are several methodological problems. The range of responses is large and the initial scale of any RTI application is likely to be small, and so measurement of change will be difficult. It also seems likely that many changes will not be measurable in the terms outlined here as the driver may choose to ignore the advice given in the RTI application, or the modification of behaviour and consumer satisfaction may be marginal, or two people when presented with the same information may react differently.

How much would you make use of each of the following if it was installed in your car?	A great deal	A fair amount	A little	Not at all
Parking guidance systems to tell you where parking is available in a town or city centre	45	32	12	10
A talking computer which advises you of failures such as lights or braking systems before you would normally be aware of them	38	30	12	19
A system which automatically keeps you a safe distance from the car in front	38	31	15	16
A system which alerted you to road works in a 30 mile radius from where you are	37	33	17	12
A system which adjusted your speed for road conditions or weather conditions	37	30	15	18
A system which planned your route and guided you without needing to use a map	27	25	22	26
A system which adjusts your speed automatically as you entered a lower speed limit zone	26	30	18	25
A car telephone	8	10	18	63
An in car office including a computer and fax machine	1	3	6	89

Table 4 : New Technology in the Car
Note   : About 1 percent of respondents had no opinion
Base   : All drivers (1277)
Source : Lex Motoring (1992)

With respect to at least two areas of RTI application (Traffic and Travel Information and Driver Assistance and Cooperation), effective implementation will only take place above particular thresholds of acceptance. Imaginative means to increase market penetration and measurement will be required:

* EC standards for all RTI applications will have to be established
* The possibility of free installation of RTI in vehicles, at public transport termini, and in homes may be considered together with leasing the equipment
* Publicity and marketing programmes will be required to raise public awareness and acceptance of the need for RTI

* Careful analysis is required of the exact information and guidance specifications needed by the users
* An understanding of the range of reactions from the car driver and passenger to route guidance advice or instructions will have to be researched. Many of these reactions cannot be covered by conventional demand analysis and new qualitative methods will be required

Behind all these concerns is the role and the symbolism of the car which should not be underestimated. Much of the attraction of the car has been its ability to give the user freedom and the opportunity to make their own decisions. Many RTI applications in driver assistance and cooperation can reduce that independence. This may result in rejection and the user making the deliberate decision to ignore the advice given, hence eliminating many of the benefits from RTI.

4.   The Future
The inevitable conclusion reached in this chapter is that the likely impact of RTI on transport congestion will be limited. The most effective forms of RTI will be those which improve traffic management in the system (including public transport management). These passive systems require no action from the user of the system, but increases the reliability and efficiency of the system itself. The second area of significant potential is in logistics and in the organisation of production and distribution systems, principally in the road freight sector. Here, competitive principles can be applied to ensure the operational efficiency of companies is maintained, and RTI may be a crucial part of that competitive advantage.

Where most uncertainty occurs is in the user response to RTI, and how they may react to "smart vehicles" (Figure 2). Diffusion of innovation takes time, the technology itself often changes rapidly, and access to the technology is limited by knowledge and price. A major barrier to the acceptance of RTI technology is consumer awareness, the knowledge base required, and the realisation of the full potential advantages that the technology will bring. At the end of the DRIVE II Programme there will be clear indications on the technical feasibility of the range of RTI applications being tested, and some assessment will also have been made of the overall consumer benefits of RTI in road transport. New borders and new frontiers will have been explored. RTI will result in a more flexible approach to decision making at the individual user or firm level, and this in turn may result in greater variability in the performance of the transport system as a whole. Patterns of routinised behaviour, typical of many traditional transport studies will be replaced by flexible dynamic choices which result from different decisions being made by people, even those faced with the same choices. The barriers facing RTI in road transport are not technological, but relate to political and organisational issues, and to questions of social and economic acceptability.

REFERENCES

Banister, D. and D. Bayliss, Structural Changes in Population and Impact on Passenger Transport Demand, European Conference of Ministers of Transport, Round Table 88, Paris, 1991.

Bernard, M.J., Problems in Predicting Market Response to New Transportation Technology, **New Horizons in Travel Behaviour Research** (P.R. Stopher, A.H. Meyburg and W. Brog, eds.), Lexington Books, 1981, pp 465-87.

Chen, K., Driver Information Systems: A North American Perspective, **Transportation**, 17(3), 1990, pp 251-62.

Commission of the European Communities, The DRIVE Programme in 1991, DGXIII - Telecommunications, **Information Industries and Innovation**, DR1202, Brussels, April, 1991.

Department of Transport, Transport Statistics Great Britain 1979-1989, London: HMSO, 1990.

EC DRIVE II BATT Consortium, Initial Ideas on Defining Objectives, Internal Working Note 1, January, 1992.

Hepworth, M. and K. Ducatel, **Transport in the Information Age: Wheels and Wires**, Belhaven, London, 1992.

Kashima, S., Advanced Traffic Information Systems in Tokyo, **Built Environment** 15(3/4), 1989, pp. 244-50.

Kawashima, H., Japanese Perspective of Driver Information Systems, **Transportation**, 17(3), 1990, pp 263-84.

Khattak, A.J., J.L. Schofer and F.S. Koppelman, **Commuters' Enroute Diversion and Return Decisions: IVHS Design Implications**, Proceedings of the 6th International Conference on Travel Behaviour, Quebec, May, 1991, pp 362-76.

Lex Motoring, **Lex Report on Motoring 1992**, Report Produced by MORI for Lex Motoring, London, January, 1992.

Organisation for Economic Cooperation and Development, **Environmental Indicators**, Paris: OECD, 1991.

Pangalos, S., Prominent Applications and Software, Paper Presented at the DRIVE-EUROFRET Workshop on Freight and Fleet Management, Brussels, November, 1989.

Tanaka, M., Dealing with Unanticipated Events, **The Wheel Extended** 76, 1991. p. 30.

Toffler, A., **Power Shift: Knowledge, Wealth and Violence at the Edge of the 21st Century**, Bantam, London, 1991.

Vogel, S. and I. Rowlands, The Challenges and Opportunities Facing the European Electronics Information Industry, **The Single European Market and the Information and Communication Technologies** (G. Locksley, ed.), Belhaven, London, 1991.

CHAPTER 16

BARRIERS IN PROBLEM SOLVING: EPILOGUE

1.   Methodological Barriers, Uncertainly and Scenarios

In many disciplines, methodologies used to design, verify and promote theories, models and techniques are developed from the perspective of the conceptual framework which is the dominant one in the discipline. Approaches dealing with past, current and new challenges in society, involve "disciplinary based and subject matter oriented techniques as well as problem-solving methods" (Johnson, 1986, pp. 12-14). Problems arise, when the nature of the problem appears to defy known and proven explanatory frameworks.   Then the nature of the problem provides the researcher and the policy maker with a challenge which cannot be overcome by improving theories, their models and techniques. It has become increasingly noticeable that the conceptual frameworks most often used, are in a state of transition. Clarity in terms of what the new conceptual framework is, is not readily available. To focus on the methodology involved in understanding the nature of problems, may be a first step in the process of developing appropriate explanatory frameworks. Variables such as technology and institutions are often used as scapegoats when problems cannot be solved. However, information, its nature, its organization and its management are areas worthy of investigation.[1] The role of information and information management are emerging as areas which will likely provide the researcher with knowledge to solve problems.

When various groups, including researchers and decision-makers, who are interested in, and concerned with designing policies and policy tools, engage in research activities, it often appears that the complexity of the areas they are dealing with defies the typical approach to reduce the problem to a smaller number of variables.[2] Variables used are normally determined by the fields of study and the disciplinary background of the researcher.[3] As a rule, this involves, both in the past and at present, an assumed relationship between those variables.[4] Continued attempts to understand the nature of problems, natural systems, society, and the linkages and interactions between these are characterized by a high degree of uncertainty. At the same time the need to increase knowledge about the changed and changing nature of problems, and the need to prescribe solutions as part of policies and plans, highlight the degree of uncertainty involved. The dynamic nature of the challenges and the impacts in socio-economic, political-institutional and environmental terms, only serve to increase the apparent uncertainty as to how to approach problems, and how to design policies aimed at solving problems.[5] Increasingly, some problems are perceived as characteristic of their specific cultural context. Although this may allow for a less abstract way[6] of designing "generic solutions for generic problems", this approach still constitutes only a step (albeit an important one) in the direction of understanding the nature of problems. Moreover, the prescriptive aspect, so much part of the science-based decision making part of economics, is still very much prevalent in this "cultural context" approach. Many contemporary problems show a number of common properties: they exhibit a high degree of complexity and they display what appears to be an overwhelming amount of information in assorted degrees and forms of organization. Such current problems appear to defy known problem solving methods and techniques which are discipline based.[7] Subject-matter based methodologies, which are often more inter-disciplinary based, are experiencing similar difficulties. For example, in attempts to understand "the environmental problem" a succession of approaches has been tried, including: improving disciplinary based methodologies, multi-disciplinary research and team-work, as well as inter-disciplinary based research and team-work. I refer to this method of inclusion of a previously not acknowledged problem, as the internalization of the environmental problem.[8] With regard to economics, such environmental problems have become problems to be treated as if they were a problem of inefficient production methods, unequal income distribution or resource management. In any case, not a unique problem, but subject to the conceptual framework of the "appropriating discipline". However, it is becoming clear that such traditional approaches aimed at understanding and solving problems are inadequate at best and in-appropriate at worst, particularly for environmental problems, and it is my contention that we need to look at the nature of such problems. Because of the changed and changing nature of these problems, it has become necessary to concentrate on moving away from traditional methodologies. The focus of research needs to be on finding solutions for complex problems and the methodology needed to do so. The nature of many of today's problems, particularly of the environmental problems is that we are desperately in need of new ways to understand what the nature of the problem is and how we can devise ways and means to solve them outside of traditional disciplinary and interdisciplinary lines. Thus, this entails designing new methodologies as the changed and changing nature of the problem cannot be accommodated within disciplinary or inter-disciplinary methodologies.[9]

To date, reliance has been on the analysis of data, trends and increased knowledge to provide a better picture of what researchers and policy makers were attempting to understand. The expectation was that this would provide reduced uncertainty in society and increase clarity in different policy fields. To do so, the focus is on collecting more and more data (both in quantity and quality) and on perfecting models and soothsayer's techniques. That is to say, analysis of the past provides understanding and knowledge in the present and increased knowledge and certainty to predict the future. This has led to the development of sophisticated methods and techniques and associated continuing efforts to improve on these, while rarely questioning whether to do so does in fact facilitate policy design and management of our resources.[10]

In addition to the difficulties with solving problems from a disciplinary or inter-disciplinary perspective in the traditional manner, there is an area which many disciplines do not deal with at all. According to Simon (1969):

"The central task of a natural science is to make the wonderful commonplace: to show that complexity, correctly viewed, is only a mask for simplicity; to find pattern hidden in apparent chaos...The world we live in today is much more a man-made [sic], or *artificial*, world than it is a natural world. Almost every element in our environment shows evidence of man's [sic] artifice...If science is to encompass these objects and phenomena in which human purpose as well as natural law are embodied, it must have means for relating these two disparate components" (pp. 1-4)[italics mine].

He proposes that not only should there be a science for the natural phenomena, but also for the "artificial objects and phenomena" (Simm, 1968, p. 4). This brings into question the foundations of economics as a discipline. In this discipline, as in many other disciplines, the theories, models and techniques are based on, or modelled after the natural science method, specifically physics. A science of the artificial does not exist. That is to say, a science chiefly designed for all those artificial objects and phenomena such as infrastructure, information technologies, urban-regions, institutions, and their interactions with people and natural environments.[11] For example, we treat people-made problems ranging from traffic jams to warfare as if they are natural phenomena.[12] Once again there is a reliance on physics here. Our solutions are often discipline based, and they shape our policy design and as they are derived from the natural sciences, by implication we treat people-made problems as if they were natural problems. I argue, that part of the changed nature of the problem and the complexity are the "artificial objects and phenomena" (1968,4) aspect referred to earlier. To design solutions one needs to understand this and re-examine the disciplines.[13] One needs to identify what their exact field of study is, and examine in what manner the discipline deals with the interface of the natural and the artificial.[14] The next phase would be to examine what should be involved in the design of a "science of the artificial".[15]

During this time of transition, a possible first step is to concentrate on scenario building, specifically on the methodology involved in the creation of such scenarios and the decision-making which occurs. To utilize scenario building and the methodology involved, is relevant for several reasons. First, although:

"Scenarios are not predictions. It is simply not possible to predict the future with certainty... scenarios are vehicles for helping people learn...they present alternatives images; they do not merely extrapolate the trends of the present...scenarios allow a manager to say, 'I am prepared for whatever happens."(Schwartz,1991, p. 6).

Second, the process which is involved in scenario building is one of the areas to concentrate on when designing methodologies appropriate for the nature of contemporary problems. This may provide a particularly interesting methodology to begin to understand the complexity of people-made environments. It will also constitute a start to the design of methodologies capable of addressing Simon's artificial objects and phenomena (1969, pp. 1-4). Included in this could be the function and role of cultural context. Third, scenario building will allow us to distinguish between what Simon refers to as the outer and inner environment (Simon, 1969, p.7). That is to say, the interface between these two environments which are what Simon refers to the artifacts:

"An artifact can be thought of as a meeting point - an "interface" in today's terms - between an "inner" environment, the substance and organization of the artifact itself, and an "outer" environment, the surroundings in which it operates. If the inner environment is appropriate to the outer environment, or vice versa, the artifact will serve its intended purpose" (Simon, 1969, p.7).

Scenario building must make this distinction explicit and emphasize the interactions between the various systems. This would then concern itself with a number of areas which disciplines traditionally deal with in a discrete manner. This approach does not constitute a multi-disciplinary or inter-disciplinary approach. It is different in so far as it focuses on the interface and the steps needed to take to achieve desirable goals and objectives. More importantly, scenario building does not assume *a priori* cause and effect; it is dynamic (and not static posing as dynamic), and it is not mechanistic. It will develop as it progresses. It draws on myths, stories and cognitive parameters. The methodology which would emerge from the scenario building process, could serve as a first step toward understanding and solving the complexity of the economy-ecology interactive systems.[16]

2.   An Illustration: The Environmental Problem

Over the last four decades the perception of what is the "environmental problem" has undergone several metamorphoses. Environmental systems, in the sixties and seventies, were thought to be subject to the so called negative[17] impacts of economic development. A variety of disciplines became involved in attempts, to not only identify what the problems were, but to also design ways and means to solve them. Often, known methods and techniques were used to solve these "new" problems.[18] People from a variety of backgrounds, thought they had an understanding of the problems and their disciplines and could provide the models and techniques to solve these problems. The body of knowledge referred to as economics had its own way of doing this: it now viewed the environment as part of the market system and as such it "drew the environment" into its analytical framework simply as another variable. Negative impacts were treated as externalities and, once internalized into the discipline, economic solutions were thought to be the answer.[19]

By the eighties, it became clear that the problems created by economic development, could not be solved simplistically and so an interdisciplinary approach was tried. This consisted of a merging of various problem-solving techniques from a mix of disciplines. For example, an economic cost benefit analysis now would include environmental criteria and would be used in the evaluation of development projects. In reality, not much progress was made. Whereas previously the economic system had been viewed as the dominant system, during the eighties the ecological system was viewed as the dominant one. At present many people view the economic and the ecological system as integrated systems and happily continue to develop but now in a "sustainable manner".[20] But what that means is that we use the term "development" (sustainable or not) as a synonym for the explicit concept of "economic" development. Economic in this sense also encompasses social well being criteria such as equity, equality and access. However, when the concept of environment is explicitly introduced in a development framework then it becomes a resource economics issue. Development now simply includes so-called "environmental resources".[21] This internalizes the environment into the economic discipline (or for that matter into several other disciplines) and allows for the application of the models and techniques developed for the market system, to the integrated economic/environmental problem.

To date, environmental problems are predominantly approached in the following manner:

"..environmental problems can be analysed in economic terms on three major levels:

(1) **The general policy level**, where the links to environmental damage may not be particularly obvious, but nevertheless at times quite strong;

(2) **The environmental policy level**, where conscious decisions are made to limit environmental degradation through regulation, taxation, subsidies, etc.;

(3) **The project level**, where adjustments can be made to optimize [sic[22]] environmental damage.

The three approaches should be seen as complements; one without the others may not do much good. Much of the environmental degradation is the result of large numbers of individuals engaging in destructive (but privately rational) actions. We cannot hope to reach them all by area-based projects. These must be complemented and supported by sound general economic policies" (Bojo et al., 1990, p.2).

The basis for this approach is the neo-classical economics framework. Despite its shortcomings, it is used as a benchmark and anything that deviates from the model is seen as market or policy failure (Bojo et al., 1989, p.2). This is a clear example of how economists and their discipline are **out of tune with the economy**. The economy is not simply a "the market system". It is a complex dynamic, probabilistic system comprising ecological/biological, socio/economic and political/institutional systems which are linked through technology. Not much is known about the interactions of these systems. Many economist in an attempt to understand the dynamics of the market system, reduce the number of variables to a manageable level, assume a relationship between variables, and perceive this reductionist approach as the best suitable methodology which will increase understanding of the functioning of the economy.

But there are signs of a changing perspective on the nature of environmental problems, according to Wiman (1992):

"The new paradigm stresses quite a different perspective: Nature Non-Linear (or Nature Complex). Whereas the Nature Benign [wait-and-see] view emphasizes the existence of stabilizing (homeostatic, geophysiological, gaian)...properties of natural systems, the Nature

Non-Linear school of thought highlights the potential that systems complexity implies destabilizing properties, rather than stabilizing ones. Such properties can be generated by non-linear dependencies between system components, conducive to flip-flop, threshold, or runaway tendencies...the complexity of natural systems ...is seen partly as a safe-guard against anthropogenic stress and partly as a trapdoor that can change the **modus operandi** on natural systems. These extremes lead to very different environmental policies" (p. 27).

Questions such as, what phenomena are emerging, what relationships are there between these phenomena, are the ones which require more research.[23] Methodology to address these questions does not exists within the social sciences.

3.   **Methodology**

According to Johnson, there are three kinds of research practiced by economists: "...disciplinary, subject-matter, and problem-solving...different kinds of information are acquired in doing each, and acquisition of the information requires different methods." (Johnson, 1986, p.11). Such different methods arise out of different underlying philosophies. It is important to make this distinction, although of course research often involves and contributes to all three methodologies as it reflects a particular form of conceptualization and, in cases where research is done specifically for policy design purposes, it may involve changing the nature of policies significantly.[24] Johnson provides the following descriptions of what each kind of research is:

> **Disciplinary research** is research designed to improve the discipline. In economics, it consists largely of research to develop and improve economic theorics, quantitative techniques of economists, and the measurement of basic economic phenomena and parameters...[involving at times] a group of ancillary disciplines that provide it with research tools...
>
> **Subject-matter research** is multidisciplinary research on a subject of interest to a *set* of decision makers facing a *set* of practical problems. Well-defined subject-matter research is germane to well-defined sets of decision makers and practical problems. It is the relationship of the different disciplines to the set of problems involved that makes the multidisciplinarity of subject-matter research so different from the multidisciplinarity of the relationship between economics and its ancillary disciplines...
>
> **Problem-solving research** is research designed to solve a specific problem for a specific decision maker, though in some instances it is possible to find several decision makers with exactly the same problem. In this case, the research can be designed to solve a problem faced by more than one decision maker. Problem-solving research, like subject-matter research, is typically multidisciplinary. The practical problems of real-world decision makers respect neither the organizational charts of universities and research institutes not the academic disciplines

around which universities and institutes are organized (pp. 12-14) [underlining mine].

One of the problems which this leads to is what Daly and Cobb (1989), describe as "the fallacy of misplaced concreteness" (p. 35). This refers to the abstraction which occurs in the way economics organizes its knowledge. Although the argument, that abstraction may lead to fallacies, is not new, both writers have brought forth a comprehensive and compelling argument, particularly in relation to the way economics as a discipline deals with land and hence with natural resources.[25] They further argue that the way "markets" are dealt with in the discipline is an abstraction which is based in the physics' model (and methodology) of science. This means that social conditions, dynamic relationships and other fluctuations in societies, are treated as causal, linear, mechanistic relationships and deviations from the standard model, are treated as aberrations to be brought in line by means of various "market" interventions. Combined, this creates as it has done since Ricardo's Corn Model, a problem, and the: "...result is that conclusions are drawn about the real world by deduction from abstractions with little awareness of the danger [misplaced concreteness] involved." (Daly and Cobb, 1989, p. 35). Efforts are made to mitigate this: first through rigorous empiricism and the subsequent adjustments of the theories and models. Second, through the development of conceptual frameworks[26] from the "bottom up". Third, sustainable development is proposed as a new paradigm and as mentioned earlier, has come to mean for many, the appropriate development of "environmental resources" in addition to the more traditional resources. Fourth, the development of new conceptual frameworks such as for example the energy-matter based ones. Fifth, an in-depth examination of the nature, function and organization of information. Information management based conceptual frameworks may provide a way to increase knowledge regarding the interactive areas of systems and their components.[27]

4.   Information

It is striking that often papers presented at a meeting on a certain specific topic have several commonalities. Many of them are focussing on a "descrambling" of a variety of information with regard to a particular topic[28]. The ways and means applied to collect and interpret such information are usually those as taught by the disciplinary background, experience and knowledge of the researchers. Despite the fact that disciplines[29] demarcate the areas of research and the methodology used in gaining and organizing information, it is clear that "de-ciphering" the information is not an easy task. What information is and does and how and why is not necessarily an easy question to answer: "Information is a word which has never been easy to pin down." (Campbell, 1982, p. 15).

Is it a word which changes its meaning over time and as such perhaps should be put on the endangered species list? In the words of Wright, both the words "information" and "message" are at risk as not only has academia over-used them, but:

"Even in popular parlance these terms have run the risk of excessive application for some time now. At the turn of the century they already referred to everything from classified ads to love letters, and they have since expanded to encompass the eleven o'clock news and junk mail. But more striking than the growing number of technological things that everyone puts under these labels is the growing number of **biological** things that scientists put there. This century, as human societies have spent more and more time making information, and making things that make information, more and more scientific emphasis has been placed on the information that makes people and the information that is people-and, indeed, the information that makes and is, all living things" (Wright, 1988, pp. 83-84).

Information of this type includes everything. In that sense one could distinguish between organized and unorganized information[30]. Knowledge is a particular form of organized (coded, emerging) information. How we increase this is determined by our methodologies. However, the problem is that our past knowledge and methodologies used to increase what we know and how we organize this knowledge, will encourage us to interpret emerging information in a pre-determined way.

According to Johnson, knowledge can be broadly categorized into the following forms of knowledge: "...positivistic knowledge, normative knowledge, knowledge of values and prescriptive knowledge." (Johnson, 1986, p. 16). Whereby:

Normative knowledge...is regarded as including prescriptive knowledge as well as knowledge about values-about goodness and badness. The adjective "normative" then covers propositions about goodness and badness as well as prescriptive propositions having to do with what ought not or ought to be done, whether the latter are stated as laws, recipes, regulations, social mores and norms, or ethical imperatives...

Knowledge of values...[has] to do with the goodness and badness of conditions, situations, and things...

Positivistic knowledge is synthetic knowledge that deals with the characteristics of conditions, situation, or things in the real world...

Prescriptive knowledge is knowledge about what ought or ought not to have been done, or ought or ought not be done. Prescriptions are sometimes expressed in the future tense as goals or targets. They are also expressed as actions in the present tense; at times they are stated imperatively as laws, regulations, social mores, and norms enforced with sanctions...[etc.]" (Johnson, 1986, pp. 16-18).

In short, to gain more knowledge, information in a variety of forms in a variety of areas is gathered and interpreted to either always hold true (natural laws) or to be the best manner to achieve desirable futures. The information is collected and interpreted according to established methodologies. The methodologies themselves are determined by the disciplinary conceptual framework and standards. In addition, organized information (e.g. knowledge) as it occurs within disciplines[31] and as it is taught, discourages the crossing of the disciplinary barriers and throws veils over areas with which we are not already familiar.

Problems appear when faced with information for which there are no apparent mechanisms of deciphering. In such a case one can either improve on known theories, methods and techniques or look for altogether new management of information. However, before such new approaches are tried, it appears that during this period of uncertainty, before designing new methodologies becomes more commonly accepted, a "time of blame" occurs. That is to say, a scapegoat [32] is often identified to explain the inability to read and manage information properly. I suggest that this is a usual problem in times of transition: when new methodologies are not yet available and the inability to solve problems may be perceived as something which is due to an aberration and hence the result of a temporary malfunction of the overall system. Aberration may be caused by something identifiable and this gives rise to the naming of scapegoats and it is frequently technology which is assigned this role. Scientific methods and techniques have taught us the importance of causal relations; particularly with regard to "the environmental problem" many people tend to see application and use of technology in development, as one of the main causes of negative impacts on the natural environment. This of course is closely related to industrialization and the negative environmental impacts associated with this process. Technology as an enabler, is perceived to be crucial to continued economic growth in order to maintain and increase a supply of goods and services for an increasing population within a world of limited resources. Technology is seen as the way and means to provide the potential to increase the availability and use of resources. In addition, technology is seen as reinforcing itself; its use creates further demand for it. For example, the creation of a transportation infrastructure to support motor vehicles may lead to specific forms of urbanization. In turn, this leads to the development of other parts of the infrastructure, such as shopping malls, improved road systems, as well as allocation of land use driven by transportation. In the early stages of development technology is experienced as beneficial but in later stages it is associated with negative impacts. One can find examples of technology[33] as the culprit of all kinds of wrongs in all kinds of areas. Information technology in particular is not a neutral form of technology. For example, it changes the way we work and organize institutions and organizations. Information technology also changes decision-making in the domain where it is applied. As a result perceptions regarding the impact, function and use of this form of technology may lead some people to feel "trapped", whereas other people will perceive it as the panacea to all problems: the "techno-fix" approach.

Neither is completely true. First, technology comes in different forms: industrial and information technologies. The nature and impact of both are substantially different. Second, technology is a particular form of organized information and as such it is a tool. Third, technology is not an institution. Technology **links** a variety of areas: political/institutional, socio/economic and ecological. As such technology can be managed. Fourth, technology is **the artificial**. That is to say, it is part of what has shaped the artificial objects and phenomena within society[34]. It is very much part of the interface of which Simon refers to as the 'inner and outer environment (1969, p. 7). Technology provides a direct link between energy, information and matter and thus it has a very important function. In addition, technology is a particular form of organized information. It may be argued that it embodies the "visible" link between energy, information and matter. Utilizing technology may cause information to emerge, as well as influence the nature and the direction of the emerging information.[35] Economists know relatively little about information management and even less about emerging information and the rules are which govern it.[36]

5. The Nature of a Discipline

Economists often perceive the natural environment as a system which is organized in a manner similar to economic systems, albeit containing different variables. Many economists forget that as economists they know very little about economic systems and what they know is rooted in "misplaced concreteness".[37] Subsequently improvements in the discipline are attempted (e.g. Pearce and Turner, 1989; Bojo et al., 1990; Daly and Cobb, 1989), with all that that implies (different and new or improved expanded theories, better models, improved techniques) and this correction would then make the abstract models a better reflection of reality. This does not address underlying methodology (science based, reductionist etc).

In essence, many economists assume that their methodologies are the appropriate ones for solving the problems. This can be interpreted as making the problem fit the methods and techniques of the discipline.

"In the modern university, knowledge is organized into academic disciplines. There are clear norms establishing what such disciplines must be. These provide criteria that divide subject matter among the disciplines and establish goals for the internal structure of each one. This organization of knowledge has been brilliantly productive, but it also has built-in limitations and dangers, especially the danger of committing what Alfred North Whitehead called "the fallacy of misplaced concreteness." This fallacy flourishes because the disciplinary organization of knowledge requires a high level of abstraction; and the more successfully a discipline fulfills the criteria established for it, the higher is the level of abstraction involved. Inevitably, many practitioners of successful disciplines, socialized to think in these abstractions, apply their conclusions to the real world without recognizing the degree of abstraction involved" (Daly and Cobb, 1989, p. 25).

Many of the scientific disciplines as we know them have been developed within the science paradigm. A paradigm according to Kuhn, is related "closely to "normal science"" (1970, p. 10). When Kuhn referred to normal science he meant "research firmly based upon one or more past scientific achievements, achievements that some particular scientific community acknowledges for a time as supplying the foundation for its further practice." (1970, p. 10). Transformations in paradigms are referred to by Kuhn as "scientific revolutions" (1970, p. 12). In other words when there is a set of common beliefs based on a particular conceptual framework, this leads to a generally acceptable approach in the choice of problems to be solved, how to best go about doing so, and how to interpret the results. Within this "both fact collection and theory articulation became highly directed activities" (Kuhn, 1970, p.

18). While emerging new paradigms have an impact on "the structure of the group that practices the field" (Kuhn, 1970, p. 18), the choice of what is considered important and in need of research, is determined by the the dominant paradigm. This leads to the following:

"that one of the things a scientific community acquires with a paradigm is a criterion for choosing problems that, while the paradigm is taken for granted, can be assumed to have solutions. To a great extent these are the only problems that the community will admit as scientific or encourage its members to undertake. Other problems, including many that had previously been standard, are rejected as metaphysical, as the concern of another discipline, or sometimes as just too problematic to be worth the time" (Kuhn, 1970, p. 37).

Accepting Kuhn's arguments, there are several elements relevant here with regard to economics as a science-based discipline, methodology and the emerging nature of problems. First, according to Routh (1989):

"the paradigm that provides the inner framework for economic thought has not changed since the seventeenth century; that neither the advent of marginalism that distinguishes classical from neo-classical economics, nor the admission of the possibility of involuntary unemployment, that distinguishes Keynesian from neo-classical economics were revolutions in the Kuhnian sense. On the other contrary, they were the means by which the survival of the existing paradigm was ensured.[38]" (1989, p. 27).

This view is supported by Daly and Cobb (1989), as well as by Pearce and Turner (1989). These writers argue, that the conceptual framework underlying economics as a discipline, needs expanding, because the discipline as it has evolved, cannot deal properly with either development in a more sustainable manner or with externalities. But they argue that the paradigm in use is able to accommodate contemporary problems with current analytical methods, provided the number of variables researched is extended to include the natural environment. The writers recognize some difficulties, such as the misplaced concreteness and the perception of values, but these they say, can be solved. The difficulty I have with their arguments, is that in essence they practice what I referred to earlier as the internalizing of the problem. Although Daly and Cobb (1989) argue strongly for the abandonment of the "misplaced concreteness" as part of the analytical framework in economics, they do not fully recognize that the nature of contemporary problems is such, that a new approach is required as argued above. To solve such problems, scenario building should be used as a step in the process of understanding the changed and changing nature of contemporary problems.

Scenario building involves a number of variables and steps. First, scenarios involve:

"The world of facts and the world of perceptions. They explore for facts but they aim at perceptions inside the heads of decision makers. Their purpose is to gather and transform information of strategic significance into fresh perceptions" (Schwartz, 1991, p. 38).

This form of organization uses scientific information which has been gathered previously, while collecting more data as needed in response to specific questions. It also utilizes the cultural context within which the problem occurs and within which decision-makers and researchers function. Computer simulation models incorporate this view to some degree.[39] Second, scenario building uses "the language of stories and myths" (Schwartz, 1991, p. 40), in order to design possible futures. This is not as far-fetched as it may initially appear as it is a possible way of addressing the uncertainty of the future. Given that "Stories are an old way of organizing knowledge...they are about meaning; they help explain why things could happen in a certain way..." (Schwartz, 1991, p. 40); they draw on and use, the qualitative aspects of information. Third, scenario building involves **inter alia** determining which are the driving forces within a society; what variables are pre-determined; what are some of the critical uncertainties in society or of the problem situation being researched; and what are some of the underlying assumptions of and about some of these trends and variables which are prevalent within a society, or within the specific research area. Fourth, scenario building enables researchers and policy makers, to gain a broad overview[40] of the situation at hand and to detect and analyze emerging phenomena within the bounded field. This is another step in understanding complexity. Fifth, scenarios do not establish **a priori** cause and effect. They do not predict the future but they fascilitate the creation of a vision about the future. Scenarios incorporate flexibility and allow for action to be taken when more information emerges, thereby preventing unduly long waiting time for scientific confirmation. Focus on emerging phenomena will also allow researchers to gather data on such phenomena rather than on pre-determined variables and assumed relationships.[41]

In conclusion, because most of the current methodologies are incapable of dealing with the changed and changing nature of problems, the use of scenario building is a logical approach to take during this time of transition. Although it may not be suitable for all problems, it is a useful methodology to decipher some of the unorganized information in a way which is not deterministic and discipline bound. It will increase knowledge about current problems and the nature of such problems. It will also allow us to start dealing with the role of Simon's artificial objects and phenomena within a cultural context.

Notes

1. Technology, particularly information technology, as a form of organized information is a good indicator both in use and as part of their function, of the complexity of problems. As such it is linked with the difficulties of solving problems and hence its recurring use as "scapegoat".

2. I will use "the environmental problem" throughout this paper as a "case-study", and I also use it as an illustration of a complex problem, meaning the areas of interaction between an economic system and an ecological system. Although both systems are constructs, and their properties are very different. It is the nature of the interaction between the variables within these two systems which I refer to as the environmental problem. It is also the area about which we know relatively little, other than the fact that it is a complex problem.

3. See Ely Devons and Max Gluckman (1982).

4. Many of the relationships are based on what appears to have been the case in the past. As well, they are based on what may have been proven empirically. These relationships may also be based on what is the norm within a discipline, what society perceives the relationship to be or what the researcher hypothesis what the relationship could or should be.

5. Implicitly I may be conveying the message here that all research and policies are done and designed to solve problems. Not so, first and foremost one needs a conceptual framework, problem-solving is but one of the research methodologies. I am simply making a generalization at this point.

6. I refer here specifically to Economics: abstracting from society still forms the basis for many models and techniques used in Economics.

7. This has certainly to be the case in Economics. It holds true for several other disciplines as well, such as Geography, Ecology.

8. That is to say, problems were either not dealt with at all within such disciplines, or they were perceived as being the area of research of other disciplines. Once recognized as falling within the domain of a particular discipline, the problem will be analyzed according to the analytical methods of such a discipline. At that point, they have become part of the general research domain.

9. I examine Economics only.

10. I will not argue here whether research increases disciplinary knowledge or not. It is my contention that in the case of Economics it would not make much difference whether one does or does not. The discipline itself is out of tune with society (witness the divergence between Economics textbooks and the Economy) and real world knowledge about the Economy is often turned into abstractions and vice versa.

11. In doing this, we limit ourselves to solutions which have been designed within and for a discipline and are bound by the way fields of study have been demarcated.

12. There are some exceptions to this. Some sciences, such as Engineering and Architecture, deal in part with artificial objects: "Synthetic or artificial objects-and more specifically, prospective artificial objects having desired properties- are the central objective of engineering activity and skill...Hence, a science of the artificial will be closely akin to a science of engineering-but very different...from what goes currently by the name of 'engineering science'." (Simon, 1969, p.5).

13. At least this is the case for Economics. I understand that many other disciplines are experiencing similar difficulties.

14. Such as planning, design and management which together are the domain of decision making.

15. Neither time nor space permits a detailed examination of this particular topic here.

16. And of course be applicable in many other problem-solving areas with a high degree of complexity, such as transportation, telecommunication and urban-regions.

17.   The term "negative" refers to unanticipated costs related to production and consumption and not accounted for in the price of goods and services.

18.   Cost Benefit Analysis is a clear example of this.

19.   There is a large body of literature available from this period. At the policy level, during the sixties and seventies there were a variety of attempts to prevent further pollution, and to clean up already polluted areas. Industry was perceived as the main cause of pollution and when requested to "clean up", one of the more common arguments heard, was that the associated cost would be too high. To accommodate the negative cost of development would have to involve either cost cutting in other areas of such companies or closing down of plants or companies involved threatened to move their operations to other countries. This resulted often in governments backing out of proposed regulations, proposed deadlines and so on. The common term for these kind of practices was referred to as "industrial blackmail". In other words use the threat of "jobloss" in order to convince other parties not to take action against the "offender".

20.   I will not enter the debate on how sustainable development should be defined. Suffice it to say, that it is a conceptual framework. The crucial part of it being the need to maintain the world' life support systems.

21.   See Delfgaauw and Tyler (1991).

22.   I believe that this should read "minimize".

23.   For example, innovative perspectives are presented by Bo Wiman, in Svedin and Aniansson (eds.) (1992). Although not much attention is given to methodology, many of the authors in this book provide insightful perspectives on the changed and changing nature of problems, and in particular the environmental problem.

24.   This is particularly relevant for two reasons: policies are guidelines aimed at achieving desirable results, and policy tools (as well as the choice of which one) may differ substantionally depending on the conceptual framework underlying the policy design.

25.   See Daly and Cobb (1989, Chapter 5), they argue convincingly that: "the abstractions by which land has been represented as a distinctive aspect of the economy have faded to the periphery or disappeared altogether [in Economics]" (p. 97) and that this caused land to be viewed as "..merely one commodity among others." (p. 99), leading to the forces of nature "and therefore nature in general...[disappearing] from the physical world." (p. 99).

26.   And the theories, models and techniques that this would give rise to, such as the development of conceptual frameworks through comparative analysis or increased knowledge about community development.

27.   Some of this is evident in the approach taken by Ten Brink (1991).

28.   I refer in this case to the workshop "EUROPE ON THE MOVE, New Borders, Old Barriers." NIAS, Wassenaar, March 17, 1992.

29.   This includes multi-disciplinary and inter-disciplinary approaches.

30.   Alternatively: coded or uncoded information or emerging and inherent information.

31.   This includes multi-disciplinary and inter-disciplinary approaches.

32.   I use the term "scapegoat" here as I want a relatively neutral word to indicate that responsibility is being shifted away from people, organizations and nature.

33.   See Zuboff (1988).

34.   Although it also contains natural elements (Simon, 1969).

35.   This is a term used by Campbell (1982), meaning information which is still in chaotic state.

36.   This is partly so, because information is studied in a separate, disciplinary approach. Although e.g. some economists may be familiar with some aspects of information, it is collected and interpreted using the methodologies of the relevant discipline. For more information on this topic see for example Machlup and Mansfield (1983).

37.   This term is used by Daly and Cobb (1989).

38.   This footnote is an existing one in Routh's book (1989) and reads as follows: "'But economics has never had a major revolution; its basic maximizing model has never been replaced. "Donald F. Gordon, op. cit. p. 124."

39.   See for example Ten Brink (1991).

40.   Of course scenarios can be used for micro and macro situations.

41.   For a complete overview of scenario building, see Schwartz (1991).

REFERENCES

Bojo, J., K.G. Mäler, and L. Unemo, **Environment and Development: An Economic Approach**, Kluwer Academic Publishers, Dordrecht, 1990.

Campbell, J., **Grammatical Man, Information, Entropy, Language, and Life**, Simon & Schuster, Inc., New York, 1982.

Daly, H.E. and J.B. Cobb Jr., **For the Common Good: Redirecting the Economy toward Community, the Environment and a Sustainable Future**. Beacon Press, Boston, 1989.

Delfgaauw, M. C. Th., and M.E. Tyler, **A Baysian Approach to Problem Solving**, Unpublished paper, 1991.

Devons, E. and M. Gluckman, Procedures for Demarcating a Field of Study, **Field Research: a Sourcebook and Field Manual** (R.G. Burgess, ed.), George Allen & Unwin, London, 1982.

Johnson, G.L., **Research Methodology for Economists, Philosophy and Practice**, MacMillan Publishing Company, New York, 1986.

262

Kuhn, T.S., **The Structure of Scientific Revolutions**, University of Chicago Press, Chicago, Second Edition, Enlarged, 1970.

Machlup, F. and U. Mansfield (eds.), **The Study of Information: Interdisciplinary Messages**, John Wiley & Sons, New York, 1983.

Pearce, D.W. and K.R. Turner, **Economics of Natural Resources and the Environment**. The Johns Hopkins University Press, Baltimore, Maryland, 1990.

Routh, G., **The Origin of Economic Ideas**. Sheridan House Inc., Second Edition, Dobbs Ferry, NY., 1989.

Schwartz, P., **The Art of the Long View, Planning for the Future in an Uncertain World**, Doubleday, New York, 1991.

Simon, H.A., **The Sciences of the Artificial**. The M.I.T. Press, Cambridge, Mass., 1969.

Ten Brink, B. The AMOEBA Approach as a Useful Tool for Establishing Sustainable Development?, **In Search of Indicators of Sustainable Development**, (O. Kuik and H. Verbruggen, eds.), Kluwer Academic Publishers, Dordrecht, 1991.

Wiman, B.L.B. Designing Resource Systems for Sustainability: Safe-Fail versus Fail-Safe Strategies, **Society and the Environment: A Swedish Research Perspective**, (U. Svedin and B.H. Aniansson, eds.), Kluwer Academic Publishers, Dordrecht, 1992.

Wright, R., **Three Scientists and Their Gods, Looking for Meaning in an Age of Information**. Harper & Row, New York, 1988.

Zuboff, S., **In the Age of the Smart Machine, The Future of Work and Power**. Basic Books, Inc., New York, 1988.

List of Contributors

David Banister
University College London, Wates House
22 Gordon Street
London WC1H OQB
England

Ulrich Blum
Technical University of Dresden
George-Bährstrasse 7
D-8027 Dresden
Germany

Frank Bruinsma
Department of Economics, Free University
De Boelelaan 1105
1081 HV Amsterdam
The Netherlands

Roberta Capello
Universita Commerciale Luigi Bocconi
Via R. Sarfatti 25
20136 Milano
Italy

Mieke C. Th. Delfgaauw
Faculty of Environmental Studies of Waterloo
200 University Ave
Waterloo, Ont. N2L 3GL
Canada

Maria Giaoutzi
Department of Geography, National Technical University
Zographou Campus
Athens
Greece

Alexander Granberg
Advisor to President of the Russian Federation
The Kremlin
Vavilov Street 7
Moscow 117822
Russia

264

Niles Hansen
Department of Economics, University of Texas at Austin
Austin, Texas 78712
USA

Dirk-Jan Kamann
Department of Economics, State University Groningen
Paddepoel, W.S.N. Building
Groningen
The Netherlands

Kai Lamberg
Sundvanget 9
DK 2900 Hellerup
Denmark

Rico Maggi
Sozialökonomisches Seminar, University of Zurich
Ramistrasse 71
CH-8006 Zurich
Switzerland

Peter Nijkamp
Department of Economics, Free University
De Boelelaan 1105
1081 HV Amsterdam
The Netherlands

Remigio Ratti
Economic Research, Cantone Ticino
Stabile Torerreta
CH-6501 Bellinzona
Switzerland

Piet Rietveld
Department of Economics, Free University
De Boelelaan 1105
1081 HV Amsterdam
The Netherlands

Ilan Salomon
Department of Geography, Hebrew University
Mount Scopus
Jerusalem 91905
Israel

Boaz Tsairi
Department of Geography, Hebrew University
Mount Scopus
Jerusalem 91905
Israel

Roger Vickerman
Channel Tunnel Research Unit, University of Kent
Canterbury
Kent CT2 7NF
England

Jaap de Wit
Faculty of Regional Economics, University of Amsterdam
Roeterstraat 11
1018 WB Amsterdam
The Netherlands